John Stuart Blackie

Scottish Song

Its Wealth, Wisdom and Social Significance

John Stuart Blackie

Scottish Song
Its Wealth, Wisdom and Social Significance

ISBN/EAN: 9783744774604

Printed in Europe, USA, Canada, Australia, Japan

Cover: Foto ©Thomas Meinert / pixelio.de

More available books at **www.hansebooks.com**

SCOTTISH SONG

Wo man singt da lass dich ruhig nieder,
Böse Menschen haben keine Lieder.
—*German Proverb.*

SCOTTISH SONG

ITS WEALTH, WISDOM, AND
SOCIAL SIGNIFICANCE

BY

JOHN STUART BLACKIE

EMERITUS PROFESSOR OF GREEK IN THE UNIVERSITY OF
EDINBURGH; AUTHOR OF 'LAYS AND LEGENDS
OF ANCIENT GREECE,' ETC.

WILLIAM BLACKWOOD AND SONS
EDINBURGH AND LONDON
MDCCCLXXXIX

TO

DR A. C. MACKENZIE,
PRINCIPAL OF THE ROYAL ACADEMY OF MUSIC, LONDON,

THIS HUMBLE ATTEMPT

TO EXHIBIT THE WEALTH, STIMULATE THE STUDY,

AND EXTEND THE INFLUENCE

OF OUR NATIVE SCOTTISH SONG,

IS WITH SINCERE ESTEEM

𝔇𝔢𝔡𝔦𝔠𝔞𝔱𝔢𝔡 𝔟𝔶

JOHN STUART BLACKIE.

PREFATORY NOTE.

THE title which this little volume bears, sufficiently explains the reason of its appearance, and whatever small claims it may be able to advance for originality in a theme so often and so ably handled by experts in the folk-lore and the popular music of their country. I have no pretensions either to the scientific knowledge or to the curious literary research which might enable me to compete with these men of skill, and to share in any part of the praise which they have so justly earned; I only thought I might do some good, in an age urged by various stimulating forces to seek after what is new rather than to hold by what is true, if I should present, in a sort of dramatic totality, the wealth of moral, intellectual, and æsthetical nutriment of the best kind that lies stored in our heritage of national song. My task, therefore, was simply one of collection and selection, and presenting, so to speak, in a moral nosegay the lyrical blossoms that stood around me, as thick as flowers in the green meadow, or trouts in the amber pool. My selection was guided in the main by the currency which the songs had obtained in the life of the great mass of the people; though sometimes also I had to complete the picture by productions equally significant of what is best in Scottish life, but which had not found their way so widely into the popular ear. In making my selections, with accompanying historical remarks where they might appear useful or pleasant, I have used a great variety of the best authorities, which will be found acknowledged in the text; specially, however, I have to return thanks to those eminent musical publishers who have, with the greatest liberality, allowed me to make free use of those musical illustrations which had not yet passed from their special protectorship into the large arena of unclaimed melody. These gentlemen are, Messrs Paterson & Sons, Edinburgh; J. Muir Wood, Joseph Ferrie, and John Cameron, Glasgow; Messrs Field & Tuer, J. Blockley, and Swan & Sons, London. I have also particularly to acknowledge the valuable assistance which I have received from Mr Alan Reid, Edinburgh, in the revision of the airs.

9 DOUGLAS CRESCENT, EDINBURGH,
    20th December 1888.

CONTENTS.

CHAP.		PAGE
I.	SCOTTISH SONG, ITS VALUE AND SIGNIFICANCE,	1
II.	SONGS OF LOVE, COURTSHIP, AND MARRIAGE,	29
III.	PATRIOTIC SONGS, WAR-SONGS, JACOBITE BALLADS,	142
IV.	SONGS OF CHARACTER AND INCIDENT IN DAILY LIFE,	248
V.	DRINKING-SONGS, CONVIVIAL SONGS,	296
VI.	SEA-SONGS, NAVAL SONGS, AND BOAT-SONGS,	334
VII.	SONGS OF THOUGHT AND SENTIMENT,	357
	GLOSSARY,	385

SCOTTISH SONG.

CHAPTER I.

SCOTTISH SONG, ITS VALUE AND SIGNIFICANCE.

"A people which takes no pride in the noble achievements of remote ancestors will never achieve anything worthy to be remembered by remote descendants. Such pride is a sentiment which belongs to the higher and nobler part of human nature, and which adds not a little to the strength of states."—MACAULAY.

WE have long been troubled with the feeling that there is something radically wrong in the place which Music holds in the moral life and social atmosphere of the people of these islands, especially of Scotland. It is more of an exhibition and an accomplishment, less of an educative force, than it ought to be in a well-balanced system of national culture. It is looked upon too much as an outside affair, belonging to a professional or specially gifted few, not as a healthy atmosphere which all ought to breathe, and a girdle of strength to brace the manhood of the people. With the Greeks, who are our models in all the higher culture, it was not so. With them Music —Μουσική—occupied the whole field of artistic expression for the mass of the people, except what was covered by the eloquence of the popular assemblies and the law courts; and even their prose, as we see from the writings of the rhetoricians, was cultivated with a rhythmical curiousness which distinctly pointed to the musical cradle in which it had been nursed. When Homer, or any of the grand old school of Chian minstrels who gave circulation to his heroic cantos, commenced their recital with the words, "Sing, O Muse," they were not using a phrase as unmeaning as when a proud man signs himself at the bottom of a letter "your humble servant." They did sing. And the great festal compositions which we call the Greek drama or the Greek tragedy were in fact more lyrical than dramatic in their nature, and, if they are to bear a name expressive of their true character and significance, ought rather to be called sacred and patriotic operas. That they were accepted by the people as song, not as drama, followed naturally from the stirring power of the μέλος, or melody, as distinguished from the somewhat formal and stately attitude of the λέξις, or prose dialogue—an effect of which a striking witness remains to the present day in the word τραγούδι, or *tragedy*, which in modern Greek simply means a *song*. But in Great Britain, both north and south of the Tweed, we are compelled to say, not without sorrow, and we may hope also with a certain shame, that our great store of sacred and secular tradition has not been used, as the Greeks would have used it, to enrich the blood and to brace the nerve of the people; and, though our splendid oratorios compensate in some degree for the loss of that happy union between the pulpit and the stage indicated by the mysteries of the middle ages, and do give us, only without the scenic accompaniment, what may well be called the soul of a sacred opera, yet these grand efforts of professional skill are more of the nature of a brilliant exhibition for the few than of a popular delight for the many. Our hymns, psalms, and spiritual songs also, in the weekly temple services, present to us the most solemn lessons, in strains not less popularly effective than the most sublime moralising in the choruses of Æschylus and Sophocles; but neither in the magnificent harmonies of the oratorio nor in the solemn soothings of the cathedral chant is there any place found for the native, national, and patriotic element so strongly pronounced in the national drama, or opera, of the Greeks. Shakespeare's historical plays, no doubt, as the Baron von Bunsen well remarked, are the true Iliad of the English people; but they are dramas, not operas. Not less notable in the æsthetical use of historical and heroic tradition are the "Lady of the Lake" and other poems of Scott; but they are read, not sung. For the purely native, patriotic, and national element so potent in Greek art we seek in vain, except in the sphere of the popular song or *Volkslied* — a domain of musical expression, therefore, which has peculiar claims on our attention, as retaining those charms of native growth, native atmosphere, native incident, and native heroism, from which the higher branches of the art have so unfortunately been divorced.

It is natural in a certain class of persons of high culture, or who move on a certain elevated social platform, to look with indifference or contempt on the ballads of the people that are hawked about the street, and sung in rainy weather by ragged minstrels with a cracked voice; but it is not wise. The songs that please the great mass of the people are the songs that flowed most directly and most potently from the heart of the people; and whosoever wishes to know the people, must know to love their songs. If, as Richter with his usual wisdom said, the way to a mother's heart is through her children, and the way to a people's heart is through their mother-tongue, the utterance of this mother-tongue which goes most directly to the popular heart is the popular song; and whoever has to do with the people—whether as politician, landlord, or spiritual guide—will find that a single well-timed verse from a popular ballad will prove more effective to point his address, and to strengthen his influence, than the most weighty sentence from an infallible Aristotle or a universal Shakespeare. Nor is this without reason,—the people do not feed on soap-bubbles: the songs which they sing are not pretty fancies or dainty conceits, but have a root in fact, a growth in experience, a blossom in the dramatic incidents, and a fruit in the ripe wisdom of life. They are the stuff of which Homer is made,—Homer who may be anybody, or nobody, as the Wolfians will have it, but is always the Greek people. So the Scottish songs are not the songs of Ramsay, or Burns, or Ballantine, as men with a special personality to reveal, but the songs of the Scottish people, of whom Ramsay, and Burns, and a host of others, were merely the spokesmen for the nonce. It is quite otherwise with the poetry of such men as Milton, Shelley, Southey, Byron, Wordsworth, Browning. These men, however diverse in the distinctive type of their genius, speak mainly for themselves: they not only do not declare the genius of the people in whose language they sing, but, like the prophets among the Jews, they not seldom deliver themselves of a burden directly antagonistic to it. Individual genius has its sphere of exalted influence among the sympathetic few; but unless its productions be, like Shakespeare's, as popular as they are peculiar, they never can compete in interest with the poetry which is the glowing expression and the typical embodiment of the higher life, and the notable fates of a whole people. This poetry, though it cannot boast the rarity, the novelty, or the originality of a few extraordinary and brilliantly abnormal men, is, like the heather on the hills and the birch in the glen, the more agreeable the more catholic it is in its diffusion, and the more characteristic in its graces.

Of all the species of the genus *Volkslied*, so generally appreciated since Cowper and Wordsworth brought poetry back to Nature, the most extensively known and the most largely acknowledged is the Scotch. This extensive recognition it owes, no doubt, in some degree, to the far-travelled habits of the people to whom it belongs; partly to the crown put upon its glory by the fervid genius of Burns and the wide human sympathies of Scott, but unquestionably also, in no small degree, to its own intrinsic excellence. Had there been no Scottish song of real excellence before him and round about him, even the strong intellect of that inspired ploughman might not have prevailed to give a world-wide circulation to the Scottish *Volkslied*. It would have been Burns in that case that the world would have admired, not Scotland. But the simplest glance at any of our collections of popular Scottish songs will show that, though the Ayrshire singer stands out naturally as the Corypheus of the chorus, not a few of the individual members of that tuneful band are in no wise inferior to their leader, either in force or in tenderness, in keen perception of character, in sound sense, in shrewd humour, in dramatic effectiveness of incident, or in picturesque environment of scenery. His national poetry, therefore, is a heritage of which every loyal-hearted Scot ought to be proud; a heritage which, taken along with the evangelic constructiveness of Knox, the mechanical inventiveness of Watt, the economic subtlety of Smith, and the large human catholicity of Scott, has obtained for him a place among the independent nationalities of Europe which it will be his own shame if he shall lose.

Is there, then, any danger that the charm of such an ignoble self-disownment may fall in these days on a people that has so long been known for the fervour of its national sentiment and the strength of its sturdy self-esteem? Yes, unquestionably; and that not only from the operation of the truth contained in the well-known saying that "far birds have fair feathers," which causes the eyes of fools to wander to the end of the earth for flowers which bloom more fairly at their feet, but from the combination of a number of causes that tend to make the Scotsman of the present hour less a Scot than he was in the day when the Baroness Nairne sang the praises of "the auld house," when Burns gave new wings to the memory of the Bruce as he paced the field of Bannockburn, and Scott raised to worthy fellowship with Chaucer and Shakespeare the local heroism of the Lowland straths and the Highland lochs. The first of these causes lies in the natural influence which a large country exercises on a smaller country when united to it politically for the purposes of common action, in virtue of which a certain process of assimilation will take place, tending to rub off the more salient features of the smaller body, and replace it with a superinduced paste of imperial uniformity. Such a smoothing over and wiping out of national peculiarities we see, to a considerable extent, in the Germanisation of Hungary, notwithstanding its possession of a local parliament and national guarantees of a very strong kind, but which must manifest itself much more strikingly when the union of the smaller with the greater kingdom has been accompanied with a complete transfer of all legislative and governmental machinery to the capital of the larger factor in the contract. In this view the framers of the Union of 1707, while they deserve all praise for preserving our dearly bought ecclesiastical, legal, and educational organisation intact, in divesting Edinburgh of its historical position as a centre of national life cannot be acquitted of the charge of sapping the roots of our national character by formally depriving us of all *locus standi* in the political world. The evil effects of this ill-advised centralisation of all British business in the English capital soon became apparent. The nobility, who, for various reasons, are generally the least national class of society, were taught to look upon London, not Edinburgh, as the headquarters of their social life, and felt themselves more at home dangling about the purlieus of St James's than in faithful service to the country by whose industry they were supported, and by whose manhood they had been ennobled. This general faithlessness to the local interests of Scotland received an additional impetus, so far as the Highland gentry were concerned, by the unfortunate rising of the 1745—a sentimental blunder soon followed by the penalty of diminished importance in the local gentry, absenteeism with factorial management, and the substitution of a purely mercantile-minded economy for the kindly personal superintendence of a resident gentry. Less prominently before the eyes of the public, but not less effectively than these political and social forces, were certain great defects in the Scottish scholastic system, tending towards the Anglification of an influential section of the rising youth of the country. Born north of the Tweed, but not bred, after five years' English training at Harrow, and other five, it may be, at Oxford, they returned to the land whence they drew their blood utterly innocent of all patriotic fervour, prepared to doubt whether, after all, Wallace might not be a myth, roundly to assert that John Knox was a boor, and to believe firmly with Charles II. of pious memory that "Episcopacy is the only religion for a gentleman." All this educative transmuting of stout young Scotsmen into fine young Englishmen took place, and is taking place more and more every day, as the natural and necessary result of the neglect of the middle, or, as the Germans call it, learned school organism, as a middle stage between the university and the primary or parochial schools. Under such a perverse system, or rather lack of system, the gentry were scarcely to be blamed for sending their hopeful progeny to schools where alone an education and a society was offered them which they had a right to claim; though they might have been to blame certainly, judged by the highest standard of patriotic duty, for not having done anything to enable their countrymen to clothe with living bone and sinew the well-ordered scheme of educational gradation laid down by Knox in the 'First Book of Discipline.'[1] But this was not the only great neglect of the Scottish people, which worked, and is

[1] Chap. VII., Of Schools and Universities.

working slowly and surely, to the undermining of the foundations of their noble nationality. Whether from their comparative poverty in the time when universities were being founded, or from the prepossession of the public mind by the revived learning of Greece and Rome, uniting as it did at that time the charm of novelty with the grace of inherent excellence, certain it is that in the course of study laid down for the aspirants to academical degrees, no provision was made except here and there in the most superficial and elementary style for any historical teaching, much less for any special indoctrination in the pregnant facts and heroic memories of the history of the fatherland—insomuch that in the University of Edinburgh, which in some departments is more richly provided with chairs than the sister institutions, the hopeful youth of Scotland are regularly trained, according to a rigid routine, to take the highest honours in arts, without the slightest taste of native historical criticism, or the slightest breath of patriotic inspiration. And so it has come to pass that a knowledge of the history and archæology of his own country, which ought to be the household furniture, so to speak, of every educated Scotsman, was left to be sought after by a few antiquarian specialists like Skene, Anderson, and Mitchell, or patriotic enthusiasts like Walter Scott and William Burns. Compare this with any scheme of lectures in the meanest and most ill-furnished

German university, and then say whether what a distinguished English writer calls our "insular ignorance" is not more than matched by our educational absurdity. In the primary schools, which in some respects may have been more conformable to nature than the university curriculum, how much or how little of what I should call a Scottish, or in the Highlands a Celtic Plutarch, occupies its just position under the operation of the recent London-made codes, I cannot say: but in schools of higher pretensions I am afraid it is a universal fact that a youth of good parts shall sooner be able to tell you what Miltiades and Themistocles did for Greece more than two thousand years ago, than what Bruce and Wallace did to give Scotsmen a firm tread and a manly footing on the heather of their native hills. And if a general patriotic foundation is thus neglected in the more earnest domain of historical prose, it is not to be expected that the national music and the popular song should have received any recognition from a race of pedagogues who had been taught to believe that the one orthodox discipline for a young human Scottish soul is to conjugate an irregular Greek verb, or to twist a nice Ciceronian sentence into shape. For here not only the vulgar prejudice for a smattering of the two learned languages—a forced growth, all thorns and no berries—must be taken into account, but the yet more dangerous notion from which we started, that music is habitually regarded in Scotland rather as an amusing accomplishment than as an educative force, and in a scholastic point of view is looked upon exceptionally as the refined luxury of the few, not as the healthy diet of the many. In this respect our national culture has certainly notably declined from the days—now three hundred years ago—when the indoctrination of the youthhood in music was held to be of such importance as to call forth a special Act of Parliament for its encouragement and enforcement.[1] This low estimate of the educative value of the divinest of the arts is no doubt to be attributed, in no small degree, to the hardness of the severe struggle which the nation had to go through in the defence of its liberties against the despotism of the Stuarts, and to the excess of severe and ungenial antagonism into which it was driven as a revolt against their intrusive Episcopacy: anyhow, it was a great loss to Scotland that the rich tradition of choicest Scottish song should have been left to the exercitation of a wandering ballad-singer, or the exhilaration of a company of village topers. I remember in a mixed company, some forty or fifty years ago, to have been reproved by a young lady for singing a Scotch song, not because it was Scotch, but because it was a song, and because the practice of singing had a tendency to bring

[1] Scottish Acts, 1579, chap. 98.

people into bad company! This observation, silly as it may appear, was only the natural fruit of the idea, still so common in Scotland, that popular song, while it does nothing for the higher culture, may, like wine and women, often lead a man into very slippery proximities. The three generations that have seen the wonderful changes of the nineteenth century have doubtless done not a little to render the expression of such prosaic ideas as ridiculous as it is unreasonable, and to claim for national music and national song the same place in Scotland that they maintained in Palestine under King David, and as they continuously maintained in Protestant Germany from the days of Martin Luther to the present hour. In the primary schools especially, I have good reason to believe that music is generally looked upon and handled as an educative force, though I doubt if even there the distinctive elements of Scottish patriotic tradition, shrewd Scottish wisdom, tender Scottish sentiment, and thoughtful Scottish humour, receive that prominence which, in a healthy national system of youthful training, they deserve; and certain I am that the higher we rise in the scale of Scottish schools, even where music receives its just place in the curriculum, the less shall we expect to find anything distinctively Scotch in the educational equipment of a Scottish gentleman.

So much for our political and educational position as

regards our national songs. We may now cast a glance more in detail at the operation of the principle mentioned above, that "far birds have fair feathers." It is not an uncommon occurrence that, when you ask a Scottish young lady in a Scottish West-End drawing-room to fill with a little sweet vocalism the void which nature abhors, she will sing a German or an Italian song, or a light French ariette, but she will not sing a Scotch song—at least, she will not sing it unless exceptionally, and by special desire, and with special urgency on the part of the petitioner. What is the reason of this? She has more reasons than one,—some which she will be prone to confess; others that, from your own knowledge of female nature or fashionable life, you will find it not difficult to supply. In the first place, she will likely say, with a very pretty modesty no doubt, she thinks that she cannot sing Scotch songs, they are so difficult: they go so low and mount so high, that it is impossible for a voice of ordinary compass to embrace them. This is true of some Scotch songs, perhaps, because many of them were originally adapted for the fiddle; but it is not true of the whole of them, or even the majority of them—certainly not true with regard to some of the most popular. It is true of "Caller Herrin'," of "Gloomy Winter's noo awa'," "Lady Keith's Lament," and others; but it is not true of "Ye Banks and Braes o' Bonnie Doon," "Jock o'

Hazeldean," "Ae Fond Kiss and then we sever," and many others. Besides, every singer knows that the same air may be set to various keys, so as to suit the quality and the compass of every variety of voice. Driven from this position, if strongly pressed the fair performer may be led to say there is such a range of various feeling, and such a power of dramatic expression and character, in Scottish songs, that it requires a touch of the histrionic art beyond the mere craft of a good voice to represent them. So far as this is true, it merely proves the utter shallowness and falsehood of the musical training to which the fair objectors may have been submitted: it proves that they have been taught to sing with their throat only, and not with their soul—a very different style of singing from that practised by the merle and the mavis in the month of May, we may depend on it. In a good song the throat is only the instrument—the soul is always the performer. A song without the soul is as a flower without the fragrance, like a pudding without the seasoning, like a word without the accent, or like beautiful features with no expression. Self-exhibition in some shape, instead of the true presentation of nature, is the besetting sin of all art; and he who sings with his throat mainly, and not with his soul, is making an exhibition of his dexterity as a musical artist, not an utterance of his emotions as a man. As to the alleged dramatic talent necessary for singing a Scotch song, it is enough to say that man is naturally a dramatic, or, as Aristotle has it, a mimetic animal; and that a certain amount of dramatic feeling and gesture belongs to every healthy-minded human being, from the chief of a Red Indian tribe to a popular orator or a street preacher. And, if it be the effect of any education, musical or academical, to make a public singer or a speaker the slave of a piece of printed paper, instead of being the free master of his emotions and his movements, one can only say that such training strangles the nature which it should have nursed; and that it is far better for all moral purposes to sing or to speak naturally, without any training at all, than to be trained to a force without fervour and a dexterity without soul. But again, our poor disnatured young victim of false methods may allege that she would gladly sing Scotch songs if they were only written in English; but the Scotch language is too broad and guttural for her, and so with a wise abstention she early makes up her mind to let it drop. Poor creature! sweet little sophist! who has been trained away from the sweetness and the roundness of her native Scottish dialect, and trained into the clippings and the mincings and the sibilations of the unmusical English tongue; who, perhaps, while she eschews a Scotch song for the difficulty of saying *loch* instead of *lake*, will trill you off a German *Volkslied* in which the same guttural occurs six times for once that it occurs in the Scotch; and whose organs are too refined, she deems, for broad Scotch, at the very moment when she is learning Italian in order to improve her voice with the musical broad Italian *a*, which is at the same time the distinctive and dominant vowel-sound in every popular Scotch song! Nothing can be more silly, indeed, and more significant of the false culture and gross ignorance so common in what is called "fashionable society," than the manner in which they talk of the beautiful Scotch language, which indeed is not, properly speaking, a different language, but only the most uncorrupted and the most musical dialect of our common English tongue—"that noble Doric which," as a fine poetical genius did not hesitate to say, is "at once rustic and dignified, heroic and vernacular."[1] It is sad, indeed, and shameful, that well-dressed young gentlemen and ladies with Scottish blood in their veins should allow themselves to talk contemptuously of a language which one of the most original and most cultured of modern English poet-thinkers is proud to imitate; but this is only one of the unfortunate results of the process of denationalising our upper classes by making them pendants to a centralising metropolis out-

[1] Sydney Dobell, in a note to the "Market-Wife Song" in 'England in Time of War.'

side of their natural home, and of the lamentable omission of the national element in our schools and colleges noted above, which leaves to the chance fancy of an occasional amateur what ought to have been the sacred care of a united people. The Greeks whom we profess to honour acted otherwise. They placed their vulgar Doric in the front van of their choral music: we look on quietly, and allow ours to die.

Along with these political and educational influences, tending to give to English far feathers a wider acceptance with native Scots than Scottish fair ones, we must notice specially the vanity of mothers—especially of those whose highest ambition for their children is that they should be able to figure with all the conceits and conventions of the hour in what is called fashionable society. What is fashionable society? A phase of human aggregation somewhat difficult to define. But if fashion in social intercourse has any kinship with the same potency as we see it operating in ladies' bonnets and in ladies' skirts, we shall not expect to find reason one of its dominant elements. So far as I have been able to generalise on the subject, I perceive in fashionable society a habit of mind and life which inclines to put a value on outward form and display, gold and gewgaws, pedigrees and coronets, and all sorts of glittering and imposing externalities, rather than on the breezy atmosphere of a stirring and manly soul, the radiance of a pure and noble inspiration, and the spontaneous flow of living waters from within; and the fashionable man, taken overhead—for of course, here as elsewhere, there are big trouts plashing among the minnows of the pool—is a creature who habitually sacrifices strength to polish, substance to show, nature to convention, and a fervid instinct to a cold propriety. Now the mother who wishes her daughter to shine in such society will naturally seek out for her some fellowship with the brilliant displays of Italian and German music which a great metropolis commands, rather than with the commonness, the homeliness, and what she may possibly call the vulgarity, of Scottish songs. It would be in vain to ask such a mother what she means by vulgarity. Is it vulgar to be true to nature, to hate all affectation, and to call a spade a spade roundly, as Shakespeare did, and the English Bible, and Robert Burns? Is it vulgar to be patriotic, and to love the land which came to you from your father's blood and with your mother's milk? Is it vulgar to pour forth from the heart melody of native growth as fresh and bright and strong as the heather on the Scottish braes, or the fountains that leap from the rim of Scottish crags, instead of piping forth soap-bells of shallow sentiment to tickle the ear of dreamy girls and shallow foplings in a drawing-room? She would not understand the question. My Lord B. or my Lady C. are to-night to have a grand reception, with the famous Italian cantatrice of the season to exhibit her splendid tuneful somersets: my daughter shall take her model from that. Italian, German, and Hungarian airs belong to good society; but let "Bonnie Jean" and "Bessy Bell," and even the classical "Newhaven Fishwives," be left to the streets and to the ballad-singers!

. Leaving these devotees of a spurious gentility in the West-End paradise where they delight to display their painted faces and their gilded fans, we shall now endeavour to state articulately the peculiar features of excellence in the *Volkslied*, or popular song, which have always secured to it a place of honour in the hearts of the wise and the good and the healthy-minded of all nations. And here, generally, we may say that the song of the people is natural, not artistical; catholic, not special, breathing always the common breath of humanity modified by nationality, but affording no field for the display of individual talent, abnormal genius, or brilliant transcendentalism. In Shelley's poetry you always see Shelley, and in Byron's Byron; but in "Bonnie Jean" and "Wandering Willie," though you may know that there was a Burns, you never feel personally that he is there. In his songs, whatever he may be in his letters, Scotland is everywhere, Burns nowhere. Art, of course, and personality, in one sense, there must be in all excellent presentation of the beautiful; but in popular song it is an art which does not parade itself, and a personality in the human love that stirred it.[1] Popular song is opposed to what is called literature, as the rich melodious roll of full joyous vitality from the throat of a mavis or a blackbird in the month of May is to the deft execution of agile fingers on the keynotes of a piano; or as the roll and the swell and the swirl of waters in a Highland stream is to the start, and the leap, and the dash of an artificial waterfall at a German Wilhelmshöhe, or other prettily got up display of the non-natural picturesque; or again, we may say that the poetry of the people is to the poetry of sentimental young gentlemen saying pretty things, as the native dances of the peasantry in any country are to the exhibition of highly strained muscle and curiously supple joints in the dances of professional ballet-dancers, which no doubt are wonderful performances, but are apt to sin as much against the simplicity of true art as the

---

[1] This subordination of the personal element explains the fact, so noticeable in some of the best of our Scotch songs, that nobody knows who wrote them; or as Chambers has it (Poetry before Burns, ch. xii.), in looking over the roll of the most popular of our old songs, we constantly stumble on the phenomenon of "striking incidents inimitably crystallised into verse through the medium of some mind that was poetical without knowing what poetry was;"—only another illustration of what the sweet singer of Israel said (Psalm viii. 2), "Out of the mouth of babes and sucklings Thou hast perfected praise."

modesty of nature. Then as to personal peculiarities, individuals may easily deflect from the line of typical truth in nature, either by some congenital want of balance, or in the delight in the exhibition of a strong point which turns art into mannerism and caricature; but the seduction which leads the professional artist, or the original genius of a literary age, into this aberration, for the maker of a popular song does not exist. He is always true in tone, because he has no motive to be false; he must stir the popular heart by touching a universally human heartstring, otherwise he is nothing. He does not live in an age or move in an atmosphere where literary cliques will make a pet of his foibles, and pay an idol-worship to his eccentricities. In this way he is practically infallible, because nature is infallible; and whosoever is moved simply and singly by the direct indication and inspiration of nature cannot go wrong. It is with poetry as with philosophy and morals, as Cicero has it,—not the novelty which makes people stare, but the truth which makes people feel, is most agreeable to the nature of man: "*quod verum simplex, sincerumque sit, id est naturæ hominis aptissimum.*"[1] And as nature in her normal presentation always means health, and health means cheerfulness, so the song of the people is never falsely delicate, or sentimentally morbid, or artificially sublime, but healthy and vigor-

[1] Cicero, Off., i. 4.

ous, of fine texture, strong nerve, and ruddy hue, manly and valorous, ever wise to temper laughter with grace and to sweeten sorrow with resignation. A second notable point in the poetry of the people, and eminently of our Scottish popular song, is its practical wisdom and thoughtful humour: for the general mass of the people, trained as they are in the school of stern work and honest struggle, have too much stout earnestness in their habit to find any satisfaction in the dainty conceits and petty affectations that flatter the vanity, or tickle the ears, or dangle about the skirts of persons with whom life has no sequence of earnest work to ennoble it. The poetry of the people, like their life, must be intensely real; and practical wisdom, or the harmonious dealing with the facts of life, is the only form of reality that has any claim to shape itself into song. As for the humour which we find so abundant in our Scottish national songs, that is a part of the wisdom of life with which an earnest people like the Scotch could not do without; for as a sportive play with the high and the low, the great and the small, in human fates, it acts as a foil of fence against the serious invasion of sad thoughts that, if allowed full swing, might seriously incommode, overload, and overwhelm us. We may say, indeed, of the humour of a true Scotsman, as it appears in his popular songs and in his representative men, what Wolfgang Menzel said in reply to certain of his countrymen who spoke contemptuously of the English as a people having no philosophy. "Excuse me, sirs," said the great German critic—"*Verzeihen sie mir. John Bull ist ein grosser Philosoph: sein Humor ist seine Philosophie.*" "John Bull is a great philosopher: his humour is his philosophy."

I conclude these remarks on the general literary value and social significance of popular, and specially Scottish, song, by giving the opinion of two very different men— but both, from their special field of experience, entitled to speak on this subject with an authority that will weigh more with the intelligent than whole volumes of commendatory dissertation. The first is that great spokesman of our thoughtful cousins, the Germans, whom Matthew Arnold has quaintly and truly characterised as the greatest poet of our times, and the greatest critic of all times.

"POETRY AND POPULAR LIFE—THE GREEKS—BURNS.

"We admire the tragedies of the ancient Greeks; but, to take a correct view of the case, we ought to admire the period and the nation in which their production was possible, rather than the individual authors; for, though these pieces differ in some points from each other, and though one of these poets appears somewhat greater and more finished than the other, still, taking all things together, only one decided character runs through the whole. This is the character of grandeur, fitness, soundness, human perfection, elevated wisdom, sublime thought, pure strong intuition, and other qualities one might enumerate. But when we find all these qualities, not only in the dramatic works which have come down to us, but also in their lyrical and epic works—in the philosophers, orators, and historians—and in an equally high degree in the works of plastic art that have come down to us,—we must feel convinced that such qualities did not merely belong to individuals, but were the current property of the nation and the period.

"Now, take up Burns. How is he great, except through the circumstance that the songs of his predecessors lived in the mouth of the people—that they were, so to speak, sung at his cradle; that, as a boy, he grew up amongst them, and the high excellence of these models so pervaded him that he had therein a living basis on which he could proceed further? Again, why is he great but from this, that his own songs at once found susceptible ears amongst his compatriots; that, sung by reapers and sheaf-binders, they at once greeted him in the field; and that his boon-companions sang them to welcome him at the alehouse?

"POPULAR SONGS AND BALLADS.

"The special value of what we call national songs, or ballads, is that their inspiration comes fresh from nature.

They are never got up; they flow from a pure spring. The poet of a literary age might avail himself of this advantage, if he only knew how. There is always one thing, however, in which the former assert their advantage. The unsophisticated man is more the master of direct effective expression in few words than he who has received a regular literary training." [1]

My second witness is from an altogether opposite quarter of the literary world, as far below the common platform of cultivated intellect as Goethe was above it—a poor Aberdeenshire weaver, and for one stretch of his short career a wandering penniless pedlar,—William Thom of Inverury, one of that noble army of untitled and untutored minstrels whose productions have done, and are still doing, more to make rich the blood and strong the pulse of Scotland than all the vaunted Greek and Latin of the schools.

"Moore was doing all he could for love-sick boys and girls, yet they never had enough. Nearer and dearer to hearts like ours was the Ettrick Shepherd, then in his full tide of song and story; but nearer and dearer still than he or any tuneful songster was our ill-fated fellow-craftsman Tannahill! Poor weaver child, what we owe to you!

[1] Wisdom of Goethe, by J. S. B., pp. 110, 136, from Eckermann's Conversations.

Your 'Braes o' Balquhidder,' and 'Yon Burnside,' and 'Gloomy Winter,' and the minstrel's wailing ditty, and the noble 'Gleniffer,'—oh, how did they ring above the rattle of a thousand shuttles! Let me again proclaim the debt we owe to these song-spirits, as they walked in melody from loom to loom, ministering to the lone-hearted; and, when the breast was filled with everything but hope and happiness, let only break out the healthy and vigorous chorus, 'A man's a man for a' that,' and the fagged weaver brightens up. Who dare measure the restraining influences of these songs? To us all they were instead of sermons. Had one of us been bold enough to enter a church, he must have been ejected for the sake of decency. His forlorn and curiously patched habiliments would have contested the point of attraction with the ordinary pulpit eloquence of that period. Church bells rang not for us. Poets were indeed our priests: but for these, the last relics of moral existence would have passed away. Song was the dewdrop which gathered during the long night of despondency, and was sure to glitter in the very first blink of the sun. You might have seen 'Auld Robin Gray' melt the eyes that could be tearless amid cold and hunger, and weariness and pain."[1]

[1] Rhymes and Recollections of a Handloom Weaver, in Murray's Ballads and Songs of Scotland. London: 1874.

CHAPTER II.

SONGS OF LOVE, COURTSHIP, AND MARRIAGE.

> Ἔρως ἀνίκατε μάχαν,
> σε οὔτ' ἀθανάτων φύξιμος οὐδεὶς
> οὔθ' ἀμερίων ἀνθρώπων,
> ὁ δ' ἔχων μέμηνεν.
>
> SOPHOCLES.

IN the popular poetry of all countries, love-songs occupy a prominent place—generally, in fact, in one shape or other, stand in the van; and whosoever looks reverently into human motives, and the constitution of the universe, will find there a very good reason for this. Nearly three thousand years ago now, the old Bœotian theologer, Hesiod, with the close insight into the nature of things which distinguishes the genial mythology of the Greeks, sang of the creation, or, as they preferred to express it, generation of the world, to the effect that out of the primordial CHAOS the first two potencies to emerge were EARTH and HADES, and after them came forth "EROS or

LOVE; the most beautiful of all the immortals, whose thrilling power subdues the limbs of all gods and all men, and prevails even to control the soul, and to confound the counsel of the wisest sages."[1] This primeval theological Eros is a very different character from the little wanton boy with wings on his shoulders, and bow and arrows in his hand, who, from the days of Sappho and Alcæus downwards, has played such harmful sport with the hearts of susceptible young ladies, fervid young gentlemen, and Platonic young poets; but a theologico-philosophical figure as real as any in the creeds, and believed in as potently by the most profound thinkers and the most accurate scientists of the present day, as by any protesting Scot that ever talked of shooting himself for the sake of an Annie Laurie or a Bonnie Jean. It is, in fact, nothing less than what in the physical world we call attraction,—the power which gives electric affinities in the laboratory of the chemist, and the monogynic and polyandric alliances of the vegetable inflorescence. In the moral world, as a higher platform for the display of cognate divine mysteries, the same force dominates everywhere. An absolutely single self-contained loveless human soul, a Mephistopheles made up of sneering all round, is a monster of the most rare occurrence; and we must say roundly that in the great

[1] Hesiod, Theog., 116.

symphony of kindred existences which we call life, every human being instinctively seeks some cognate other to make his complement, just as one note in music demands another to make a harmony. The most impassioned poets, and the most stoical philosophers, have agreed in enunciating this great law of love, which pervades the universe, as, in fact, the great selecting and appropriating power which makes a universe possible, and, as the good old Bœotian plainly means, causes the hubbub of confusion in chaos to blossom into an orderly cosmos. So the most metaphysical of our poets, Percy Bysshe Shelley, has it—

> "Nothing in the world is single:
> All things by a law divine
> In one another's being mingle;
> Then why not I with thine?"

So the grand old imperial Stoic, Marcus Aurelius: "We are born for one another, as the teeth of the upper jaw for the teeth of the under jaw;"—a common illustration, no doubt, but conveying a profound truth, which Whig and Tory, and other antagonistic parties in Church and State, would do well to recognise. One other witness I will adduce from the wisest of the wise poets of the Greeks—for with the Greeks a poet was always a σοφός—to prove not only the universality but the sovereignty of this noble affection—a sovereignty so absolute as to make the persons who are the subjects of it, when contrasted with those not under its sway, appear mad; and mad indeed they are, not with the human madness which disturbs the machinery, but with the divine madness that intensifies the steam force of the brain. Sophocles in the "Antigone" sings thus:—

> "O, Love unvanquished in the fight,
> Then when thou puttest forth thy might
> O'er hearts and homes of men;
> Or where the gloss is soft and fair
> On maiden's cheek, thou lodgest there,
> Or o'er wide seas dost bravely swim,
> Breasting the billows foamy rim,
> Or watching by a wattled pen
> With shepherds in a grassy glen;
> Whate'er thy place, whate'er thy shape,
> Thy craft no being can escape,
> Nor man, nor god, nor lass, nor lad;
> And he who owns thy sway is MAD!"

And if so, then we certainly have to do not only with a very sacred matter which demands pious cherishing, but with a delicate affair which requires careful regulation—for the more divine the draught, the greater the danger that poor human nature may drink to intoxication; and the stronger the steam, the greater need to guard against explosion. But, though nature forbids excess, she does not enjoin abstinence: she triumphs in control. In love, as in all other matters, total abstinence is the shield of weakness, and the despair of virtue. If you have no nerve to run any risk, better not try the game. Better not fight at all, than fight to encounter an adversary to whom you are sure you must succumb. But this chief and wholesale way of avoiding the dangers of falling in love, Nature generally does not allow. The great principle to hold by here is, as Aristotle has it, that man must always love according to the characteristic excellency of his human nature, as a reasonable being made in the image of the Supreme Reason, as a self-dominant Power, not a mere servile devotee of an instinct which he shares with the lowest animals. This is an idea common to Aristotle and Moses, from which not only love but all human emotions must receive their legitimate consecration. In the somewhat severe religiousness of Scotland, devout consecration is popularly connected only with the stern sanction of the moral law; the admiration of beauty is left to poetical fancy, which has nothing to do with the sanctifying power of the Gospel. But this is a mistake. The True, the Beautiful, and the Good,—these three, a sort of natural Trinity,—are equally divine, but not equally necessary. The blossom of Beauty is appropriated by Love; the facts of growth by science; the fruit of growth by goodness: but all equally have their root in God. Divorced from God, love degenerates into lust, science into a cold calculation of heartless and purposeless forces; and goodness becomes impossible. In other words, there must always be in man, so long as he does not disown himself, an aristocratic element that justly holds rule,— what the Stoics, those grand gospellers of antiquity, called the ἡγεμονικόν. There is a spiritual and a carnal or material element in all existence, of which the one is the natural lord of the other. Wherever this relationship is reversed, wherever the servant usurps the mastership (Eccles. x. 7) on his own motive, as if no master were necessary, there we have divorce, rebellion, and usurpation, with the natural sequence of degradation and ruin. Love in its human nobility can no more be separated from holiness than beauty from health. Undermine the health, and the beauty vanishes. As the paint from a thousand rouge-boxes cannot restore the divine virtue of the vital flush which belongs to health, so no attractions, no graces, no endearments, no accomplishments, no witchery of smiles, no fascination of glances, can confer dignity on that love which has disowned the supremacy of a moral ideal. It is better to be cool and creeping with the most prosaic of earth-treading mortals, than to be winged with a rapture that does not bring us nearer to the gods.

Love, therefore, in the wide and philosophical sense of the term, is the name for those emotional feelers, so to speak, with which the God-created soul of man rapturously and reverentially lays hold of the God-created beauty which blossoms and burgeons everywhere in this beautiful world; and the love with which we have to do in our popular love-songs, the love of fair women, is for obvious reasons the most popular and universally appreciated species of the genus. If we may define love in the widest sense to be the impassioned admiration of congenial excellence, or the rapturous recognition of an ideal, where can we find this ideal more potently operating than in that fair being, the necessary complement of the sinless Adam, in whom the beauty that charms every sense in the rose and the lily and the violet of the fields is elevated by intellect, harmonised by grace, and ennobled by character? The man, if there be such a creature, who is not moved by this display of the matchless skill of the great Fountain of all being, is a poor creature, and less than a brute; for brute creatures, as Darwin teaches, make selection of fair feathers for procreative purposes sometimes; but such a loveless, unimpassioned, unfeathered human biped, capable only as a scientist of registering dry bones, or as a gentleman of fashion surrounding himself with the glittering show of the mere externalities of life, is a monster of whom nothing can be expected in any wise worthy of the human name which he bears. Truly Anacreon was right when he sang—what the history of many wars and of many courts, of many evangelists and of many wise men, largely proves—that there is no power on earth in the hand of God sometimes more mighty for achieving the noblest ends in the most pleasant way than a beautiful woman, when she is a woman indeed in all the completeness of her divine dual nature,—not a mere well-put-together, well-chiselled, well-coloured, and well-dressed piece of flesh and blood, in which virtues she may be matched, and overmatched, by many a plumy bird, or light-footed fawn upon the mountains. Hear what the merry old bard of Teos says in the Iambic lines beginning with Φύσις κέρατα ταόροις, which, while translating, we shall venture to expand by way of adaptation to our modern life:—

>Nature gave hoofs to horses, horns to bulls,
>Far-ranging thought to men, laughter to fools,
>To birds fleet pinions, a sharp nose to dogs,
>Running to hares, and leaping power to frogs,
>To fishes fins, to monkeys nimble tails,
>Talons to eagles, mighty jaws to whales,
>To lawyers tongues, to dancing girls agility,
>To editorial scribes infallibility,
>Learning to scholars, to good boys apple-pies,
>To churchmen pride, to politicians lies,
>Money to brewers, shopkeepers, and bankers,
>To the wise man a heart that's free from cankers,
>To woman, what? so slender, slim, and slight,
>'Mid coarse-grained things of masterdom and might;
>She gave weak woman *Beauty*, with a power
>More strong than fire or iron, as her dower.

And, if the voluptuous old singer of sunny Ionia felt this power so strongly, our own Robert Burns, the stout son of the cloudy North, owed the greater part of his literary reputation to the wise worship, and some part of his social offences to the unwise worship, of the fair sex. In reference to this dominant passion of the man who has been baptised by one of his admirers "the Laureate of love," his sister, Mrs Begg, with equal humour and truth, remarked, "Robin had aye an unco wark wi' the lasses. I wonder what he saw in them. I prefer a lad to the whole lot of them!" No doubt; for the element of sex comes in here, as also the important principle enunciated by Plato in The Banquet, that the grand attractive force of love in the physical and in the moral world makes itself felt by contraries in some points, as much as by correspondence in others. The poet himself, who is always honest in his confessions, and given to use language as a song-writer with a strong lyrical accentuation, has expressed himself on this subject in several notable passages. In one short phrase he calls woman "the blood-royal of creation"; and in one of his impassioned letters to Clarinda we read, "He who sees you and does not love you, deserves to be damned for his stupidity; and he who loves you and would injure you, to be doubly damned for his villainy." Not less strong is the language with which he expresses his admiration of the beautiful Miss Burnet, daughter of the celebrated scholar and philosopher, Lord Monboddo, one of that bright array of beauty and culture to which the ploughman bard was introduced during his visit to Edinburgh, and whose aristocratic splendour caused the ill-starred adventure with "Bonnie Jean" to be thought of with less regret for a season. "The heavenly Miss Burnet," says he in a letter to Mr Chalmers, written in December 1786; "there has not been anything nearly like her in all the combinations of beauty, grace, and goodness the great Creator has formed since Milton's Eve on the first day of her existence." But with these glowing superlatives for this unequalled specimen of the Divine workmanship in the shape of woman, the taste of Burns was as remarkable for its catholicity as for its intensity. "When I meet," he writes to one of his fair female correspondents, "with a person after my own heart, I positively feel what an orthodox Protestant would call a species of idolatry, which works on my fancy like inspiration; and I can no more resist rhyming than an Æolian harp can refuse its tones to the streaming air. A distich or two would be the consequence, though the object which hit my fancy were grey-bearded age; but when my theme is youth and beauty,—a young lady whose personal charms, wit, and sentiment are equally striking and unaffected,—ye heavens! though I had lived threescore years a married man, and threescore years before I was married, my imagination would hallow the very idea!"[1]—a passage which gives us a penetrating glance into the inmost heart of our great ploughman's inspiration, and which at the same time carries with it the most important moral, that fair ladies given to be touched by the mean passion of jealousy should never marry poets.

We see, therefore, there is a double reason for giving love-songs the leading place in this little book—the general reason of the catholicity of the passion in all well-constituted minds, and the special reason of these songs having been placed by the genius of our great national lyrist on a pedestal of classicality overtopped by none in the rich repertory of popular song. Wherever a love-song of the purest and best quality is felt and understood, from the Ganges to the St Lawrence—wherever the sun shines on the wide empire of Queen Victoria—there the name of Burns is named with the first. But we must not suppose that in this chapter we have to deal only, or mainly, with the songs of the farmer of Ellisland. The love-songs of Scotland are as rich and various as the flowers of the field, and poured out from all quarters as spontaneously and as sweetly as the song of

[1] Burns to Miss Davies—Currie, ii. No. lxi.

the mavis in May. Of course, in the midst of such abundance I could only form a bouquet of the choicest gems of song that had either laid strong hold of my fancy, or had struck deep roots in the popular affection; and when I had chalked out my scheme of classification, I was not a little surprised, and at the same time delighted, to find that only a small proportion of the whole belonged to the Coryphæus of the Choir. This, of course, proves the extraordinary wealth of our lyrical vegetation. Burns, in fact, never would have been the man he was, had he not derived an inspiration from the people, and breathed an atmosphere of popular song from the cradle; and to stand before his countrymen in the solitary sublimity of a Shelley or a Byron, would have been as hateful to his nature as it was foreign from his genius. I will therefore, in this bouquet of love-lilts, give no preference to Burns, except where he comes in unsought for as the first among equals, the most prominent, and the most popular specimen of the class which he is called on to illustrate; and the classes under which all love-songs naturally arrange themselves are four: love-songs of joy; love-songs of sadness; love-songs of wooing and courtship; and lastly, love-songs of marriage and connubial life.

I begin then now with—

Love-Songs of Joy,

—as indeed joy is the end of all existence; and love, as the rapturous recognition of an ideal, is, and must ever be, the potentiation of the highest human joy; and if there be any that would give a preference to woful ballads and sentimental sighs in their singing of love-songs, let them know that they are out of tune with the great harmonies of Nature, and that, though it be the divine virtue of love-songs, in certain cases, to sweeten sorrow, their primary purpose is to give wings to joy. As an example of the sweetness of soul and sereneness of delight that belong to the Scottish love-song, we cannot do better than commence here with—

When the Kye comes Hame.

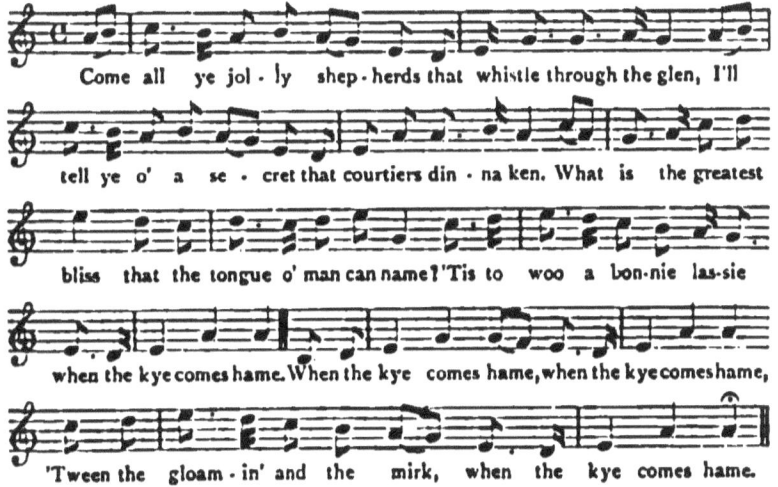

Come all ye jol-ly shep-herds that whistle through the glen, I'll tell ye o' a se-cret that courtiers din-na ken. What is the greatest bliss that the tongue o' man can name? 'Tis to woo a bon-nie las-sie when the kye comes hame. When the kye comes hame, when the kye comes hame, 'Tween the gloam-in' and the mirk, when the kye comes hame.

'Tis not beneath the burgonet, nor yet beneath the crown,
'Tis not on couch of velvet, nor yet on bed of down:
'Tis beneath the spreading birch, in the dell without a name,
Wi' a bonnie, bonnie lassie, when the kye comes hame.

Then the eye shines sae bright, the haill soul to beguile,
There's love in every whisper, and joy in every smile;
O who would choose a crown, wi' its perils and its fame,
And miss a bonnie lassie when the kye comes hame.

See yonder pawky shepherd that lingers on the hill—
His yowes are in the fauld, and his lambs are lying still;
Yet he downa gang to rest, for his heart is in a flame
To meet his bonnie lassie when the kye comes hame.

Awa' wi' fame and fortune—what comfort can they gie?—
And a' the arts that prey on man's life and libertie!
Gie me the highest joy that the heart o' man can frame,
My bonnie, bonnie lassie, when the kye comes hame.

In this beautiful lyric observe three things—the persons, the scenery, and the season of the year. It was long a fashion to identify lovers with shepherds or swains, till the affectation and the triteness of the notion made the Muse sick of it; but it nevertheless had reason in it, as the life of a shepherd is far more favourable both to thoughtful meditation and to tender contemplation than professions that put forth their energies amid the bustle of business, the whir of industrial wheels, or the parade of public life. The man who composed this song was a shepherd living in a land of shepherds, and in him it could be no affectation; but whether shepherd or not, the man who wishes to compose or quietly to enjoy a love-song, or, what is better, a loving soul, will more naturally transport himself to the green slopes and the broomy knowes of a quiet land of shepherds, than to the splendid roll of chariots in the Park at London, or the motley whirl of holiday-keepers on Hampstead Heath. The scenery of the best love-songs in all languages is decidedly rural. No doubt there may be love, and very wise love too, in a London lane, as "Sally in our Alley" and other songs abundantly testify; but they will want something to stamp on them the type of the highest classicality, and that something will be found not far from Yarrow braes and Ettrick shaws, "when the kye comes hame." Love in a green glade, or by a river side, or on a heather brae, is poetical; for there the living glory of the raptured soul within finds itself harmonised with the glory of the living mantle of the Godhead without: whereas love in a fashionable saloon, a gay drawing-room, or a glittering train of coaching gentility, is both less congruous on account of its artificial surroundings, and apt to degenerate into flirtation, which is a half-earnest imitation of the least earnest half of love. Observe also the season of the year, though indicated only by a single word in the song: "'Tis beneath the spreading birch," the most graceful, the most fragrant, and the most Scottish of all trees; and the birch spreads its tresses not till May or June. It is, therefore, in May, "when the birds sing a welcome to May, sweet May," and the "zephyrs as they pass make a pause to make love to the flowers,"[1] that love-songs should be aired and marriages made, if they are meant to be touched with the finest bloom of the poetry of Nature.

The author of this song, we said, was a shepherd, and we need scarcely say that the shepherd was Hogg—a name that will go down in literary tradition, along with Burns and Scott, John Wilson and Lord Cockburn, as typical representatives of the best virtues of the Scottish character in an age when Scotland had not begun to be ashamed of her native Muse, and to lose herself amid the splendid gentilities of the big metropolis on the Thames. In outward condition and social circumstance, Hogg was more nearly allied to Burns than to Scott: if Burns was a ploughman on the banks of Doon in Ayrshire, Hogg was first a cowherd, then a shepherd, and then a farmer, first in his own native parish of Ettrick, in the high land of Selkirkshire, and afterwards on Yarrow braes, not far from the sweet pastoral seclusion of St Mary's Loch. But in the tone of his mind, as well as the traditional influences of his birthplace, he belonged to Scott. In literature they

---

[1] Sweet May: words by J. Little. Music by A. Hume. Lyric Gems of Scotland, i. 96.

were both story-tellers rather than song-writers; and in politics they were both Conservatives, nourishing their souls in a sweet-blooded way on the heroic traditions and pleasant memories of their forefathers. The moving tales and strange legends from the fertile pen of the Shepherd, for generations to come, will help innocently to entertain the fancy of many an honest cottar's fireside in the long winter nights; while the strange unearthly weirdness of his " Fife Witch's " nocturnal ride, and the spiritual sweetness of his " Bonnie Kilmeny," will secure their author a high place among the classical masters of imaginative narrative in British literature; but his appearance on the field of narrative poetry in the same age with the more rich and powerful genius of Scott, was unfavourable to his asserting a permanent position as a poetical story-teller. It is as a song-writer, therefore, that he is likely to remain best known to the general public; for, though in this department he has no pretensions to the wealth or the power or the fire of Burns, he has prevailed to strike out a few strains of no common excellence, that have touched a chord in the popular heart and found an echo in the public ear: and this, indeed, is the special boast of good popular songs, that they are carried about as jewels and as charms in the breast of every man that has a heart, while intellectual works of a more imposing magnitude, like palatial castles, are seen only by the few who purposely go to see them or accidentally pass by them. Small songs are the circulating medium of the people. The big bullion lies in the bank.[1]

We proceed to instance a few other classical examples of that sweet pensive musing of the lover, quietly feeding upon beauty as the honey-bee feeds on the flower,—a cheerfulness and a lusciousness of pure emotion much more chaste, much more safe, and much more permanent than the passion which glows like a furnace, or the steam which threatens to explode. Take first one of Tannahill's, perhaps not the best, but certainly at one time the most popular of his love-songs:—

JESSIE, THE FLOWER O' DUNBLANE.

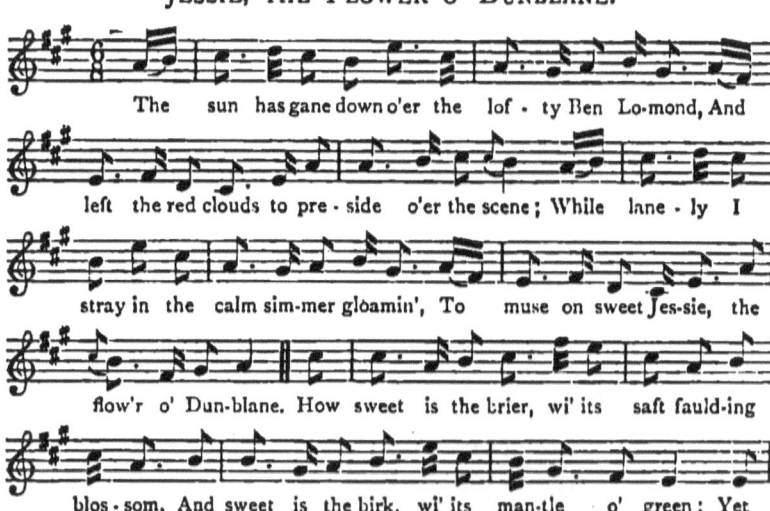

The sun has gane down o'er the lof-ty Ben Lo-mond, And left the red clouds to pre-side o'er the scene; While lane-ly I stray in the calm sim-mer gloamin', To muse on sweet Jes-sie, the flow'r o' Dun-blane. How sweet is the brier, wi' its saft fauld-ing blos-som, And sweet is the birk, wi' its man-tle o' green; Yet

---

[1] An excellent Life of Hogg will be found in Rogers's Scottish Minstrel, Edinburgh, 1870.

"Jessie o' Dunblane."

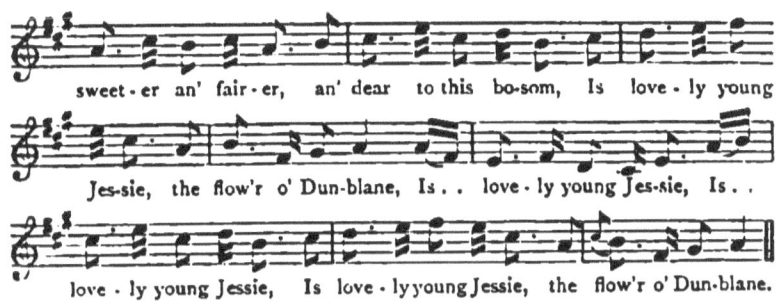

sweet-er an' fair-er, an' dear to this bo-som, Is love-ly young Jes-sie, the flow'r o' Dun-blane, Is .. love-ly young Jes-sie, Is .. love-ly young Jessie, Is love-ly young Jessie, the flow'r o' Dun-blane.

    She's modest as ony, an' blythe as she's bonnie,
        For guileless simplicity marks her its ain;
    An' far be the villain, divested o' feeling,
        Wha'd blight in its bloom the sweet flow'r o' Dunblane.
    Sing on, thou sweet mavis, thy hymn to the e'enin',
        Thou'rt dear to the echoes o' Calderwood glen;
    Sae dear to this bosom, sae artless and winning,
        Is charming young Jessie, the flow'r o' Dunblane.

It is recorded by those who are versed in the detailed history of Scottish song, that there never was such a Jessie beneath the shade of Leighton's grand old cathedral, and that Ben Lomond is not visible from that venerable haunt of Scottish Episcopacy called Dunblane,—a fact worthy of note, not because it in any wise detracts from the singable excellence of the song, but because it is in this respect an exception to the general character of Scottish songs, which always spring from a strong root in reality, never deal with imaginary persons,—an Amaryllis or an Amanda for the nonce,—and are in fact as true as a photograph to the person and place celebrated. Here is another ditty in a similar strain, composed by the poet under the immediate inspiration of the grassy slopes, wooded hills, dewy dells, and wimpling brooks of his own beautiful Renfrewshire; a poem which, for picturesqueness of pastoral scenery, is, I will venture to say, unsurpassed in the lyrical literature of any language, ancient or modern:—

GLOOMY WINTER'S NOO AWA'.

Gloom-y win-ter's noo a-wa', Saft the west-lin' breez-es blaw,
'Mang the birks o' Stan-ley shaw The ma-vis sings fu' cheer-ie, O.
Sweet the craw-flower's ear-ly bell, Decks Glen-if-fer's dew-y dell,
Bloom-in' like thy bon-nie sel', My young, my art-less dear-ie, O.
Come, my las-sie, let us stray O'er Glenkilloch's sun-ny brae,
Blythe-ly spend the gowden day, 'Midst joys that ne-ver wea-ry, O.

    Tow'ring o'er the Newton woods,
    Lav'rocks fan the snaw-white clouds,
    Siller saughs, wi' downy buds,
        Adorn the banks sae briery, O.

> Round the sylvan fairy nooks,
> Feath'ry breckans fringe the rocks,
> 'Neath the brae the burnie jouks,
>   And ilka thing is cheerie, O.
> Trees may bud, and birds may sing,
> Flowers may bloom and verdure spring,
> Joy to me they canna bring,
>   Unless wi' thee, my dearie, O.

Poor Tannahill! Paisley truly has good reason to be proud of her handloom weaver, who knew to mingle the whir of his busy loom, not with the jarring notes of political fret or atheistic pseudo-philosophy, but with the sweet music of Nature in the most melodious season of the year. Sad to think that the author of this song, one of the most lovable, kindly, and human-hearted of mortals, and who, in spite of the deficiencies of his early culture, had achieved a reputation second only to Burns among the song-writers of his tuneful fatherland, should have bade farewell to the sweet light of the sun and the fair greenery of his native glens at the early age of thirty-six—drowning himself, poor fellow! in a pool not far from the place of his birth. "Frail race of mortals, these poets!" some one will be quick to exclaim. "Burns and Byron died at thirty-seven, Shelley at thirty, Keats at twenty-six, and Kirke White even younger. Let no man envy the gift of song, and seek to batten on the delicious food that is seasoned with poison and sauced with death!" But this is a mistake. Many poets live long, and the biggest often the longest. Anacreon lived long, Sophocles lived long, Chaucer lived long, Goethe lived long, Wordsworth lived long, Southey lived long, Wilson lived within a year of the legitimate seventy, and Scott, had it not been for unfortunate commercial mishaps, which caused him to overstrain his powers, with another decade added to his years, had stuff in him to rival that rich union of mellow thought and melodious verse which all men admire in the octogenarian poet-thinker of Weimar. It is not poets, but a particular kind of poets, that die early: they had some unhappy ferment in their blood, that would have made them die early, as men, had they never written a verse. It was not poetry that killed Robert Burns; it was untempered passion: it was not poetry that drowned Tannahill; it was constitutional weakness.

It would be unfair, in recalling the image of the great Paisley songster, not to mention the distinguished musical composer to whose friendly aid he owed no small share of his abiding popularity. Robert Archibald Smith, though born in Reading, was of Scotch descent, and restored to his native country in the year 1800, when he was twenty years of age. A native of East Kilbride, his father had followed the profession of silk-weaving at Paisley; and on his return from Reading, betook himself to the weaving of muslin in that town. The son, following the father's lines, commenced likewise as a weaver of webs; but he was too often found scratching crotchets and quavers on the framework of the loom, when he ought to have been watching the interlacings or the snappings of the thread. The starvation of his intellectual strivings by the monotony of the loom operated disadvantageously on a constitution not naturally strong; and the depression of spirits into which he was falling acted as a wise warning for his father to let the poor bird out of the cage, and be free to flap his wings in the musical atmosphere for which he was born. He accordingly threw the loom aside, and commenced a distinguished musical career, first as leader of the choir in the Abbey Church, Paisley, and then in St George's Church, Edinburgh, where he enjoyed the stimulating and influential fellowship of Dr Andrew Thomson, a theologian distinguished not less for his refined musical taste than for the warmth of his evangelical zeal, and the slashing vigour of his polemics. While holding this situation, he sent forth a series of well-known and highly esteemed musical publications, both in the sacred and secular sphere of the noble art which he professed; and, though he had but finished half what might have been prophesied as his destined career, he achieved enough to cause his name to be remembered in the history of Scottish culture as the pioneer of a new era, and the first mover in a necessary reform. The church service of Scotland had suffered too long from the barbarism of a certain Puritanical severity that had no better reason for the neglect of music in religious worship than that it was cherished by the Romanists and the Episcopalians; and the name of R. A. Smith, the friend and fellow-songster of Tannahill, will live in the grateful memory of the Scottish people as the herald of the advent of a wiser age which reconciles devotion to her natural ally music, and removes from Presbytery the reproach of cultivating only the bald prose of the temple service, while the graces of the divinest of the arts are left in the exclusive possession of other churches, whose doctrine may be less sound, and their preaching less effective, but whose attitude is more dignified, and whose dress is more attractive.[1]

We shall content ourselves with three more specimens of this initiatory stage of present sweetness and prospective joy in love, and then pass to songs of wooing and courting, which, while they are more richly marked by dramatic situation and incident, are at the same time seldom free from difficulties and entanglements of various kinds, over which even the persistency that belongs to all strong instincts and noble passions cannot always triumph. The first is the popular Dumfriesshire song of—

---

[1] For full particulars with regard both to Tannahill and Smith, see The Works of Tannahill. A. Fullarton & Co., Edinburgh.

ANNIE LAURIE.

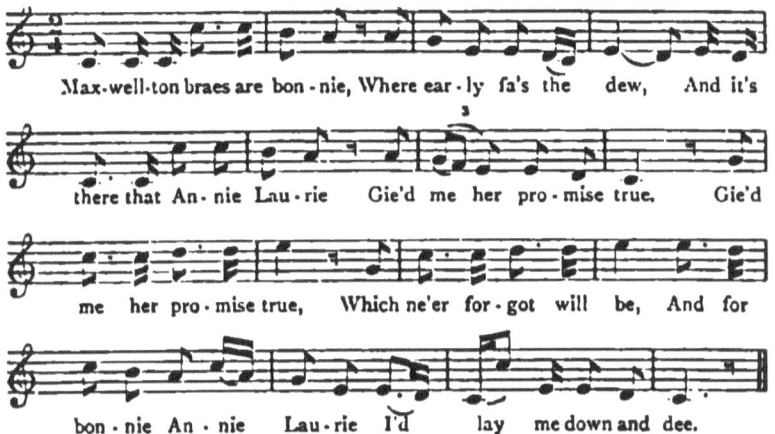

Max-well-ton braes are bon-nie, Where ear-ly fa's the dew, And it's there that An-nie Lau-rie Gie'd me her pro-mise true. Gie'd me her pro-mise true, Which ne'er for-got will be, And for bon-nie An-nie Lau-rie I'd lay me down and dee.

    Her brow is like the snaw-drift,
      Her neck is like the swan,
    Her face it is the fairest
      That e'er the sun shone on—
    That e'er the sun shone on,
      And dark blue is her e'e;
    And for bonnie Annie Laurie
      I'd lay me down and dee.

    Like dew on the gowan lying
      Is the fa' o' her fairy feet;
    And like winds in summer sighing,
      Her voice is low and sweet—
    Her voice is low and sweet,
      And she's a' the world to me;
    And for bonnie Annie Laurie
      I'd lay me down and dee.

The heroine of this song was, as Chambers informs us,[1]

[1] Chambers's Scottish Songs (Edinburgh, 1829), p. 284.

a daughter of Sir Robert Laurie, first Baronet of Maxwelton; and the devoted admirer who sang her praises was a Mr Douglas of Fingland. It may be interesting to compare the above verses, as now commonly sung, with the original verses as given by Chambers:—

>Maxwelton braes are bonnie
> Where early fa's the dew;
>Where me and Annie Laurie
> Made up the promise true—
>Made up the promise true,
> And never forget will I;
>And for bonnie Annie Laurie
> I'll lay me down and die.
>
>She's backit like the peacock,
> She's briestit like the swan;
>She's jimp about the middle,
> Her waist ye weel micht span—
>Her waist ye weel micht span,
> And she has a rolling eye;
>And for bonnie Annie Laurie
> I'll lay me down and die.

Our second is

OWRE THE MUIR AMANG THE HEATHER.

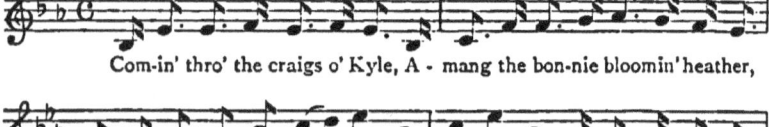
Com-in' thro' the craigs o' Kyle, A - mang the bon-nie bloomin' heather,
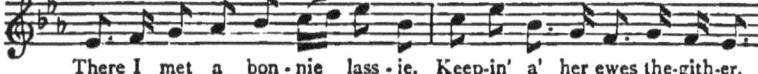
There I met a bon-nie lass-ie, Keep-in' a' her ewes the-gith-er.

Says I, my dear, where is thy hame
   In muir, or dale, pray tell me whether?
Says she, I tent thae fleecy flocks
   That feed amang the blooming heather.
                        Owre the muir, &c.

We sat us down upon a bank,
   Sae warm and sunny was the weather:
She left her flocks at large to rove
   Amang the bonnie blooming heather.
                        Owre the muir, &c.

She charmed my heart, and aye sinsyne
   I couldna think on ony ither;
By sea and sky! she shall be mine,
   The bonnie lass amang the heather.
                        Owre the muir, &c.

This song comes to us with a whiff of the mountain heather, particularly grateful and specially salubrious in an age when so much of the best music is condemned to be sung in the hot air of fashionable saloons, where the poetry of Nature is utterly ignored and the laws of health systematically violated. The authoress was Jean Glover, a Kilmarnock girl, who had the misfortune to unite her fates in life to a pleasant fellow, a strolling-player or mountebank, with whom she travelled over the country, frequenting fairs and markets, supporting herself and entertaining the public with show and song in an irregular sort of way. Burns, who picked up the song from her in one of her strolling expeditions, has spoken of her in very disparaging terms (for which see Chambers, p. 49); but his severe judgment, in Miss Tytler's delightful work on 'The Songstresses of Scotland,' receives a kindly mitigation. She died at Letterkenny, in Ireland, when not much past the middle term of life. It requires very little knowledge of human nature to know that the power of striking out a good song is no guarantee for the steady march or the fruitful issue of a well-rounded life-drama. Sensibility finds a vent in song; purpose shapes a career.

Our third song differs from this in being a song of absence of the beloved one; and yet it is a song of pure and placid enjoyment, as the arrival of the fair from her sojourn beyond the western hills was near and certain. It was written by Burns shortly after his settlement on his farm at Ellisland on the Nith, when his house was not yet ready for the reception of Jean Armour, to whom, after many plunges and variations of passion, he had at last been firmly united in the bonds of honourable wedlock. Jean was with her father at Mauchline, in Ayrshire, where the poet had first made her acquaintance, and was now preparing to make her final flitting eastward with due equipment of marriage gifts, when her expectant mate was crooning these beautiful lines with his face to the west :—

O' A' THE AIRTS THE WIND CAN BLAW.

O' a' the airts the wind can blaw, I dearly lo'e the west; For there the bonnie lassie lives, The lass that I lo'e best; Tho' wild woods grow, an' rivers row, Wi' mony a hill between, Baith day and night my fancy's flight Is ever wi' my Jean.

I see her in the dewy flow'r, Sae lovely sweet an' fair; I hear her voice in ilka bird, Wi' music charms the air; There's no' a bonnie flow'r that springs By fountain, shaw, or green, Nor yet a bonnie bird that sings, But minds me o' my Jean.

    O blaw, ye westlin' winds, blaw saft,
        Amang the leafy trees;
    Wi' gentle gale, frae muir and dale,
        Bring hame the laden bees;

An' bring the lassie back to me
    That's aye sae neat an' clean;
Ae blink o' her wad banish care,
    Sae lovely is my Jean.

What sighs an' vows amang the knowes
    Ha'e past atween us twa;
How fain to meet, how wae to part,
    That day she gaed awa'.
The powers aboon can only ken,
    To whom this heart is seen,
That nane can be sae dear to me
    As my sweet lovely Jean.

We now advance to the incidents of courtship, and the stages that lead towards matrimony. By the law of Nature, the man, as the more energetic creature, makes the advance; but, though he is more forward to march, the woman, as of a more sensitive and specially loving nature, is often more quick to feel; and so, from the time of Solomon downwards, in all lyrico-dramatic expressions of the divine passion of love, she is put forward as a principal speaker. Of this we have in our Scottish repertory some admirable examples, in which the quiet, graceful, sly humour so characteristic of our people gleams forth in all its fascinating simplicity. The persons who are called in to work out the dramatic situation here are the persons most nearly allied to the prospective bride, and most interested in her proposed change of state—the mother and the sisters; interested nobly and wisely no doubt, in many cases, partly as experienced in the serious step about to be taken, partly from their unimpassioned position as impartial judges of the merits of the lover; but, in some cases, also ignobly and foolishly moved to thwart the desire of the loved one, whether from a lust of dictation, unreasonable prejudice, impertinent intermeddling, or it may be even a petty jealousy. But, whatever the motive of the objectors may be, where there is real love on both sides, the impassioned sister, if she be a woman of purpose and worth having for a wife, in nine cases out of ten with a little patience and a little management will have her own way, as in the following ditty, too rarely sung, which smacks of the good old times when Nature was not afraid to be Nature, and women could express their preference for a well-accentuated kiss without being supposed to be coarse:—

KIND ROBIN LO'ES ME.

Ro-bin is my on-ly jo, For Ro-bin has the art to lo'e, So to his suit I mean to bow, Be-cause I ken he lo'es me. Hap-py, hap-py

60 Songs of Love, Courtship, and Marriage.

was the show'r, That led me to his birk-en bow'r, Where first o' love I fand the pow'r, And kenn'd that Ro-bin lo'ed me.

Old Air for last four lines, from Macfarlane MS. 1740.

O hey, Ro-bin, quo' she, O hey, Ro-bin, quo' she, O hey, Ro-bin, quo' she, Kind Ro-bin lo'es me.

They speak o' napkins, speak o' rings,
Speak o' gloves and kissing strings,
And name a thousand bonnie things,
   And ca' them signs he lo'es me.
But I'd prefer a smack o' Rob,
Sporting on the velvet fog,
To gifts as lang's a plaiden wab,
   Because I ken he lo'es me.

He's tall and sonsy, frank and free,
Lo'ed by a', and dear to me;
Wi' him I'd live, wi' him I'd dee,
   Because my Robin lo'es me!
My sister Mary said to me
Our courtship but a joke wad be,
And I, or lang, be made to see
   That Robin didna lo'e me.

But little kens she what has been
Me and my honest Rob between,
And in his wooing, O so keen
   Kind Robin is that lo'es me.

> Then fly, ye lazy hours, away,
> And hasten on the happy day,
> When "Join your hands," Mess John shall say,
>   And mak' him mine that lo'es me.
>
> Till then let every chance unite
> To weigh our love, and fix delight,
> And I'll look down on such wi' spite
>   Wha doubt that Robin lo'es me.
> O hey, Robin, quo' she,
> O hey, Robin, quo' she,
> O hey, Robin, quo' she,
>   Kind Robin lo'es me.

But it is the mother, of course, that has the principal interest in the marriage of her daughters; and acting on the wise principle of *obsta principiis*, she will naturally put herself forward with a troublesome prominence to both parties. We have one song with the burden to this effect :—

> " My mither's aye glowrin' o'er me,
>   Though she did the same before me ;
> I canna get leave to look at my love,
>   Or else she'd be like to devour me ! "

In another admirable skit of humour, the mothers are roundly declared to be "a bore." All persons versed in the fine art of osculation know that behind the door is the proper place for stealing a taste of such sweet enjoyment, and not, as Burns did to his own shame and sorrow one night near Dumfries, marching up to the fair lady of the house in the middle of the drawing-room, and giving her a fervid salute on the lips, smelling more of wine than of poetry;[1] but not even behind the door, especially when the gentleman is unwisely emphatic, can a kiss always deceive the ears of the wakeful mother within:—

The Kiss ahint the Door.

O meikle bliss is in a kiss, Whyles mair than in a score; But wae be-tak' the stou-in' smack I took a-hint the door. O laddie, whisht, for sic a fricht I ne'er was in a-fore, Fu' brawly did my mither hear The kiss a-hint the door. The wa's are thick, ye need-na fear, But gin they jeer an' mock, I'll swear it was a start-it cork, Or wyte the rus-ty lock.—Cho.

   We stappit ben, while Maggie's face
    Was like a lowin' coal,
   An' as for me, I could hae crept
    Into a mouse's hole:

---

[1] Life of Burns, by J. S. B. (London, 1888), p. 136

The mither look't, sauff's how she look't!
  Thae mithers are a bore,
An' gleg as ony cat to hear
  A kiss ahint the door.
          O meikle, &c.

The douce gudeman, though he was there,
  As weel micht been in Rome,
For by the fire he fuffed his pipe,
  And never fash'd his thoom;
But tittrin' in a corner stood
  The gawky sisters four,
A winter's nicht for me they micht
  Hae stood ahint the door.
          O meikle, &c.

"How daur ye tak' sic freedoms here?"
  The bauld gudewife began;
Wi' that a foursome yell gat up,
  I to my heels an' ran;
A besom whisket by my lug,
  An' dishclouts half-a-score,
Catch me again, though fidgin' fain,
  At kissing 'hint the door.
          O meikle, &c.

The author of this song was Thomas C. Latto, born in December 1818, in the parish of Kingsbarns, in Fife. After studying at the University of St Andrews, he obtained his livelihood first by acting as a lawyer's clerk to two well-known Edinburgh gentlemen—the late John Hunter, auditor of the Court of Session, and Professor Aytoun, the bard of the Cavaliers—and then as commission agent in Glasgow, whence he removed to the United States and occupied himself with commercial and literary work in New York.

But more delicate and daintily sly in its humour, and indicative throughout of the master-hand of Burns, is the following :—

TAM GLEN.

There's Lowrie, the laird o' Drumeller,
  "Gude day to you," coof, he comes ben;
He brags and he blaws o' his siller,
  But when will he dance like Tam Glen?
My minnie does constantly deave me,
  And bids me beware o' young men;
They flatter, she says, to deceive me—
  But wha can think sae o' Tam Glen?

My daddie says, gin I'll forsake him,
  He'll gie me gude hunder merks ten;
But, if it's ordain'd I maun tak' him,
  O wha will I get but Tam Glen?
Yestreen, at the valentines' dealin',
  My heart to my mou' gied a sten';
For thrice I drew ane without failin',
  And thrice it was written—Tam Glen.

The last Hallowe'en I was waukin'
  My drookit sark sleeve, as ye ken,
His likeness cam' up the house staukin',
  And the very grey breeks o' Tam Glen.
Come, counsel, dear tittie, don't tarry;
  I'll gie ye my bonnie black hen,
Gin ye will advise me to marry
  The lad I lo'e dearly, Tam Glen.

Scarcely inferior to this stealing approval from the dear sister is the delicate tact with which the artful maiden works upon her father in the hiring of her lover for farm service; the words by Joanna Baillie, a lady of whom we shall have something to say by-and-by, when we come to the consummation of courting in actual marriage :—

SAW YE JOHNNIE COMIN'? QUO' SHE.

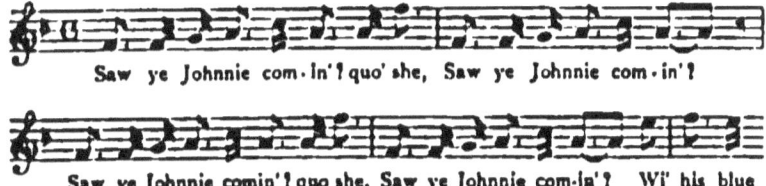

Saw ye Johnnie com-in'? quo' she, Saw ye Johnnie com-in'?
Saw ye Johnnie comin'? quo she, Saw ye Johnnie com-in'? Wi' his blue

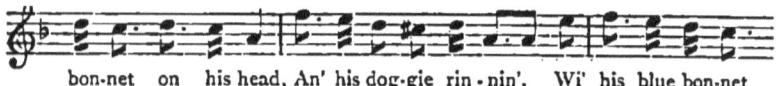
bon-net on his head, An' his dog-gie rin-nin'. Wi' his blue bon-net

on his head, An' his doggie rin-nin', quo' she, An' his dog-gie rin - nin'.

> Fee him, father, fee him, quo' she,
>   Fee him, father, fee him;
> Fee him, father, fee him, quo' she,
>   Fee him, father, fee him;
> For he is a gallant lad,
>   And a weel-doin';
> And a' the wark about the house
>   Gaes wi' me when I see him, quo' she,
>   Wi' me when I see him.
>
> What will I do wi' him, hizzie?
>   What will I do wi' him?
> He's ne'er a sark upon his back,
>   And I ha'e nane to gi'e him.
> I ha'e twa sarks into my kist,
>   And ane o' them I'll gi'e him,
> And for a merk o' mair fee
>   Dinna stand wi' him, quo' she,
>   Dinna stand wi' him.
>
> For weel do I lo'e him, quo' she,
>   Weel do I lo'e him;
> For weel do I lo'e him, quo' she,
>   Weel do I lo'e him.
> O fee him, father, fee him, quo' she,
>   Fee him, father, fee him;
> He'll haud the pleugh, thrash in the barn,
>   And crack wi' me at e'enin', quo' she,
>   And crack wi' me at e'enin'.

Let us now see how the gentlemen comport themselves. The following is a specimen in the direct old style, somewhat sudden and rough, no doubt—courtship and marriage at one bold stroke—but not the less honest for that, and not the less happy in its results. A brave woman likes a bold lover:—

MUIRLAND WILLIE.

O hearken and I will tell you how Young Muirland Willie cam' here to woo, Tho' he could neither say nor do; The truth I tell to you... But aye he cries what-e'er be-tide, Maggie I'se hae to be my bride, With a fal da ra, fal lal da ra la, fal lal da ra lal da ral la. . . .

On his gray yade as he did ride,
Wi' dirk and pistol by his side,
He prick'd her on wi' meikle pride,
    Wi' meikle mirth and glee,
Out o'er yon moss, out o'er yon muir,
Till he cam' to her daddie's door,
    With a fal da ra, &c.

Gudeman, quoth he, be ye within?
I'm come your dochter's love to win,
I carena for making meikle din;
    What answer gi'e ye me?
Now wooer, quoth he, would ye light down,
I'll gi'e ye my dochter's love to win,
    With a fal da ra, &c.

Now, wooer, sin' ye are lighted down,
Where do ye won, or in what town?
I think my dochter winna gloom
    On sic a lad as ye.
The wooer he stepp'd up the house,
And wow but he was wondrous crouse,
    With a fal da ra, &c.

The maid put on her kirtle brown;
She was the brawest in a' the town:
I wat on him she didna gloom,
    But blinkit bonnilie.
The lover he stended up in haste,
And gript her hard about the waist,
    With a fal da ra, &c.

The maiden blush'd and bing'd fu' law,
She hadna will to say him na,
But to her daddie she left it a',
    As they twa could agree.
The lover gi'ed her the tither kiss,
Syne ran to her daddie, and tell'd him this,
    With a fal da ra, &c.

The bridal day it came to pass,
Wi' mony a blithesome lad and lass;

"The Cauldrife Wooer."

But siccan a day there never was,
  Sic mirth was never seen.
This winsome couple straiked hands,
Mess John ty'd up the marriage bands,
  With a fal da ra, &c.

Our next presents the opposite picture, of a backward and cool, and therefore a bungling lover; for love, like war, is ever a hot business, in which to feel or to show indifference is the sure pledge of defeat :—

THE CAULDRIFE WOOER.

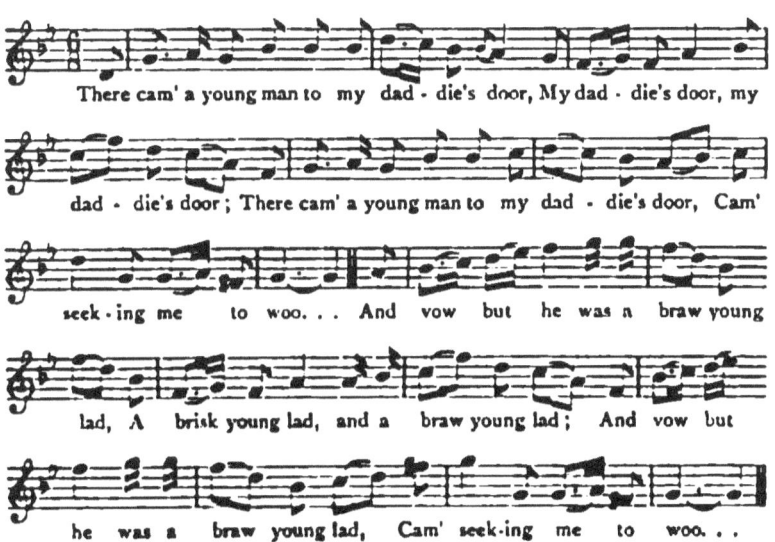

There cam' a young man to my dad-die's door, My dad-die's door, my dad-die's door; There cam' a young man to my dad-die's door, Cam' seek-ing me to woo... And vow but he was a braw young lad, A brisk young lad, and a braw young lad; And vow but he was a braw young lad, Cam' seek-ing me to woo...

But I was bakin' when he cam',
  When he cam', when he cam';
I took him in and gied him a scone,
  To thowe his frozen mou'.—And, &c.

I set him in aside the bink,
I gied him bread and ale to drink;
But ne'er a blythe styme wad he blink
    Until his wame was fou.—And, &c.

Gae get you gane, you cauldrife wooer,
Ye sour-looking cauldrife wooer !
I straightway showed him to the door,
    Saying, Come nae mair to woo.—And, &c.

There lay a deuk-dub before the door,
Before the door, before the door;
There lay a deuk-dub before the door,
    And there fell he, I trow.—And, &c.

Out cam' the gudeman, and heigh he shouted,
Out cam' the gudewife, and laigh she louted;
And a' the toun-neebors were gathered about it,
    And there lay he, I trow.—And, &c.

Then out cam' I, and sneer'd and smil'd,
Ye cam' to woo, but ye're a' beguil'd;
Ye've fa'en i' the dirt, and ye're a' befyl'd;
    We'll ha'e nae mair o' you.—And, &c.

Willie, whose name is connected with Melville Castle, is a quite different character, both from the rude and rough Muirland Willie and from the well-dressed low-spirited diver into the deuk-dub before the door. He was a cavalier and a gallant of the first water, and with a blithe confidence in himself—ready to carry off, not one fair willing maiden only, but half-a-dozen, or a score, had it been his fortune to have been born an old Hebrew monarch, or a Zulu chief, or a

Turk. But as things are here, he had to content himself with one; and there was a great competition for him among the ladies, as the song most dramatically sets forth :—

WILLIE'S GANE TO MELVILLE CASTLE.[1]

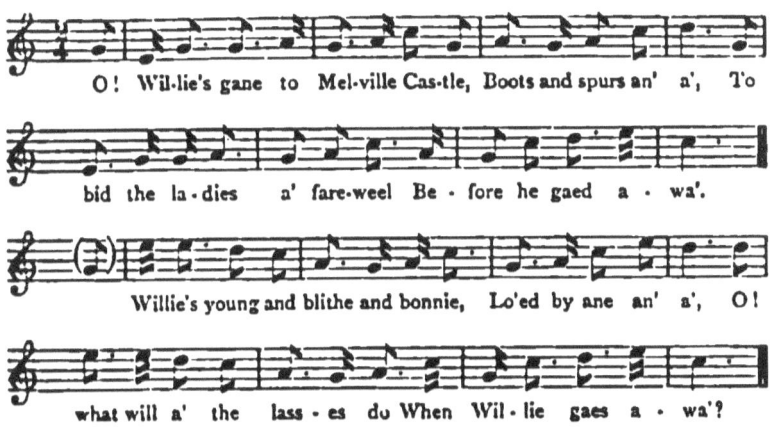

The first he met was Lady Kate,
    She led him thro' the ha',
And wi' a sad and sorry heart
    She let the tear doon fa';
Beside the fire stood Lady Grace,
    Said ne'er a word ava—
She thocht that she was sure o' him
    Before he gaed awa'.

Then ben the hoose cam' Lady Bell—
    "Gude troth, ye needna craw,
Maybe the lad will fancy me,
    An' disappoint ye a'!"

---

[1] *Air* by kind permission of J. Blockley, Argyll Street, Regent Street, London.

Down the stair trip't Lady Jean,
　　The flow'r amang them a'—
"Oh! lasses, trust in Providence,
　　And ye'll get husbands a'!"

When on his horse he rode awa',
　　They gaithered roond the door,
He gaily waved his bonnet blue,
　　They set up sic a roar!
Their cries, their tears, brocht Willie back,
　　He kissed them ane an' a';
"Oh! lasses, bide till I come hame,
　　And then I'll wed ye a'!"

The excellence of love never appears in stronger relief than when it is contrasted with money—two forces as naturally diverse as the ballast of a ship from the sails, but which must learn to act in some not uncomfortable way together, the moment courtship takes the decisive step into a proposal of marriage. A man falls in love—a most significant phrase—without knowing it, as a traveller through a Sahara stumbles on an oasis, or a botanist on some rare flower in a dell; a delicious luxury, and a stimulating surprise: but marriage is a business, and, like other kinds of business, cannot be managed wisely without the help of bankers and lawyers—two classes of men the most difficult of all to be made to interflow with the passion of the song-writer or the meditation of the sonneteer. It is a general principle in the constitution of things that the union of contraries is perfection, as when Apollo, the favourite deity of the Greeks, unites the strength of the archer god with the grace of the leader of the Muses; and in this fashion, where love and money unite, we have the ecstasy of an unselfish passion perfected in the just course of things by a comfortable settlement and pleasant surroundings; whereas, love rushing with its single strength into marriage leads lightly into discomfort, and may often end in ruin, as, on the other hand, single-handed money without love, making a contract of marriage, as it commenced with baseness, so in baseness it must end. Love is the great magician divinely commissioned to disenthrall the world in the vestibule of manhood from the grasp of the triform demon composed of a tiger, a fox, and a bear, called in moral philosophy φιλαυτία, or love of self; and the man who at the first serious step in life has allowed himself to be defrauded of the opportunity to do an act of pure disinterestedness, when the will to do was most natural and most imperious, is, we may truly say, in Scripture language, "damned already," and no good thing can be expected from him; and whosoever, with a profession of love in his mouth, secretly knows, or even is not ashamed publicly to own, that he marries, not the woman with the money, but the money with the woman, falls under the curse which the fervid apostle pronounced on Simon Magus, when that vainglorious Samaritan mountebank offered money to buy the gift of the Holy Ghost to eke out the legerdemain tricks of his professional platform: "*Thy money perish with thee, because thou hast thought that the gift of God may be purchased with money. Thou hast neither part nor lot in this matter.*" And so it must be ever; as in the matter of evangelic apostleship, so, in the constitution of the family bond, the man who marries for money, or worldly status in any form, has neither part nor lot in the best emotions of the heart or the best songs of the people. Money represents only the exchangeable value of things external, the mere furnishings and trappings of human life; it is utterly destitute of any originating force or creative inspiration: at best it supplies only the tools with which the workman works, and can neither project for him a worthy field for his operations, nor guide him to fruitful issues when the work is found. It has, in fact, altogether an ancillary and a servile function; and the moment it pretends to anything higher, its dominion becomes a usurpation, as much as when the saddle of the knight is mounted by the groom, or the throne of Majesty by the master of ceremonies. In this view the love of money is condemned both by apostles and philosophers as the root of all evil; and if it be so even in matters of trade, where money is in its natural place, it must be doubly so in love, where neither the passion nor the object of the passion has any money value. The man who marries for money, when you gauge him truly, is not a lover but a merchant, not a husband but a huckster; and as such, never fails to be estimated at his true value, if not in the hollow society which he courts, certainly in the true-hearted song of the people, where he is systematically set forth as a man who meddles with what does not belong to him, and has no more to do with love than an atheist in the Church of God, or a pig in a drawing-room.

In Scottish song the antagonism between true love and marriage for money and worldly position is often put into the mouth of the fair maid who has fixed her affections on some honest labourer of the district, while her ambitious parents are eager for her union with a man of more lofty pretensions, more costly furnishings, and a weightier money-bag. This is natural enough, no doubt, in papa and mamma; but the song always takes the side of the daughter:—

LOGIE O' BUCHAN.

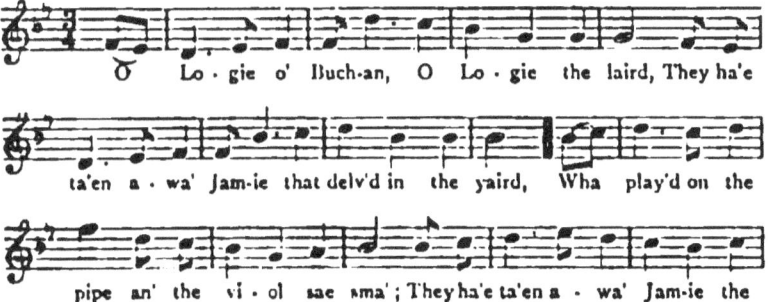

O Logie o' Buchan, O Logie the laird, They ha'e ta'en awa' Jamie that delv'd in the yaird, Wha play'd on the pipe an' the viol sae sma'; They ha'e ta'en awa' Jamie the

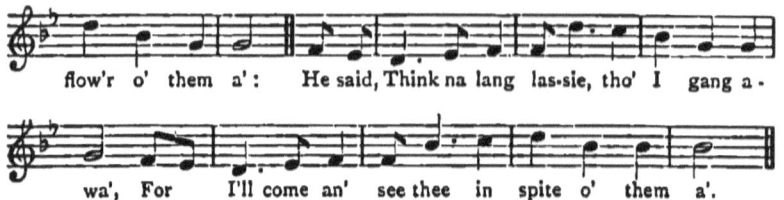

flow'r o' them a': He said, Think na lang lassie, tho' I gang awa', For I'll come an' see thee in spite o' them a'.

Tho' Sandy has owsen, has gear, and has kye,
A house and a haddin, and siller forbye;
Yet I'd tak' my ain lad wi' his staff in his hand,
Before I'd hae him wi' his houses and land.
    But simmer is comin', cauld winter's awa',
    An' he'll come an' see me in spite o' them a'.

My daddy looks sulky, my minny looks sour,
They frown upon Jamie because he is poor;
Though I like them as weel as a dochter should do,
They're nae hauf so dear to me, Jamie, as you.
    He said, Think na lang, lassie, tho' I gang awa',
    For I'll come an' see thee in spite o' them a'.

I sit on my creepie and spin at my wheel,
And think on the laddie that lo'ed me sae weel;
He had but ae saxpence, he brake it in twa,
And he gied me the half o't when he gaed awa'.
    But the simmer is comin', cauld winter's awa',
    An' he'll come an' see me in spite o' them a'.

This excellent song, in its simplicity, its sweetness, and its picturesqueness quite worthy of Burns, was composed, we are informed, by an Aberdeenshire schoolmaster, who died in the year 1756, three years before Burns was born.[1] It

[1] See Bards of Bon Accord, by Walker (Aberdeen, 1887), p. 798.

is one of the few popular songs that date from the somewhat cold atmosphere of the granite city,—in this respect contrasting unfavourably with the lyric fertility of Glasgow, Paisley, and the fervid West.

Our next specimen, "Jenny's Bawbee," is a composition in which the lovers of the money and the lover of the maid are humorously contrasted in pictorial detail. The author was Sir Alexander Boswell of Auchinleck, in Ayrshire, son of the well-known biographer of the stout father of English dictionaries, and known less creditably for his death in a duel with James Stuart of Dunearn, brought on by ill-considered and hasty language towards that gentleman used by the song-maker in one of his fiery humours:[1]—

JENNY'S BAWBEE.

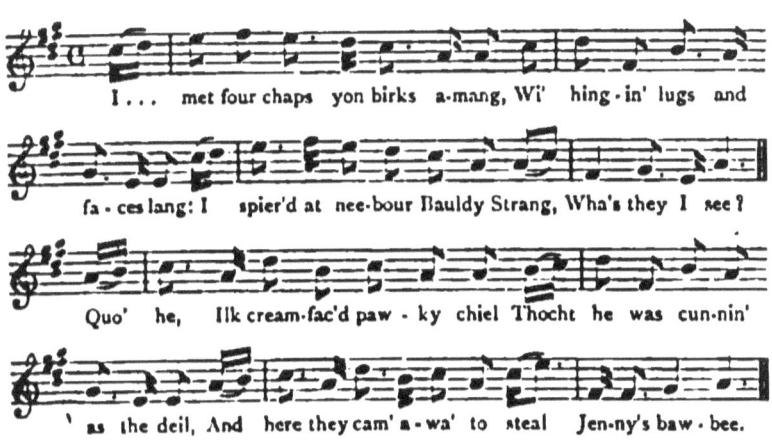

I... met four chaps yon birks a-mang, Wi' hing-in' lugs and fa-ces lang: I spier'd at nee-bour Bauldy Strang, Wha's they I see? Quo' he, Ilk cream-fac'd paw-ky chiel Thocht he was cun-nin' as the deil, And here they cam' a-wa' to steal Jen-ny's baw-bee.

[1] See Lord Cockburn's Personal Memoirs (Edinburgh, 1856), chap. vi.

The first, a Captain to his trade,
Wi' skull ill-lined, but back weel-clad,
March'd round the barn, and by the shed,
    And pappit on his knee :
Quo' he, " My goddess, nymph, and queen,
Your beauty's dazzled baith my een ! "
But deil a beauty he had seen
    But—Jenny's bawbee.

A Lawyer neist, wi' blatherin' gab,
Wha speeches wove like ony wab,
In ilk ane's corn aye took a dab,
    And a' for a fee.
Accounts he owed through a' the toun
And tradesmen's tongues nae mair could drown
But now he thocht to clout his gown
    Wi' Jenny's bawbee.

A Norland Laird neist trotted up,
Wi' bawsand naig and siller whup,
Cried, "There's my beast, lad, haud the grup,
    Or tie't till a tree ;
What's gowd to me ?—I've walth o' lan' !
Bestow on ane o' worth your han' ! "—
He thocht to pay what he was *awn*
    Wi' Jenny's bawbee.

Drest up just like the knave o' clubs,
A THING came neist, (but life has rubs,)
Foul were the roads, and fu' the dubs,
    And jaupit a' was he.
He danc'd up, squinting thro' a glass,
And grinn'd, " I' faith, a bonnie lass ! "
He thought to win, wi' front o' brass,
    Jenny's bawbee.

She bade the Laird gae kame his wig,
The Sodger no' to strut sae big,
The Lawyer no' to be a prig,
    The fool, he cried, "Tehee!
I kenn'd that·I could never fail!"
But she preen'd the dishclout to his tail,
And soused him wi' the water-pail,
    And kept her bawbee.

Then Johnnie cam', a lad o' sense,
Although he had na mony pence,
And took young Jenny to the spence,
    Wi' her to crack a wee.
Now Johnnie was a clever chiel,
And here his suit he press'd sae weel,
That Jenny's heart grew saft as jeel,
    And she birl'd her bawbee.

In this song the lady is master of the position, and having plenty of money of her own, and plenty of good sense, she gives both her beauty and her bawbee to the man who is most worthy of her love. This happy case, however, is apt to be reversed when Jenny has no bawbee, and when the parents on both sides, like Jean Armour's father, when Burns entangled himself with her, see that there is a poor outlook for the daughter, if blithe young Johnnie, without a penny in his pocket, is preferred to rich old Donald with a fine house, and a chaise to ride in, and flunkeys to wait upon her call. In this case the sacrifice of love to position on the part of the damsel is made so much the more tragic, or virtuous in a worldly sense if you please, by the difference between thirty and sixty years of age. This is the state of the case in the favourite old song of "Come under my Plaidie," written by Hector M'Neill, one of the most notable of our Scottish song-writers. He was born in October 1746, near Roslin, in Mid-Lothian, and after education in the grammar-school, Stirling, went out to the West Indies, where he engaged in commercial business; and returned to Scotland in 1795, and, after publishing "Scotland's Scaith" and other classical pieces, died at Edinburgh in the year 1818, having reached the ripe age of seventy-two:[1]—

COME UNDER MY PLAIDIE.

---

[1] Irving, Book of Eminent Scotsmen.

"Come under my Plaidie."

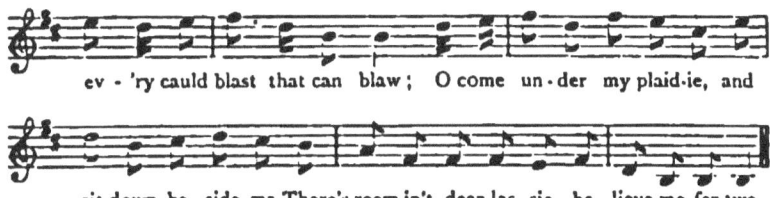

ev-'ry cauld blast that can blaw; O come un-der my plaid-ie, and
sit down be-side me, There's room in't, dear las-sie, be-lieve me for twa.

"Gae 'wa wi' yer plaidie! auld Donald, gae 'wa;
I fear na the cauld blast, the drift, nor the snaw!
Gae 'wa wi' yer plaidie! I'll no' sit beside ye;
Ye micht be my gutcher! auld Donald, gae 'wa.
I'm gaun to meet Johnnie—he's young and he's bonnie;
He's been at Meg's bridal, fu' trig and fu' braw!
Nane dances sae lichtly, sae gracefu', sae tichtly,
His cheek's like the new rose, his brow's like the snaw!"

"Dear Marion, let that flee stick fast to the wa';
Your Jock's but a gowk, and has naething ava;
The hail o' his pack he has now on his back;
He's thretty, and I am but threescore and twa.
Be frank now, and kindly—I'll busk ye aye finely;
To kirk or to market there'll few gang sae braw;
A bien house to bide in, a chaise for to ride in,
And flunkeys to 'tend ye as aft as ye ca'."

"My father aye tauld me, my mither and a',
Ye'd mak' a gude husband, and keep me aye braw.
It's true I lo'e Johnnie; he's young and he's bonnie;
But, wae's me! I ken he has naething ava!
I hae little tocher; ye've made a gude offer;
I'm now mair than twenty; my time is but sma'!
Sae gie me your plaidie; I'll creep in beside ye;
I thocht ye'd been aulder than threescore and twa!"

F

She crap in ayont him, beside the stane wa',
Whare Johnnie was list'ning, and heard her tell a';
The day was appointed!—his proud heart it dunted,
And strack 'gainst his side, as if bursting in twa.
He wander'd hame weary, the nicht it was dreary,
And, thowless, he tint his gate 'mang the deep snaw:
The howlet was screamin', while Johnnie cried, "Women
Wad marry auld Nick, if he'd keep them aye braw."

The tragic sorrow of the miscalculating lover in this case causes the singer to overlook any small amount of prudential virtue that might have led the lady to prefer the cool shelter of the plaidie from a respectable old gentleman of threescore and two, to the warm refuge of the same cover from a brisk young lad of thirty; but the small amount of prudential virtue which in this case charity may be willing to allow, is elevated into a grace of self-sacrificing duty in "Auld Robin Gray," a ballad which, for piety, pathos, and popularity, stands in the very first rank of the rich lyrical repertory of the British Islands:—

Auld Robin Gray.

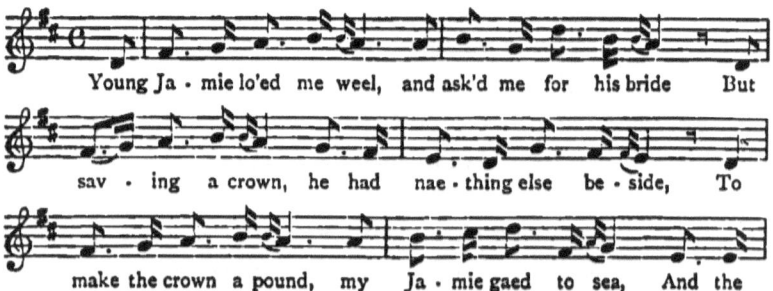

Young Jamie lo'ed me weel, and ask'd me for his bride But saving a crown, he had naething else beside, To make the crown a pound, my Jamie gaed to sea, And the

"Auld Robin Gray."

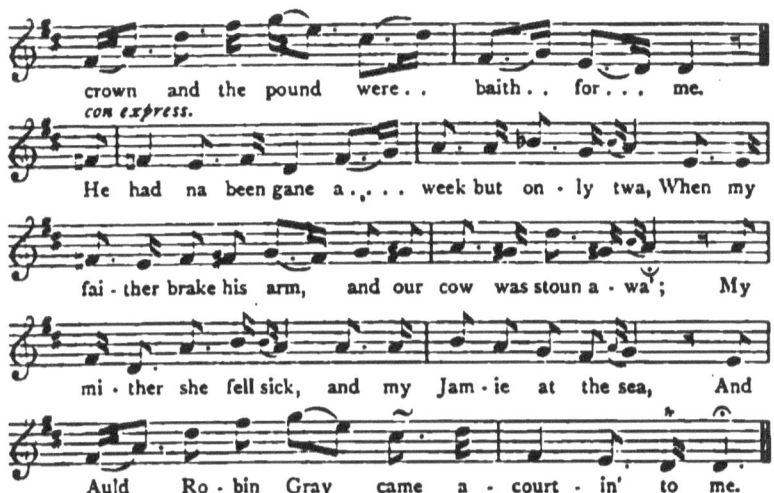

crown and the pound were.. baith.. for... me.
con express.
He had na been gane a.,.. week but on - ly twa, When my
fai - ther brake his arm, and our cow was stoun a - wa'; My
mi - ther she fell sick, and my Jam - ie at the sea, And
Auld Ro - bin Gray came a - court - in' to me.

My faither couldna work, and my mither couldna spin,
I toil'd day and night, but their bread I couldna win;
Auld Rob maintain'd them baith, and wi' tears in his e'e,
Said, Jenny, for their sakes, will ye marry me?

My heart it said nay, I look'd for Jamie back;
But the wind it blew high, and the ship it was a wrack;
The ship it was a wrack, why didna Jenny die?
And why do I live to say, wae is me!

My faither urged me sair, tho' my mither didna speak,
She looked in my face till my heart was like to break;
So I gied him my hand though my heart was on the sea,
And auld Robin Gray is gudeman to me.

I hadna been a wife a week but only four,
When sitting sae mournfully at my ain door,
I saw my Jamie's wraith, for I couldna think it he,
Till he said, I'm come back, love, to marry thee.

O sair did we greet, and mickle did we say;
We took but ae kiss, and we tore ourselves away:

I wish I were dead, but I'm no like to dee:
Oh, why do I live to say, wae is me!

I gang like a ghaist, and I carena to spin;
I darena think on Jamie, for that would be a sin;
But I'll do my best a gude wife to be,
For auld Robin Gray is kind unto me.

The authoress of this beautiful ballad, Lady Anne Barnard, like many of the most distinguished members of the Scottish peerage, belonged to a family of Norman extraction, whose name appears prominently in the political and literary history of Scotland from the time of saintly King David to the present hour. Anne, the eldest daughter of James, fifth Earl of Balcarres in Fife, had the double happiness, first of inheriting a gay and sprightly spirit from the "Lindsay's light" of the old ballads, and again of living in the good old times when Scottish lords and lairds delighted to live for the greater part of the year on the family property from which they drew their birth, and in terms of kindly intercourse and wise guidance with the people from whom they drew their rents. She was brought up accordingly, not in the luxurious style of metropolitan saloons, but with a truly Spartan maternal discipline, and a play of kindly charities at home; a healthy atmosphere, to which, along with her happy Norman temperament, she owed that rare combination of unaffected naturalness, bright intelligence, and well-seasoned hardihood, that distinguished her so favourably among the noble lady-singers of Scotland. With a wise self-reliance, and a cheerful independence not over-common in her sex, she abstained from amorous seductions and connubial entanglement till she reached the mature age of forty, and then allied herself to Andrew Barnard, Esq., son of the Bishop of Limerick, with whom she lived in quiet domestic peace and satisfaction for fourteen years, till his death in 1808. Him, in the year 1797, she accompanied to the Cape of Good Hope, whither he went in the capacity of private secretary to Lord Macartney, the first Governor of the newly acquired colony; and here, for a period of five years, she performed the duties of her official position with all that mixture of graceful dignity and homely geniality which belonged to the native Scotch aristocracy of the good old times. In the hall of ceremonial receptions in the Governor's house, or on the summit of the Table Mount amid a bevy of jolly Dutch boors, she was equally in her element. In 1802, the peace of Amiens giving the Cape Colony back to the Dutch, the secretary's wife returned to England, where, in her house in Berkeley Square, she had lived with her sister Margaret, on terms of intimacy with Horace Walpole, the Ailesburys, the Berrys, and even his Royal Highness the Prince Regent, who presented her with a gold chain, and showed the warmth of his affections in a more impressive fashion, by familiarly calling her "Sister Anne." After the death of her husband in 1808, and of her stout old mother, a bold Dalrymple, at the age of ninety-three in 1820, she continued to reside in London, with occasional visits to Balcarres and Edinburgh, till the year of her death in 1825, aged seventy-five. To the last she was distinguished for that continuity of cheerful and fruitful activity which makes her life so interesting; and among her papers we find a scrap of good advice, which, if it were acted on systematically by seekers after happiness, would save not a few human beings from the foolish snapping after excitement of various kinds with which they are fond to fill up the vacuities of their unprofitable existence. "When alone," she writes, "I am not above five-and-twenty. I can entertain myself with a succession of inventions, which would be more effective if they were fewer. I forget that I am sixty-eight; and if by chance I see myself in the glass looking very abominable, I do not care. What is the moral of this? That as far as my poor experience goes (and it is said that we must all be fools or physicians at forty), occupation is the best nostrum in the great laboratory of human life for all the pains, cares, mortifications, and *ennui* that flesh is heir to." Excellent! Plutarch, in his admirable discourse Περὶ εὐθυμίας, never wrote anything wiser.

About the famous ballad of "Auld Robin Gray" stories are told that may be worth mentioning. Like the Baroness Nairne, and other intellectual ladies of the age, Lady Anne Barnard entertained a strong aversion to the sort of publicity which accompanies the confessed fact of literary utterance in any form. She therefore for many years, long after the ballad had obtained a currency both in England and Scotland superior to any range of popularity that even the best lyrical productions of Moore or Burns could boast, still obstinately maintained her incognito, and repelled in the sharpest manner any attempt of impertinent interviewers to extract a confession from her breast. To the secretary of an antiquarian society who submitted her to a cross-examination on the point with a pertinacity only pardonable in a professional pleader at a jury trial, she replied: "The ballad in question has, in my opinion, met with an attention beyond its deserts. It is set off by having a very fine tune set to it by a doctor of music;[1] was sung by youth and beauty for five years and more; had a romance composed from it by a man of eminence; was the subject of a play, of an opera, and a pantomime; was sung by the united armies in America, and afterwards

[1] The Rev. W. Leeves, rector of Wrington, Somerset.

danced by dogs in the street; *but never more honoured than by the present investigation.*" The confession, however, at a later period of her life, was wrung from her by a very complimentary mention of herself as authoress of the poem in Sir Walter Scott's novel of 'The Pirate.'[1]

Of the hero of this famous ballad, what is known, though it will fail to gratify the minute curiosity of a certain class of inquirers, will go to prove the general truth of what Goethe said of his own poems—that all true poetry springs out of a root of real experience. Robin Gray was the name of an old shepherd at Balcarres, familiar to the young ladies, and who on one occasion had presumed to use his shepherd's staff in the way of checking their playful ramblings, instead of confining it to the guardianship of his four-footed subjects. The lady, some years afterwards, when in ripe womanhood, revisiting the haunts of her girlhood, took her revenge of the old castigator by making him enact the part of a prosaic husband in a pitiful love-ballad. This is all.

So much for the distinguished authoress of this most admired of all Scottish ballads. But it is not to be expected that the self-denying virtue here celebrated will ever become general. In all countries where women have attained to true personal dignity, and are not disposed

[1] The Pirate, chap. xxvi.

of in marriage in the way of family bargain by the paternal merchant, a young lady of spirit will not consent to be yoked for life to an old gentleman of sixty-two, for whom she does not care a straw, from a mere dutiful deference to her father's will; or to be cooped up in the ancestral hall by a monopolising mother, who, in her pride of ladyhood, forgets that she ever was a girl. Nature will not be mocked in this wise; and elopements will occasionally take place from parents who are more prudent than wise, and actuated more by the cold calculations of worldly ambition than by the kindly promptings of the human heart. To parents of this unkindly caste, Gall's song—

> " I'll never come back to my mammy again;
> I've held by her apron these aucht years and ten,
> But I'll never come back to my mammy again "—

may serve as a useful warning; and Scott's famous song of "Jock o' Hazeldean" is a text from which a useful sermon to the same effect may be preached :—

JOCK O' HAZELDEAN.

"Why weep ye by the tide, ladye? Why weep ye by the tide? I'll wed ye to my young-est son, And ye sall be his bride;

"Now let this wilfu' grief be done,
    And dry that cheek so pale;
Young Frank is chief of Errington,
    And lord of Langley dale;
His step is first in peacefu' ha',
    His sword in battle keen"—
But aye she loot the tears doon fa'
    For Jock o' Hazeldean.

"A chain o' gold ye sall not lack,
    Nor braid to bind your hair,
Nor mettled hound, nor managed hawk,
    Nor palfrey fresh and fair;
And you, the foremost o' them a',
    Shall ride our forest queen "—
But aye she loot the tears doon fa'
    For Jock o' Hazeldean.

The kirk was decked at morning-tide,
    The tapers glimmered fair;
The priest and bridegroom wait the bride,
    But ne'er a bride cam' there:
They sought her baith by bower and ha',
    The ladye wasna seen!—
She's ower the Border and awa'
    Wi' Jock o' Hazeldean!

    I will conclude this division of the subject with two humorous portraitures of the secular or prosaic lover,—the lover who either never knew what love meant, or who thinks it is a mere juvenile whim or fancy or whiff of passion with which a serious business like marriage has nothing to do. The first is the consequential or patronising suitor, the lord of the manor perhaps, what we call in Scotland the laird, who considers that any lady whom he finds it convenient to ask will be only too proud of the honour of sitting at his table-head, and being the most prominent article of furniture in his hall as often as he has occasion to enact the big man of the district before admiring dependants. The popular song "The Laird o' Cockpen" is the composition of the grand old Jacobite lady, the Baroness Nairne, of whom we shall have something more special to say by-and-by:—

THE LAIRD O' COCKPEN.

The laird o' Cock-pen he's proud and he's great, His mind is ta'en up wi' the things o' the state; He want-ed a wife his braw house to keep. But fa-vour wi' woo-in' was fashious to seek.

Doun by the dyke-side a lady did dwell,
At his table-head he thought she'd look well;
M'Cleish's ae daughter o' Claversha' Lee,
A penniless lass wi' a lang pedigree.

His wig was weel pouther'd, an' as gude as new,
His waistcoat was white, his coat it was blue;
He put on a ring, a sword, an' cock'd hat,
An' wha could refuse the Laird wi' a' that?

He took the grey mare, an' rode cannilie,
An' rapp'd at the yett o' Claversha' Lee:
"Gae tell Mistress Jean to come speedily ben;
She's wanted to speak wi' the Laird o' Cockpen."

Mistress Jean she was makin' the elder-flow'r wine:
"An' what brings the Laird at sic a like time?"
She put aff her apron, an' on her silk gown,
Her mutch wi' red ribbons, an' gaed awa' down.

An' when she cam' ben, he bowed fu' low;
An' what was his errand he soon let her know:
Amaz'd was the Laird when the lady said, Na!
An' wi' a laigh curtsie she turned awa'.

Dumfounder'd was he, but nae sigh did he gi'e,—
He mounted his mare, an' rade cannilie;
And aften he thought, as he gaed through the glen,
She's daft to refuse the Laird o' Cockpen.

An' now that the Laird his exit had made,
Mistress Jean she reflected on what she had said;
Oh, for ane I'll get better, it's waur I'll get ten,
I was daft to refuse the Laird o' Cockpen.

Neist time that the Laird and the Lady were seen,
They were gaun arm-in-arm to the kirk on the green;
Now she sits in the ha' like a crouse tappit hen,
But as yet there's nae chickens been seen in Cockpen.

It will be observed that this excellent ballad, if it be made to conclude at the end of the seventh verse, contains one moral; but if the two last are added, an altogether different one: and the fact of the matter is, that the song originally ended with the seventh verse, and the two last verses were added by Miss Ferrier, the accomplished novelist, an intimate friend of Sir Walter Scott, and aunt of the late Professor Ferrier of St Andrews, the eminent metaphysician, and son-in-law to the celebrated Christopher North. The moral of the song, as it originally stood, is doubtless the better of the two—viz., that such wooers should receive a negative answer once for all, with the cool dignity which the song indicates; but the moral of the addition that "second thoughts are best," as we have it also in Burns's "Duncan Gray," if not equally noble, is equally natural, and has been sung so often as an integral part of the song, that it can scarcely be omitted without creating a feeling of disappointment.

Our second song gives the portrait, not of a consequential person, but merely of a self-satisfied male mortal of moderate ambition, well lined as he deems, and well accoutred, and who presents himself as a shopkeeper presents his wares to any fair damsel who may have sense to accept a well-provided, well-to-do domestic article called a husband, without any of those dainty sentiments and ambitious expectations which are generally, as he deems, entertained by foolish young ladies, only to be disappointed:—

LASS, GIN YE LO'E ME, TELL ME NOO.

I ha'e laid a her-rin' in saut, Lass, gin ye lo'e me, tell me noo; I ha'e brew'd a for-pit o' maut, An' I canna come il-ka day to woo. I ha'e a calf will soon be a cow, Lass, gin ye lo'e me, tell me noo; I ha'e a pig will soon be a sow, An' I canna come il-ka day to woo.

 I ha'e a house on yonder muir,
  Lass, gin ye lo'e me, tell me noo;
 Three sparrows may dance upon the floor,
  An' I canna come ilka day to woo.
 I ha'e a but, an' I ha'e a ben,
  Lass, gin ye lo'e me, tell me noo;
 I ha'e three chickens an' a fat hen,
  An' I canna come ony mair to woo.

 I ha'e a hearth wi' a blazing log,
  Lass, gin ye lo'e me, tell me noo;
 A bawsint cat, an' a collie dog,
  An' I canna come ilka day to woo.
 I ha'e a yard wi' tawties good,
  Lass, gin ye lo'e me, tell me noo;

Wi' mint, sweet-william, and southern-wood,
    An' I canna come ony mair to woo.

I ha'e a hen wi' a happity leg,
    Lass, gin ye lo'e me, tell me noo;
An' ilka day she lays me an egg,
    An' I canna come ilka day to woo.
I ha'e a goodly kebbuck o' cheese,
    Far owre big for a single mou';
Share it wi' me, and live at your ease,
    An' bless the day when I cam' to woo!

I ha'e laid a herring in saut,
    Lass, gin ye lo'e me, tell me noo;
I ha'e brewed a forpit o' maut,
    An' I canna come ilka day to woo.
Mony a flighty fusionless goose,
    Mair fine-spun phrase would weave to you,
But I am here, and ye canna refuse
    A man like me, when I come to woo![1]

We have now to deal with the blooming crown and the midsummer heyday of love—marriage; and here at the very threshold we encounter unquestionably the noblest name among the many noble ladies who have immortalised themselves by the high place which they hold among the composers of Scottish song. Joanna Baillie,

---

[1] The oldest form of this song has been traced back to Henry VIII. (Chambers's Songs before Burns). The form now generally sung is ascribed to James Tytler, commonly called Balloon Tytler, from his having been the first in Scotland to ascend in a balloon, and described by Burns (Chambers, iv. 284). The complete form, as given in the text, contains some additions and alterations made by myself, and published in the 'Celtic Magazine.'

the authoress of the popular song, "Woo'd and Married and a'," was born in the parish of Bothwell, on the picturesque banks of the Clyde, not far from Glasgow, where her father was minister. Her name witnesses her connection with Principal Robert Baillie, a man who played a prominent part in the political and ecclesiastical history of the seventeenth century, and Baillie of Jerviswoode; while on the mother's side she claimed close connection with Dr John Hunter, the greatest anatomist of his age. On the death of her father in 1784, she removed to London, and resided there with her brother, Dr Matthew Baillie, a gentleman of high repute in the medical world. During her residence in London, at the ripe age of thirty-six, she published the first series of her 'Plays on the Passions,' which, as an exhibition of dramatic force and fervour worthy of the most masculine intellect, took the literary mind of the day by storm, and gained to the authoress, among other distinguished persons, the intimate friendship of Sir Walter Scott, who, in his introduction to the third canto of "Marmion," speaks of her as the—

"Bold Enchantress who came
With fearless hand and heart on flame;"

and, by the potent magic of her strain, made the swains of Avon deem—

"That their own Shakespeare lived again."

After her brother's marriage and her mother's death, she removed from the historical house in Great Windmill Street to Hampstead, the most picturesque old breezy suburb of London, on which the names of so many distinguished men of English and of Scottish blood have been stamped, making rich the memory of the place: here she lived in literary ease and dignity with her sister till her death in the year 1851, at the patriarchal age of eighty-nine. Her house is still shown in the upper part of the town, near the church, where her remains lie. Though her dramas can no longer boast that command of the stage which might have been anticipated from the triumph which her 'Family Legend' achieved on the Edinburgh boards early in the century, with the impersonating genius of Mrs Siddons, and the enthusiastic patronage of Sir Walter Scott, this will not be attributed by thoughtful persons so much to their want of high dramatic excellence, as to the peculiar demands of modern English theatre-goers, stimulated to such a degree by motley variety of character, startling incident, and brilliant scenic show, that the best possible drama, formed on a more chaste and classical type, with all the force of Æschylus and all the pathos of Euripides, would fall ineffective on their ears. But it is as a song-writer that we have to do with her here; and it will always be a delightful contemplation to the student of literary history, that the Scottish lady who made her ideal figures tread the stage with all the grace of a Sophocles and the majesty of a Corneille, could at the same time give utterance to the kindliest and gentlest of human feelings, with all the sly humour and shrewd merriment that belong to a masterpiece of Scottish song. In this double form of presentation she, like Burns and Scott, was bilingual in the noblest sense: while she held converse on an equal platform with the first masters of the noble English tongue, she could at the same time address the meanest peasant of her native land in the musical and expressive speech which they had imbibed with their mother's milk; and verily she has had her reward. Her plays will win the admiration of the few; her songs warm the hearts of the many:—

Woo'd and Married and A'.

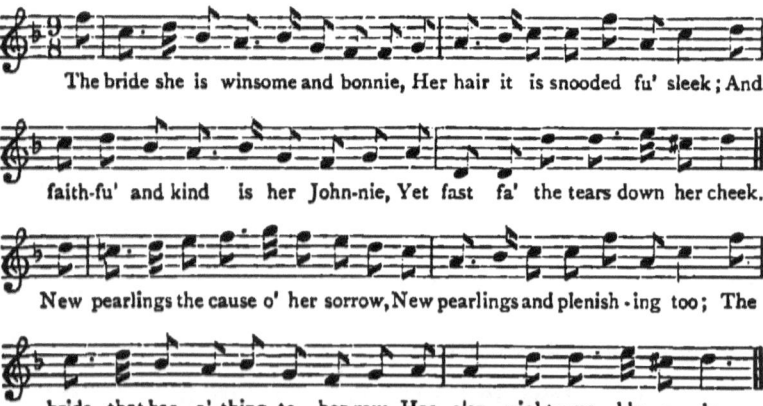

The bride she is winsome and bonnie, Her hair it is snooded fu' sleek; And faith-fu' and kind is her John-nie, Yet fast fa' the tears down her cheek. New pearlings the cause o' her sorrow, New pearlings and plenish-ing too; The bride that has a' thing to bor-row, Has e'en right muc-kle a-do.

"Woo'd and Married and a'."

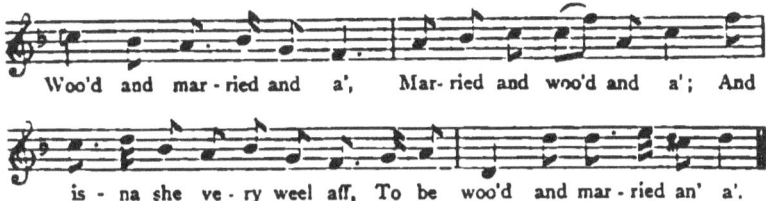

Woo'd and mar-ried and a', Mar-ried and woo'd and a'; And is-na she ve-ry weel aff, To be woo'd and mar-ried an' a'.

Her mither then hastily spak',—
  "The lassie is glaiket wi' pride;
In my pouches I hadna a plack,
  The day that I was a bride.
E'en tak' to your wheel and be clever,
  And draw out your thread in the sun;
The gear that is gifted, it never
  Will last like the gear that is won."
    Woo'd and married and a',
    Tocher and havings sae sma';
    I think ye are very weel aff,
    To be woo'd and married and a'.

"Toot, toot," quo' the gray-headed faither,
  "She's less o' a bride than a bairn;
She's ta'en like a cowt frae the heather,
  Wi' sense and discretion to learn.
Half husband, I trow, and half daddy,
  As humour inconstantly leans,
A chiel maun be constant and steady,
  That yokes wi' a lass in her teens."
    Kerchief to cover sae neat,
    Locks the wind used to blaw;
    I'm baith like to laugh and to greet,
    When I think o' her married at a'.

Then out spak' the wily bridegroom—
  Weel waled were his wordies I ween—

> "I'm rich, though my coffer be toom,
>   Wi' ae blink o' your bonnie blue een:
> I'm prouder o' you by my side,
>   Though your ruffles and ribbons be few,
> Than if Kate o' the Croft were my bride,
>   Wi' purfles and pearlings enew.
>   Dear and dearest o' ony,
>   Ye're woo'd and bookit and a';
>   And do ye think scorn o' your Johnnie,
>   And grieve to be married at a'?"
>
> She turn'd, and she blush'd, and she smil'd,
>   And she lookit sae bashfully down;
> The pride o' her heart was beguil'd,
>   And she play'd wi' the sleeve o' her gown:
> She twirl'd the tags o' her lace,
>   And she nippit her bodice sae blue;
> Syne blinket sae sweet in his face,
>   And aff like a maukin she flew.
>   Woo'd and married and a,'
>   Married and carried awa';
>   She thinks hersel' very weel aff,
>   To be woo'd and married and a'.

The original germ and general scheme of this excellent epithalamium was taken by the gifted authoress from a much older ditty, and modified with equal wisdom and good taste so as to suit the nerves of more dainty times; for who does not see that the very first verse of the song in its seventeenth-century dress—

> "The bride she cam' out o' the byre,
>   And cried as she dighted her cheeks,

> ' I'm to be married the nicht,
> And hae neither blankets nor sheets,
> Nor scarce a coverlet too ' "—

if ventilated in any West End assembly of London or Edinburgh, would cause a general fainting-fit, or a horrified symphony of screams, a soured look of displeasure, or a billowy burst of genteel laughter, through the whole length of the saloon? And the last verse, which brings the sister into the scene, and makes her declare before the public unblushingly, that she has only one desire,—viz., to be redeemed from the misery of single maidenhood, and to pass into the biform bliss of matrimony with all possible speed,—would certainly not mend the matter—

> " Out spak' the bride's sister,
> As she cam' in frae the byre,—
> ' O gin I were but married,
> It's a' that I desire :
> But we puir folk maun live single,
> And do the best that we can ;
> I dinna care what I should want
> If I could get but a man.'
> Woo'd and married," &c.

The wedding ceremony being thus completed, whether with the grave sobriety of the Presbyterian or with the hymeneal pomp of the Episcopal service, and the honeymoon having run its varied course of pleasant exhilaration, the serious business of married life commences: and here we are not to expect the same luxuriant crop of songs that festoons the courtship, partly because the security of the position renders stirring incident, and the play of fear and hope, the stimulants of song, comparatively rare; partly because, while the good a man longs for finds its natural utterance in song, the good a man possesses rests in the quiet satisfaction of the enjoyment: the bud in the spring is moved, by a certain restless eagerness, to burst into the blossom; but the blossom, once disclosed, spreads its petals to the sun, and has nothing to do but to receive. Nevertheless there are married songs, expressive of the ripe satisfaction which flows from the wise conduct of the nice and delicate relations which the married life implies. Though growing out of the same root, and fostered by the same sun, no two things, in some important respects, can be more different than love and marriage. To love is to ramble over clover meads with a pleasant companion, and no concern beyond the pleasure of the mere ramble; marriage is to draw yoked and harnessed in a wain: or, to take another simile, love is a temple for the worship of beauty; marriage is a school for the practice of mutual appreciation and sympathetic co-operation—a school in which the capacity to learn does not by any means necessarily exist in every brisk young man who, in the first transport of passion, may feel himself moved to pile a sonnet or to pour a song to the object of his affections. But the wise man, the alone true king, as the Stoics call him, will learn here as in the best of all the schools, of which human life has many; and the lesson learnt will be the ripe and mellow fruit of which young love gave only the promise. The following is one of the best specimens of this fruit, dropped from the life-experience of one of the best song-writers that the east of Scotland, less fervid than the west, has in these latter days produced:[1]—

LIZZIE.

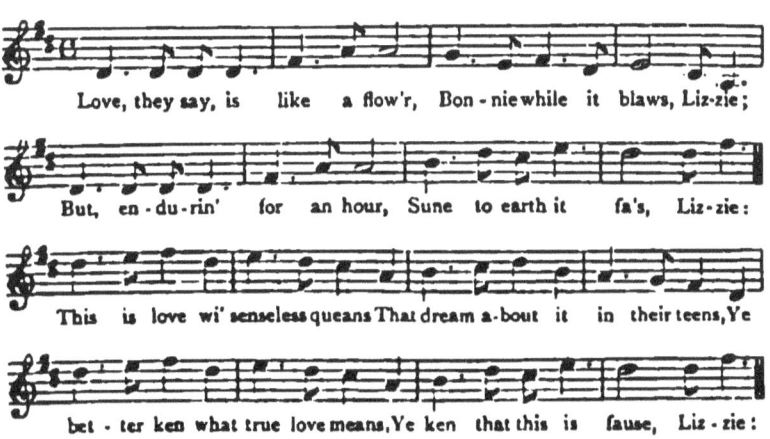

Love, they say, is like a flow'r, Bon-nie while it blaws, Liz-zie;
But, en-du-rin' for an hour, Sune to earth it fa's, Liz-zie:
This is love wi' senseless queans That dream a-bout it in their teens, Ye
bet-ter ken what true love means, Ye ken that this is fause, Liz-zie:

---

[1] Nugæ Canoræ Medicæ, by Sir Douglas Maclagan, Edinburgh, 1873. To the same happy matrimonial key is set an excellent song by a good Scotch singer, Alexander Logan—"Wifie, faithfu', fond, and bonnie," published in 'Köhler's Musical Treasury,' No. 104.

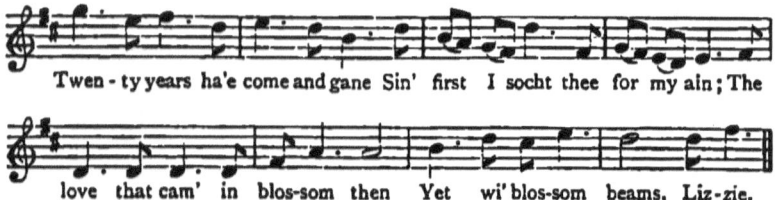

Twen-ty years ha'e come and gane Sin' first I socht thee for my ain; The love that cam' in blos-som then Yet wi' blos-som beams, Liz-zie.

Little gear we had, ye ken,
　To begin our life, Lizzie;
Treasure I had neist to nane,
　Binna in my wife, Lizzie.
To my wishes kindest Heaven
Better treasure couldna given;
Gowd wad maybe no hae thriven
　E'en had it been rife, Lizzie.
Gowd, they say, gets everything,
But true heart-love it canna bring;
Gowd is readier aye to fling
　Discord in and strife, Lizzie.

Sunshine, thanks to Heaven, has shed
　Licht within our ha', Lizzie,
Though a cloud or twa hae spread
　Shadows o'er us twa, Lizzie.
But when sorrow, grief, or care,
Frae Lizzie's ee wrang out the tear,
Our mutual love but grew the mair
　Wi' ilka watery fa', Lizzie.
Love and flowers agree in this—
A blink o' sunshine's no amiss,
But were nae rain the grun' to bless,
　They wadna grow ava, Lizzie.

Time begins to lay his han'
And to show his power, Lizzie;
We maun yield as ithers maun
To the carle dour, Lizzie.
Winter winds may round us blaw,
Our heads be white wi' winter snaw,
But warmth o' love, in spite them a',
Shall cheer our wintry hour, Lizzie.
Then, though it come stormy weather,
Gin we're spared to ane anither,
Auld and canty we'll thegither
Bide the wintry stour, Lizzie.

But there are incidents also in the routine of married life which render it as capable of dramatic representation in skilful hands as the most romantic events in the varied course of a happy or unhappy courtship; and of these unquestionably the masterpiece in our Scottish language is the universal favourite — "There's nae Luck aboot the Hoose":—

THERE'S NAE LUCK ABOOT THE HOOSE.

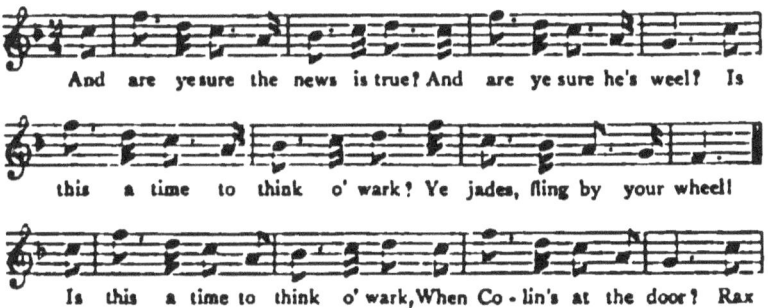

And are ye sure the news is true? And are ye sure he's weel? Is this a time to think o' wark? Ye jades, fling by your wheel! Is this a time to think o' wark, When Colin's at the door? Rax

me my cloak, I'll to the quay And see him come a-shore.

CHORUS.

For there's nae luck a-boot the hoose, There's nae luck a-va, There's lit-tle plea-sure in the hoose When oor guid-man's a-wa'!

Rise up and mak' a clean fireside,
    Put on the muckle pot;
Gie little Kate her cotton gown,
    And Jock his Sunday coat.
And mak' their shoon as black as slaes,
    Their hose as white as snaw;
It's a' to please my ain guidman,
    For he's been lang awa'.
        For there's, &c.

There's twa fat hens upon the bauk,
    They've fed this month and mair;
Mak' haste and thraw their necks about,
    That Colin weel may fare.
And spread the table neat and clean,
    Gar ilka thing look braw;
For wha can tell how Colin fared,
    When he was far awa'?
        For there's, &c.

And gie to me my bigonet,
    My bishop-satin gown;
For I maun tell the bailie's wife
    That Colin's come to town.

My Sunday's shoon they maun gae on,
  My hose o' pearl blue;
It's a' to please my ain guidman,
  For he's baith leal and true.
      For there's, &c.

Sae true his heart, sae smooth his speech,
  His breath like caller air;
His very foot has music in't,
  As he comes up the stair.
And will I see his face again?
  And will I hear him speak?
I'm downright dizzy wi' the thought,—
  In troth I'm like to greet.
      For there's, &c.

The cauld blasts o' the winter wind,
  That tirled through my heart,
They're a' blawn by, I hae him safe,
  Till death we'll never part.
But what puts parting in my head?
  It may be far awa';
The present moment is oor ain,
  The neist we never saw.
      For there's, &c.

Since Colin's weel, I'm weel content,
  I hae nae mair to crave;
Could I but live to mak' him blest,
  I'm blest aboon the lave.
And will I see his face again?
  And will I hear him speak?
I'm downright dizzy wi' the thought,—
  In troth I'm like to greet.
      For there's, &c.

The authoress of this delightful song, as seems now pretty generally recognised, was a Jean Adam, a schoolmistress[1] in Greenock, of some literary talent, who lived in the first half of the last century, before Robert Burns was born. Whether from imprudence in the conduct of life, or from misfortune, certainly without any vice, she fell into wandering ways, with very uncertain means of subsistence, and died at last in the year 1765, as an inmate of the poorhouse in Glasgow.

So much for the harmonies of married life; but we must look also to the jars and discords, which strike the ear the more that they offend against the general character of the relation, as the sins of the saints are always more noted than the sins of the sinners, and the accidental oddities that attach to the wise man more talked of than his wisdom. The causes that give rise to these jars and discords are only too obvious. The sexes being in some respects as different as in other respects they are similar, it follows that their tastes, habits, and inclinations must be not rarely antagonistic and apt to clash; whence the practice of wedded life, if it is to be a success, must in not a few cases become a delicate balance of contraries and a nice adjustment of things not naturally well fitted; and this is

[1] See her Life in the Songstresses of Scotland, vol. ii. p. 40.

a business demanding a fine feeling and a tact not to be expected from every love-sick fool, or every love-mad hero on whom an amiable young lady may have been willing to bestow her affections. Hence those explosions of temper and those scenes of back-to-back altercation, even in the course of the honeymoon, which we may have all seen occasionally in the genteel comedy of the stage. But besides faults of temper, there are men either too self-contained or of too independent habits to pay those frequent delicate attentions to the wife in which a wife delights; while, on the other hand, there are wives whose fussy affectionateness will display itself in an officious concern for the affairs and the trappings of the male, which a certain class of husbands is apt to resent as an impertinence and an offence. A connubial mis-relation of this kind is sketched with genuine Scottish humour in—

THE MARRIED MAN'S LAMENT.

I ance was a wan-ter as hap-py's a bee, I med-dled wi' nane and nane med-dled wi' me; I whiles had a crack o'er a cog o' gude yill, Whiles a bick-er o' swats, whiles a heart-heaz-ing gill. And I

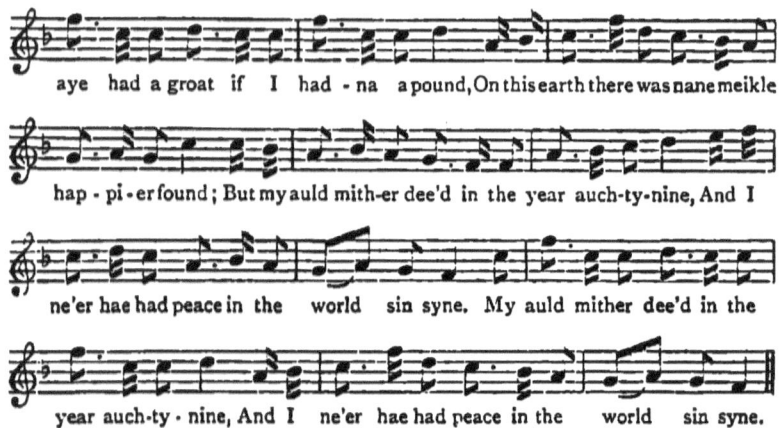

Fu' soun' may she sleep,—a douce woman was she—
Wi' her wheel, and her cat, and her cuppie o' tea.
My ingle she keepit as trig as a preen,
And she never speer'd questions as, "Where hae ye been?"
Or, "What were ye doing?" an' "Wha was ye wi'?"
We were happy thegither, my mither and me.
     But my auld, &c.

When my mither was gane, for a while I was wae,
But a young chap was I, and a wife I wad hae;
A wife I soon got, and I aye hae her yet,
An' the folks think thegither we unco weel fit;
But my ain mind hae I, tho' I daurna speak o't,
For mair than her gallop I like my ain trot.
     But my auld, &c.

When I wi' a crony am taking a drop,
She'll yammer and ca' me an auld drucken sot,
If an hour I bide out, loud she greets and she yowls,
And bans a' gude fellows, baith bodies and souls;
And yet what a care she has o' her gudeman,
You'd think I was doited—I canna but ban.
     But my auld, &c.

Now, my gilpie young dochters are looking for men,
An' I'll be a grandsire ere ever I ken;
The laddies are thinking o' ruling the roast;
Their faither, puir body, 's as deaf as a post;
But he sees their upsetting, sae crouse and sae bauld;
Oh! why did I marry, and wherefore grow auld?
          But my auld, &c.

The author of this clever piece was Robert Nicoll, in social position, as in lyrical genius, the brother of Burns, and who, like Burns, came to a premature end; not like Burns, however, by unreined strength, but by overstrained faculty. Born the son of a farmer at Auchtergaven, in Perthshire, he earned his living as a cowherd in the summer months, in order to pay for his education in the winter. Like Burns, he had a voracious appetite for books; wrote verses when he was thirteen, and when quite a youth commenced a literary life in Edinburgh, under the patronage of William Tait, the well-known Radical publisher. From Edinburgh he was transferred to Leeds, where he gained his living in the capacity of editor to a Radical newspaper called the 'Leeds Times,' the worst of all occupations for a young poet, for it not only caused him to breathe an atmosphere of narrow views and one-sided emotions, unfavourable to the human catholicity of the Muse, but it undermined his health by the constant fret and hurry of matters not to be handled without a certain robustness of nerve and coarseness of fibre, which he did not possess. He accordingly succumbed to the strain, and removed to Edinburgh, where he died at the early age of twenty-four.[1]

Miscalculations in married life, and other disappointments, turning an expected paradise into a real purgatory, as pictured in the above song, will occur now and then, so as to realise for the nonce the traditional introductory formula to the marriage ceremony credibly attributed to a certain minister of Lyne, near Peebles—"Marriage, my dear friends, is a curse to many, a blessing to few, a great risk to all!" But on the whole, we may hope that connubial couples, even when not approaching the beatitude of Sir Douglas Maclagan and his Lizzie, and in spite of considerable disparity of dispositions, manage to jog on comfortably enough, with such occasional antagonisms and altercations as, like showers in summer weather, will disturb but not destroy the serenity of the domestic firmament. Altercations of this kind offer the best possible situations for the exercise of the humorous dramatic song, so prominent in our lyrical repertory. Three of the most popular of these we will here append, with the general remark, that, however various in concep-

---

[1] See his Works, with Life, 3d edition, Paisley, 1877; and Rogers's Scottish Minstrel, p. 299.

tion, they all contain one moral—viz., that, whatever the matter in dispute may be, whether an industrial difference about connubial work, an economical one about an old cloak, or a mere point of precedence about rising from a chair and barring a door, the unbearded party in the case is sure to have her own way, if she will only keep her eye on the *mollia tempora fandi*, which she ought to know well, and use the artillery of her tongue with that nice dexterity and sly fascination for which the sex is so noted; and this not only when she is in the right—which she generally will be, for husbands are apt to be bearish—but when she is in the wrong; adding of course, in this case, to her fascinating eloquence, that persistency of purpose which is also one of her strong points, and feeling confident that the husband, whether from the love of peace, or from piety, as St Peter has it, doing honour to the weaker vessel, will yield the point rather than run the risk of a prolonged fret or a violent explosion. The first is—

JOHN GRUMLIE.

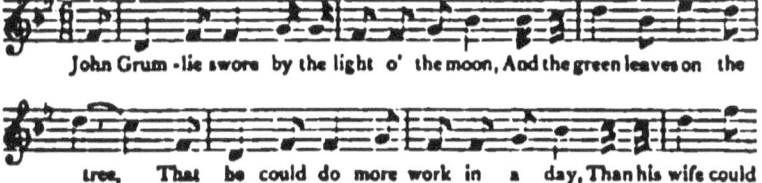

John Grum-lie swore by the light o' the moon, And the green leaves on the tree, That he could do more work in a day, Than his wife could

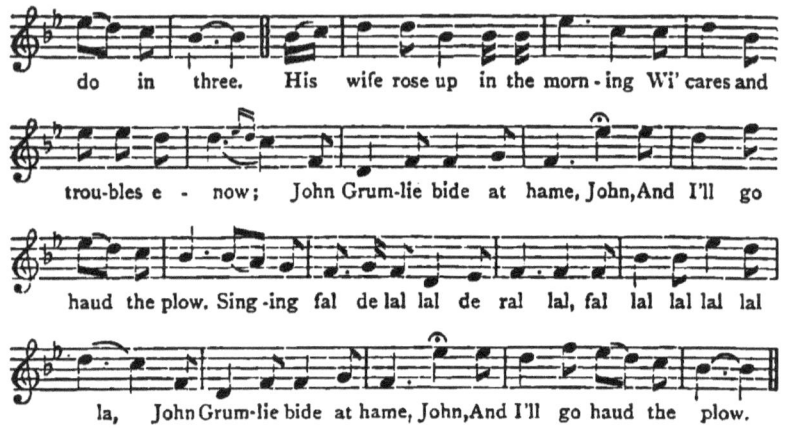

"First ye maun dress your children fair,
  And put them a' in their gear;
And ye maun turn the malt, John,
  Or else ye'll spoil the beer.
And ye maun reel the tweel, John,
  That I span yesterday;
And ye maun ca' in the hens, John,
  Else they'll a' lay away."
    Singing, fal de lal lal, &c.

O he did dress his children fair,
  And he put them a' in their gear;
But he forgot to turn the malt,
  And so he spoiled the beer.
And he sang aloud as he reel'd the tweel
  That his wife span yesterday;
But he forgot to put up the hens,
  And the hens a' lay'd away.
    Singing, fal de lal lal, &c.

The hawket crummie loot down nae milk;
  He kirned, nor butter gat;

And a' gaed wrang, and nought gaed right;
  He danced wi' rage, and grat.
Then up he ran to the head o' the knowe,
  Wi' mony a wave and shout;
She heard him as she heard him not,
  And steered the stots about.
    Singing, fal de lal lal, &c.

John Grumlie's wife cam' hame at e'en,
  And laugh'd as she'd been mad,
When she saw the house in siccan a plight,
  And John sae glum and sad.
Quoth he, "I gie up my housewifeskep,
  I'll be nae mair gudewife."
"Indeed," quo' she, "I'm weel content,
  Ye may keep it the rest o' your life."
    Singing, fal de lal lal, &c.

"The deil be in that!" quo' surly John,
  "I'll do as I've dune before."
Wi' that the gudewife took up a stout rung,
  And John made off to the door.
"Stop, stop, gudewife! I'll haud my tongue—
  I ken I'm sair to blame;
But henceforth I maun mind the plow,
  And ye maun bide at hame."
    Singing, fal de lal lal, &c.

The next is—

GET UP AND BAR THE DOOR.

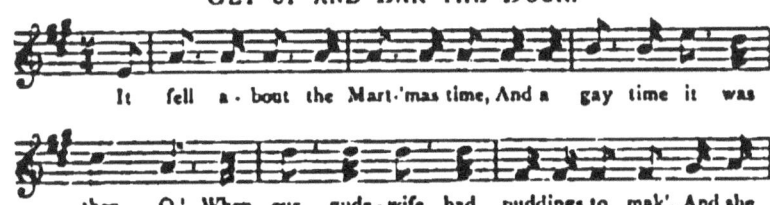

It fell a-bout the Mart.'mas time, And a gay time it was then, O! When our gude-wife had puddings to mak', And she

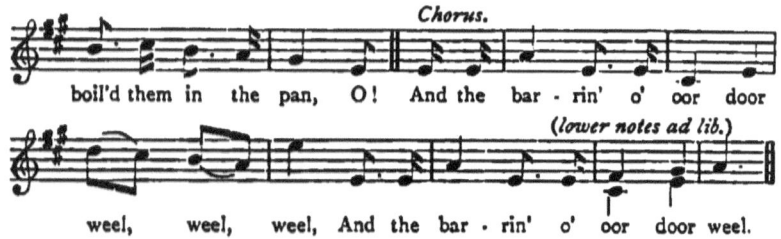

The wind blew cauld frae north to south,
    And blew in to the floor, O !
Quoth our gudeman to our gudewife,
    "Get up and bar the door, O !"

" My hand is in my housewifeskep,
    Gudeman, as ye may see, O !
An' it shouldna be barred this hunder year,
    It's no' be barred for me, O !"

They made a paction 'tween them twa,
    They made it firm and sure, O !
Whaever spak' the foremost word,
    Should rise and bar the door, O !

Then by there came twa gentlemen,
    At twelve o'clock at night, O !
And they could see nor house nor ha',
    Nor coal nor candle light, O !

Now, whether is this a rich man's house,
    Or whether is it a poor, O ?
But never a word wad ane o' them speak,
    For barring o' the door, O !

And first they ate the white puddings,
    And then they ate the black, O !
Tho' muckle thought the gudewife to hersel',
    Yet ne'er a word she spak', O !

Then said the ane unto the other—
"Here, man, tak' ye my knife, O!
Do ye tak' aff the auld man's beard,
And I'll kiss the gudewife, O!"

"But there's nae water in the house,
And what shall we do then, O?"
"What ails you at the puddin' bree
That boils into the pan, O?'

O up then started our gudeman,
And an angry man was he, O!
"Will ye kiss my wife before my een,
And scaud me wi' puddin' bree, O?"

Then up and started our gudewife,
Gied three skips on the floor, O!
"Gudeman, ye've spoken the foremost word,
Get up and bar the door, O!"[1]

---

[1] Though in strict order belonging to our next chapter, we may insert here the late Dr Norman Macleod's humorous song (the Macleods are all poets), set to the same tune, "The Waggin' o' oor Dog's Tail."

We hae a dog that wags his tail—
He's a bit o' a wag himsel', O;
A' day he wanders through the street—
At nicht he's news to tell, O.
 And the waggin' o' oor dog's tail, tail, tail,
 And the waggin' o' oor dog's tail.

He saw the provost o' the toon
Paraudin' doon the street, O;
Quo' he, "My lord, you're no' like me—
Ye canna see yer feet, O."

He saw an M.P. unco proud,
And a' thro' place and pay, O;
Quo' he, "Your tail is cockit helch—
Ilka dog has just his day, O."

Our third is decidedly the best, and the most popular, having been sung by the celebrated Scottish vocalist, John Wilson, and included in his list of the Songs of Scotland,

---

He saw the doctor drivin' aboot,
   And pu'in' at every bell, O;
Quo' he, "I've been as sick's a dog,
   But I aye could cure mysel', O."

He saw some ministers fechtin' sair—
   What an awfu' thing is pride, O;
Quo' he, "Isn't it a pity when dogs fa' out
   Aboot their ain fireside, O."

He heard a lord and lady gay
   Singin' heich a grand duet, O;
Quo' he, "I've heard a cat and dog
   Could yowl as weel as that, O."

He saw a youth gaun swaggerin' by
   Frae tap to tae sae trim, O;
Quo' he, "It's no' for a dog to lauch
   That ance was a puppy like him, O."

He saw a man grown unco puir,
   And lookin' sad and sick, O;
Quo' he, "Cheer up, for ilka dog
   Is sure o' a bane to pick, O."

He saw a man gaun staggering hame,
   His face baith black and blue, O;
Quo' he, "I think shame o' a brute like that,
   For the never a dog gets fou, O."

Our doggie he cam' hame at e'en,
   And scartit baith his lugs, O;
Quo' he, "If men had only tails,
   They're near as guid as dogs, O."

sung by him, and dedicated to Queen Victoria in the year 1842. There is a delicate touch about it which the others want, and which entitles it to the praise of classical in its kind. It has also the merit of antiquity; the original germ, if not the extended form of it in our present version, being found in Shakespeare:[1]—

TAK' YOUR AULD CLOAK ABOUT YE.

In winter when the rain rain'd cauld, And frost and snaw on ilka hill; And Boreas wi' his blasts sae bauld, Was threat'ning a' our kye to kill. Then Bell, my wife, wha lo'es nae strife, She said to me right hastily, Get up, gudeman, save Crummie's life, An' tak' your auld cloak about ye.

 My Crummie is a usefu' cow,
  An' she is come o' a gude kin';
 Aft has she wet the bairns' mou',
  An' I am laith that she should tyne.

---

[1] Othello, Act ii. sc. iii.

Get up, gudeman, it is fu' time,
    The sun shines in the lift sae hie;
Sloth never made a gracious end;
    Gae, tak' your auld cloak about ye.

My cloak was ance a gude gray cloak,
    When it was fitting for my wear;
But now it's scantly worth a groat,
    For I hae worn't this thretty year;
Let's spend the gear that we hae won,
    We little ken the day we'll dee:
Then I'll be proud, since I have sworn
    To hae a new cloak about me.

In days when our King Robert rang,
    His trews they cost but half-a-croun;
He said they were a groat owre dear,
    And ca'd the tailor thief and loon.
He was the king that wore a croun,
    And thou'rt a man o' laigh degree;
'Tis pride puts a' the country doun,
    Sae tak' your auld cloak about ye.

Ilka land has its ain lauch,
    Ilk kind o' corn has its ain hool:
I think the world is a' gane wrang,
    When ilka wife her man maun rule.
Do ye no' see Rob, Jock, and Hab,
    How they are girded gallantlie,
While I sit hurklin i' the ase?
    I'll hae a new cloak about me!

Gudeman, I wat it's thretty year
  Sin we did ane anither ken;
And we hae had atween us twa
  Of lads and bonnie lasses ten:
Now they are women grown and men,
  I wish and pray weel may they be;
If you would prove a guid husband,
  E'en tak' your auld cloak about ye.

Bell, my wife, she lo'es nae strife,
  But she would guide me, if she can;
And, to maintain an easy life,
  I aft maun yield, tho' I'm gudeman.
Nocht's to be gain'd at woman's hand,
  Unless ye gie her a' the plea;
Then I'll leave aff where I began,
  And tak' my auld cloak about me.

We conclude our sequence of marriage-songs with one which bears the same relation to the love-songs of joy, with which we started, that the mellow sweetness of the fruit in autumn bears to the exuberant flush of vegetation in the spring. Burns wrote not a few things in his best moments brighter than "John Anderson, my Jo," but none better:—

JOHN ANDERSON, MY JO.

John An-der-son, my Jo, John, When we were first ac-quent, Your locks were like the ra-ven, Your bon-nie brow was

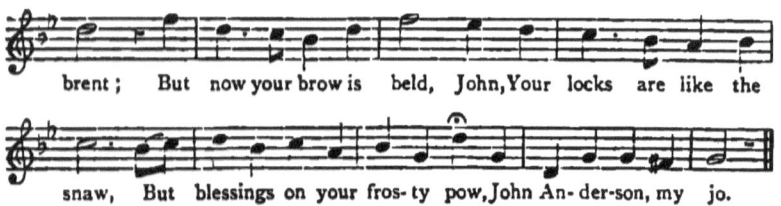

brent; But now your brow is beld, John, Your locks are like the snaw, But blessings on your fros-ty pow, John An-der-son, my jo.

> John Anderson, my jo, John,
>   We clamb the hill thegither,
> And mony a canty day, John,
>   We've had wi' ane anither;
> Now me maun totter down, John,
>   But hand in hand we'll go,
> And we'll sleep thegither at the foot,
>   John Anderson, my jo.[1]

We now come to the last division of this fertile theme—love-songs of sadness and sorrow; and here, of course, we

---

[1] The verse—

> John Anderson, my jo, John,
>   When Nature first began
> To try her canny hand, John,
>   Her maister-wark was man;
> And you, amang the lave, John,
>   Sae trig frae tap to toe—
> She prov'd hersel' nae journey-wark,
>   John Anderson, my jo—

generally interjected as the second, was not written by Burns (see Johnson's Museum, vol. iii. p. 269), nor indeed could have been, as contrary to the well-known compliment of the bard paid to his favourite sex in the lines:—

> Auld Nature swears the lovely dears
>   Her noblest work she classes, O!
> Her prentice han' she tried on man,
>   And then she made the lasses, O!

can scarcely fail to be reminded of what Shakespeare says in the well-known lines—

> "Ah me! for aught that I could ever read,
> Could ever hear by tale or history,
> The course of true love never did run smooth."

Or, as it stands in Shelley's more poignant exclamation—

> "Most wretched men
> Are cradled into poetry by wrong;
> They learn in suffering what they teach in song."

Which of course, like all lyrical utterances, is true—so far as it is true, that is, in the circumstances to which it applies, and in the degree which the intensity of impassioned sentiment demands. Curious philosophers and theologians have busied themselves with asking the question, why evil exists in a world the creation of a perfectly good Being,—they would have been wiser if they had asked how it possibly could have been avoided. In a world which, taken as a whole, is a putting forth and a play of forces, with a certain measurable momentum, it is perfectly plain that, if any force, whether moral or physical, be strained beyond its average tension, a reaction must take place which will be felt painfully in proportion to the highly potentiated pleasure which accompanied the strain; and in the case of love there is this additional element, that the rapturous pleasure is occasioned by the presence of another person whose agency acts as a responsive note, forming a harmonious chord in the sentiment of the impassioned party; the necessary consequence of which is, that, if any circumstance,—of which in this so complex world there are many,—causes the touch of the responsive note to be removed, the soul-thrilling harmony will cease altogether, or be replaced by a dissonance and a jar more painful, by contrast, than the blank occasioned by the removal. And here we have before us opened up the whole domain of those songs of sadness which modulate into sweetness the sad separation of the loved from the lover, through all the various phases which it may assume in the experience of life, from the farewell of a few days, whose cloudy aspect will certainly cease with the returning sun, to the farewell of long years in the case of the departing emigrant, and the farewell for ever on this side the grave in the awfulness of death. Of these love-songs of parting not a few of the best are by Burns, the fire and force of whose amorous passion when in full career of enjoyment was not more significant of his intensely songful and soulful nature than the deep pathos and delicate tenderness of his strains of bereavement. The following is in the person of the bereaved fair one:—

WANDERING WILLIE.

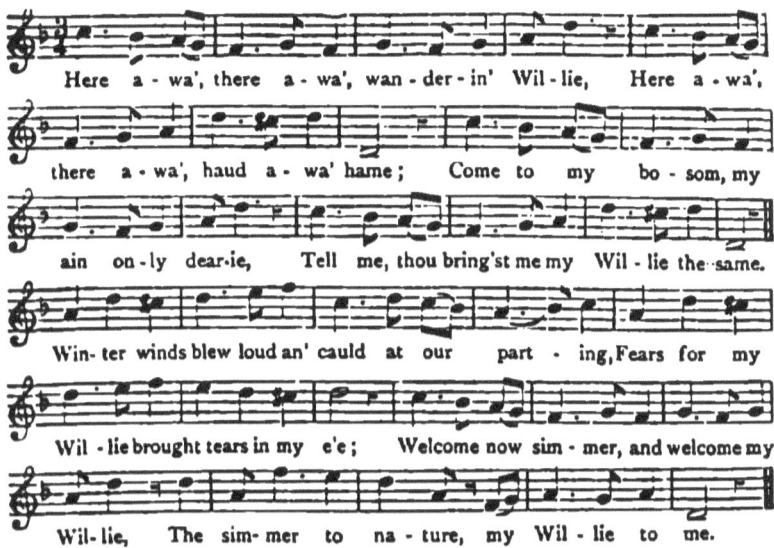

Rest, ye wild storms, in the cave of your slumbers,
  How your dread howling a lover alarms!
Wauken, ye breezes! row gently, ye billows!
  And waft my dear laddie ance mair to my arms.
But oh! if he's faithless, and minds nae his Nannie,
  Flow still between us, thou wide roaring main!
May I never see it, may I never trow it,
  But dying, believe that my Willie's my ain!

The next is in the person of the gentleman, and has been supposed to refer to Mrs Agnes Maclehose, on her departure to America to venture the dutiful but hopeless experiment of reclaiming her worthless husband; but the proof is insufficient:[1]—

[1] See the Clarinda Correspondence (Edinburgh, 1843), p. 278; and Paterson's Burns, vol. vi. p. 229.

My Nannie's Awa'.

Now in her green mantle blythe Nature arrays,
And listens the lambkins that bleat ower the braes,
While birds warble welcome in ilka green shaw;
But to me it's delightless, my Nannie's awa'.

The snaw-drap and primrose our woodlands adorn,
And violets bathe in the weet o' the morn;
They pain my sad bosom, sae sweetly they blaw!
They mind me o' Nannie—and Nannie's awa.

Thou laverock, that springs frae the dews of the lawn,
The shepherd to warn of the gray-breaking dawn,
And thou mellow mavis, that hails the night-fa';
Give over for pity—my Nannie's awa'.

Come, autumn, sae pensive, in yellow and gray,
And soothe me wi' tidings o' Nature's decay:
The dark, dreary winter, and wild-driving snaw,
Alane can delight me—my Nannie's awa.'

About the following, however, there can be no doubt, as it was enclosed in a letter to the lady, from Dumfries, dated 27th December 1791. The plaintive Highland air to which it is adapted has found an honoured place in the 'Songs of the North,' Field & Tuer, London, by whose kind permission it appears here.

AE FOND KISS.

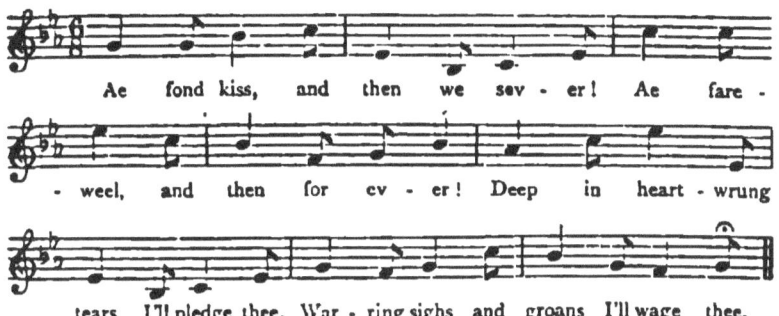

Who shall say that Fortune grieves him
While the star of hope she leaves him?
Me, nae cheerful twinkle lights me,
Dark despair around benights me.

I'll ne'er blame my partial fancy,
Naething could resist my Nancy;
But to see her was to love her,
Love but her, and love for ever.

Had we never loved sae kindly,
Had we never loved sae blindly,
Never met, or never parted,
We had ne'er been broken-hearted!

Fare thee weel, thou first and fairest,
Fare thee weel, thou best and dearest;
Thine be ilka joy and treasure,
Peace, enjoyment, love, and pleasure!

Ae fond kiss, and then we sever!
Ae farewell, alas! for ever!
Deep in heart-wrung tears I'll pledge thee,
Warring sighs and groans I'll wage thee.

Our next specimen of this class refers to that heart-rending incident in so many a Scotsman's life, his farewell to his dear-loved native land, in migrating to a far strange shore beyond the seas, in all likelihood never to return—a banishment not for seven years or fourteen, the damnatory penalty so current in the Justiciary Court, but for life. The scene of the song is a picturesque ravine with a foaming stream, in the west end of Glasgow—like the Water of Leith in the west end of Edinburgh—fifty years ago a wooded and sequestered country retreat, fit for love-making and love-songs; now, in this miraculous age, when the town marches into the country with fevered speed, part of the north-western wing of the huge metropolis of the west. The author of the song was a surgeon, Thomas Lyle, one of the illustrious roll of poetical Scotsmen who conspire in conferring on Paisley the honour of being the lyrical capital of the west. Like most poets, he does not appear to have had any special capacity for what is called making a fortune by the exercise of his profession; but besides the beautiful song of "Kelvin Grove," which will live for ever, he distinguished himself by a volume on the ancient ballads and songs of Scotland, published in 1827, which will be of permanent value to the students of Scottish poetry. He died in 1759, having attained to the respectable age of sixty-seven:—

LET US HASTE TO KELVIN GROVE.

Let us haste to Kelvin grove, bonnie lassie, O, Through its mazes let us rove, bonnie lassie, O; Where the rose in all her pride, Paints the hollow dingle side, Where the midnight fairies glide, bonnie lassie, O.

Let us wander by the mill, bonnie lassie, O,
To the cove beside the rill, bonnie lassie, O;
    Where the glens rebound the call
    Of the roaring waterfall,
Through the mountain's rocky hall, bonnie lassie, O.

O Kelvin's banks are fair, bonnie lassie, O,
When in summer we are there, bonnie lassie, O;
    There the May-pink's crimson plume
    Throws a soft but sweet perfume,
Round the yellow banks of broom, bonnie lassie, O.

Though I dare not call thee mine, bonnie lassie, O,
As the smile of fortune's thine, bonnie lassie, O;
    Yet with fortune on my side,
    I may stay thy father's pride,
And win thee for my bride, bonnie lassie, O.

But the frowns of fortune lower, bonnie lassie, O,
On thy lover at this hour, bonnie lassie, O;

  Ere yon golden orb of day
  Wake the warblers from the spray,
From this land I must away, bonnie lassie, O.

Then farewell to Kelvin grove, bonnie lassie, O,
And adieu to all I love, bonnie lassie, O;
  To the river winding clear,
  To the fragrant scented brier,
And to thee, of all most dear, bonnie lassie, O.

And when on a foreign shore, bonnie lassie, O,
Should I fall 'midst battle's roar, bonnie lassie, O,
  Then, Helen! shouldst thou hear
  Of thy lover on his bier,
To his memory drop a tear, bonnie lassie, O.

These are classical specimens of such sorrow in the separation of lovers, as every loving heart in the changeful experience of life at one time or other must have shared. But sad as they are, leaving often after many years an inward bleeding which cannot be healed, they carry nothing with them but the pang of the separation: there was no treachery in the lifelong divorce of two souls once so near and so dear; a sting there was, and a sting remained; but there was no poison on its point. A salt tear might flow ever and anon, when a significant day recurred or a speaking scene was recalled; but there was no rankling memory of fair professions falsified, or innocent confidence abused. What a beautiful thing is a rose!—for hue and fragrance, and rich broad-bosomed luxury of growth, the pride of the world of flowers; but what a sad thing, on the other hand, when the lovely and blushing petals are rudely torn away, and so scattered and trampled under foot, that only the thorn remains! Yet this is literally the treatment which a pure-minded loving girl may have received from a carnal or cowardly villain, professing to be actuated by that noblest passion which both philosophy and piety rightly declare to be the fulfilling of the law. Verily some songs are the best of sermons; and here follows one, by our great master-singer, perhaps in its shortness and simplicity the very best. A long talk, however serious, in such depth of sadness would have been out of place :—

YE BANKS AND BRAES O' BONNIE DOON.

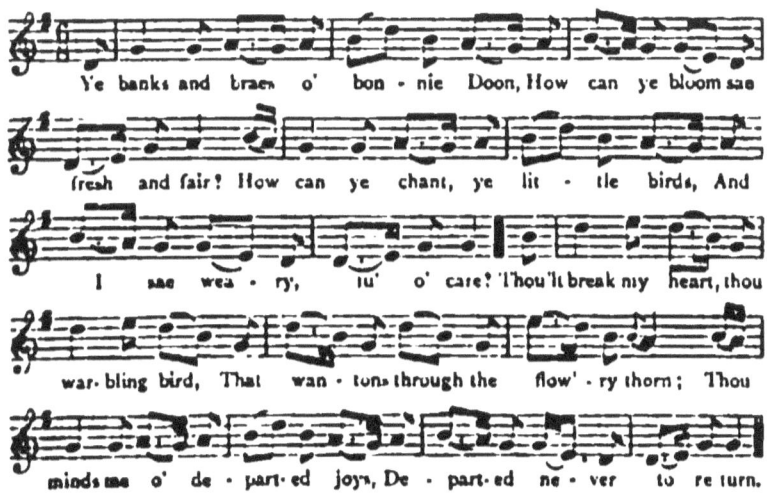

Oft have I roamed by bonnie Doon,
To see the rose and woodbine twine;
And ilka bird sang o' its love,
And fondly so sang I o' mine.
Wi' lightsome heart I pu'd a rose,
Fu' sweet upon its thorny tree;
But my false lover stole my rose,
And ah! he left the thorn to me!

Scarcely less pathetic than this gem is the following well-known love-wail, in which the allusion to Arthur's Seat and St Anthony's Well betrays its composition in the cold and stately metropolis of the east, a city whose atmosphere, partly from the larger infusion of sober Saxon blood in the inhabitants, partly, it may be, from the dominant east wind, partly also, no doubt, from the chilling influence of judicial dignity, seems to be less favourable to the inspirations of the Lyrical Muse than the regions of the west, where life is less prone to be tainted with formalism, and the race has a more liberal infusion of warm Celtic blood:—

O Waly! Waly!

O wa-ly! wa-ly! up the bank, An' wa-ly! wa-ly! down the brae; An' wa-ly! by yon burn-side, Where I an' my love wont to gae.

"O Waly! Waly!"

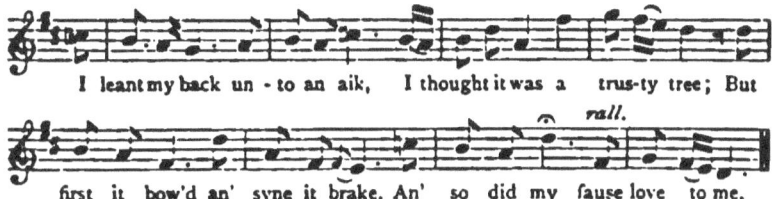

O waly, waly, but love is bonnie
  A little time while it is new;
But when it's auld, it waxes cauld,
  And fades away like morning dew.
O wherefore should I busk my heid,
  Or wherefore should I káme my hair?
For my true love has me forsook,
  And says he'll never love me mair.

Now Arthur's Seat shall be my bed,
  The sheets shall ne'er be pressed by me,
St Anton's Well shall be my drink,
  Since my true love has forsaken me.
Martinmas wind, when wilt thou blaw,
  And shake the green leaves aff the tree?
O gentle death, when wilt thou come?
  For of my life I am wearie.

Tis not the frost that freezes fell;
  Nor blawing snaw's inclemencie;
'Tis not sic cauld that makes me cry;
  But my love's heart's grown cauld to me.
When we came in by Glasgow town,
  We were a comely sicht to see;
My love was clad in the black velvet,
  And I mysel' in cramasie.

> But had I wist, before I kiss'd,
>   That love had been sae ill to win,
> I'd lock'd my heart in a case of gold,
>   And pinn'd it wi' a siller pin.
> Oh, oh! if my young babe were born,
>   And set upon the nurse's knee,
> And I myself were dead and gane,
>   And the green grass growing over me.

These are sharp sorrows indeed, piercing like a sword, in a different sense from St Paul's, even to the dividing asunder of the joints and marrow, leaving a wound in sensitive natures often incurable, and inflicting a wrong, as human laws are, often unpunishable. But the wound is not always so sharp, nor the wrong so atrocious; sometimes there may be no wrong at all, as in Carlile's[1] favourite song of "Wha's at the Window, wha, wha?"; a case in which the more fortunate lover, by natural preference of the fair one, has plucked the lovely flower which the less fortunate one had counted to plant in his bosom. Here we have only to admire the evangelical sweetness of the sorrowful resignation with which the loss is borne:—

---

[1] This is another of that group of lyrical poets that have made Paisley so illustrious in the annals of Scottish song. Mr Alexander Carlile was born at Paisley in 1788, the year in which Burns settled at Ellisland. He varied and enriched his life as a manufacturer in his native town by wooing the Lyrical Muse, and ended a life full of all sweetness at the ripe age of seventy-two.—Wilson's Poets and Poetry of Scotland, vol. ii. p. 99.

O WHA'S AT THE WINDOW, WHA, WHA?

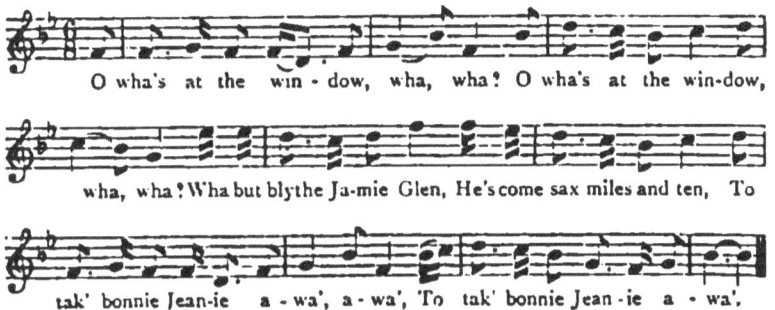

O wha's at the win-dow, wha, wha? O wha's at the win-dow, wha, wha? Wha but blythe Ja-mie Glen, He's come sax miles and ten, To tak' bonnie Jean-ie a-wa', a-wa', To tak' bonnie Jean-ie a-wa'.

He has plighted his troth an' a', an' a',
Leal love to gie an' a', an' a';
   And sae has she done,
   By a' that's aboon,
For he lo'es her, she lo'es him, 'boon a', 'boon a'.
He lo'es her, she lo'es him, 'boon a'.

Bridal maidens are braw, braw,
Bridal maidens are braw, braw;
   But the bride's modest ee,
   An' warm cheek are to me,
'Boon pearlins and brooches, an' a', an' a',
'Boon pearlins and brooches, an' a'.

There's mirth on the green, in the ha', the ha',
There's mirth on the green, in the ha', the ha',
   There's laughing, there's quaffing,
   There's jesting, there's daffing,
And the bride's father's blythest of a', of a',
And the bride's father's blythest of a'.

>It's no that she's Jamie's ava, ava,
>It's no that she's Jamie's ava, ava,
>>That my heart is sae eerie,
>>When a' the lave's cheerie,
>But it's just that she'll aye be awa', awa',
>But it's just that she'll aye be awa'.

Sometimes, when money interferes, or any other cause strong enough to produce what, in the annals of unhappy courtship, is called jilting, the pang is sharper—for no one likes to be cheated; but cases of this kind are always open to the consolation that the offending party, whether from light-heartedness, or base-heartedness, or mere feeble-heartedness, has proved himself altogether unworthy of the confidence so lightly lavished by the offended. Under the influence of such considerations, though the lost loved one may continue to lurk in some corner of the heart of the lover, the recuperative energy of a healthy nature will show itself in a certain air of gaiety and indifference, which the consciousness of honourable sentiment so naturally inspires. This gay and graceful indifference, combined with the kindliest reminiscence of the sweetness of the lost fair one, is the key-note of Mrs Grant of Carron's popular song, "Roy's Wife of Aldivalloch":[1]—

---

[1] Born at Aberlour, in Speyside, Banffshire, about 1745; married first her cousin, Mr Grant of Carron near Elchies, and then Dr Murray, a physician in Bath, where she died in 1814.—Chambers's Songs before Burns, p. 433.

ROY'S WIFE OF ALDIVALLOCH.

And O, she was a canty quean,
    And weel could dance the Highland walloch;
How happy I, had she been mine,
    Or I'd been Roy of Aldivalloch.
        Roy's wife, &c.

Her hair sae fair, her een sae clear,
    Her wee bit mou' sae sweet and bonnie;
To me she ever will be dear,
    Though she's for ever left her Johnnie.
        Roy's wife, &c.

But pleasant as is the fashion in which the air of gay and kindly indifference presents itself, here we have an older song, in which the high-hearted self-sustainment of the deserted fair one rises to a height of real heart-heroism, and evangelical charity seldom realised so perfectly in fact, and never, perhaps, expressed so happily in song:—

I'M GLAD MY HEART'S MY AIN.

It's nae ve-ry lang sin' syne, Sin'. I had a lad o' my ain; But noo he's awa' wi' an-ither, An' left me a' my lane. I'm glad my heart's my ain, I'll keep it sae a' my life, Un-til that an-ith-er casts up That has sense to wed a guid wife. I'm glad my heart's my ain!

I hae seven goons o' my ain,
And seven just lying to mak';
For a' the guid goons that I hae,
My laddie has turned his back.
I'm glad, &c.

There's nae thriftier lassie than I,
An' that a' my neebors can tell;
For a' the guid goons that I hae,
I spint them a' mysel'.
I'm glad, &c.

> But noo, sin' they're buckled thegither,
> I wish them baith happy thro' life;
> But the man that marries for siller,
> Will ne'er be guid to his wife.
> I'm glad, &c.

But there is yet another phase of the self-healing power in the breast of the wounded lover. Hope lives immortal in the human breast, it has been sung when everything else dies; and so, in the humorous song of "The Quaker's Wife," with which we wind up this chapter, the disappointed lover comforts himself with the reflection that the rich old drab-coated intruder, who ousted him of his place in the fair maid's affections, is not immortal, and may at no distant date be called upon to restore his soul to his Maker, and his mate to the original owner, from whom, by the glamour of his gold, she had been unworthily withdrawn. The words of this excellent song I have not met with in any of my collections, and I never heard any one sing it but my father, who was a Kelso man, and likely picked it up in that quarter. I enlarged it by three or four verses of my own composition, and got it published by Mr Roy Paterson, a gentleman to whom Scottish music lies under deep obligations, and by whose kind permission it appears here:—

THE QUAKER'S WIFE.

I loed a lassie lang and leal, I loed her best o' ony; But wae's my heart, she's cheated me, And thinks nae on her Johnnie. The Quaker he had 'neugh o' gear, 'Twas this that caught her fancy; And now she is the Quaker's dear Wha was my lovely Nancy.

The Quaker's wife was brisk and gay,
   And like her werena ony;
But now she wears the mantle grey,
   And thinks nae on her Johnnie.
Aye whan we met we used to be
   As blythe as lark or sparrow;
But wae's my heart, she's cheated me,
   To be the Quaker's marrow.

The Quaker's wife had ilka charm
   That Nature could allow her;
How happy I if in my arm
   Kind fortune had bestowed her.
The Quaker's wife, whene'er I see,
   It stings my heart wi' sorrow,
It gars the tears rin frae my ee,
   Like waters in a furrow.

The Quaker's wife, whene'er I see,
　I curse the fate mischancy,
A house and ha' that envied me,
　To furnish wi' my Nancy.
'Tis lack o' cash that ruins kings,
　And clips the poet's fancy;
For lack o' cash I droop my wings,
　And sigh in vain'for Nancy.

The de'il confound his wooden face,
　Wha stole frae me my Nancy,
That sic a lass o' lightsome grace
　Should touch his wooden fancy.
Wi' purple robe a beggar loon,
　A turnip wi' a pansy,
An ass that's shod wi' silver shoon,
　Is he wi' lovely Nancy.

Of all the solemn prigs that go,
　I chiefly hate the Quakers;
They're like a lump o' tasteless dough,
　That ne'er went to the baker's.
The strangest thing that earth contains
　Is this, that one so stupid
Should nurse within his sluggish veins
　So brisk an imp as Cupid.

The Quaker's wife I'll ne'er forget,
　While I can aught remember;
For I ne'er lo'ed anither yet,
　Sin' the first day I kenn'd her.
O gin the Quaker he wad dee,
　And liberty restore her,
My ain the Quaker's wife should be,
　For oh! I do adore her!

CHAPTER III.

PATRIOTIC SONGS, WAR-SONGS, JACOBITE BALLADS.

> Ἐν μύρτου κλαδὶ τὸ ξίφος φορήσω,
> ὥσπερ Ἁρμόδιος κ' Ἀριστογείτων,
> ὅτε τὸν τύραννον κτανέτην
> ἰσονόμους τ' Ἀθήνας ἐποιησάτην.

WE now come to a chapter in the record of popular poetry, not quite so rich, various, and catholic as love-songs, but in the song-literature of every healthy, vigorous, and manly people, occupying a prominent place—songs of patriotism and of war; for common love of country and common determination to assert the rights of country, are the moral forces by virtue of which loose masses of men are marshalled and organised into what we call a nation. All great nations, whatever that sweet-blooded people the Friends may say, have been cradled in war; and there is good reason for it. In a world of such complex variety of character and tendency, adverse interests and conflicting claims must exist; and where passions are strong and judgment partial, and an impartial arbiter nowhere to be found, in such circumstances the contending claims of antagonistic parties must be left to the decision of the sword; a tiger-like fashion, no doubt, in some views, of settling a dispute; but tigers and men, though they both may fight on occasions with like fierceness, are very different creatures, and fight from very different impulses, and for very different ends: the battle-field of tigers is a mere arena of ferocity; the battle-field of men is a school of manhood, and a discipline of virtue. The people which has not spirit to assert its rights, is not worthy to enjoy them; and it is a law of Nature, inherent in the system of things, that the highest goods can be enjoyed permanently by none who are not willing to hold them by their strength, and, if need be, to purchase them with their lives. But more than this. This readiness to purchase essential pleasure by accidental pain calls forth, in its realisation, every noblest quality by which a moral being can be distinguished: courage to face danger; resolution to persist in a calculated plan of action; chivalrous devotion to a noble cause; and systematic subordination of the individual to the good of the community to which he belongs. It is a bloody blossom, no doubt, a battle-field; but a battle-field like Marathon or Bannockburn is a blossom nothing the less, which, as it grows out of the deepest root of moral earnestness, so it ripens into the richest fruit of social life.

Mighty Rome and subtle Greece, holy Palestine and stout Scotland, equally grew great by battles.

All patriotic songs are not war-songs; but all war-songs, at least those which fall under the category of poetry, are patriotic songs; and as the Jacobite songs of Scotland are the finest combination of poetry, patriotism, and war that the history of literature knows, we shall give the songs in praise of the fatherland, war-songs, and the Jacobite ballads in one chapter together, as it were the positive, comparative, and superlative degrees of the same noble passion. And we cannot do better than take the start with Lord Byron, who, though he was only half a Scot, did not write Scotch, and had very little of the sweet Scotch blood in his veins, had nevertheless a soul so grandly in sympathy with some of the most picturesque features of our sublime Scottish landscape, that we shall search in vain among thoroughbred Scots for anything superior to his well-known verses, written under the inspiration of dark Loch-na-gar and the clear-flowing Dee :—

AWAY, YE GAY LANDSCAPES.

"Away, ye Gay Landscapes."

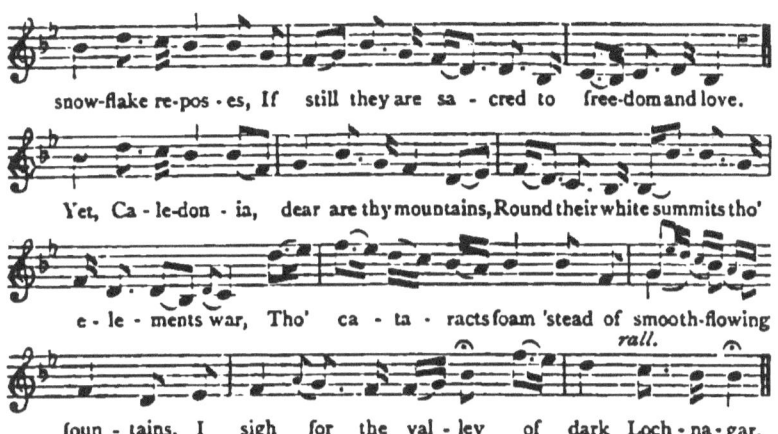

snow-flake re-pos-es, If still they are sa-cred to free-dom and love.
Yet, Ca-le-don-ia, dear are thy mountains, Round their white summits tho'
e-le-ments war, Tho' ca-ta-racts foam 'stead of smooth-flowing
foun-tains, I sigh for the val-ley of dark Loch-na-gar.

Ah! there my young footsteps in infancy wander'd,
    My cap was the bonnet, my cloak was the plaid;
On chieftains departed my memory ponder'd,
    As daily I stray'd through the pine-cover'd glade.
I sought not my home till the day's dying glory
    Gave place to the rays of the bright polar star,
For fancy was cheer'd by traditional story,
    Disclos'd by the natives of dark Loch-na-gar.

Shades of the dead, have I not heard your voices
    Rise on the night-rolling breath of the gale?
Surely the soul of the hero rejoices,
    And rides on the wind o'er his own Highland vale.
Round Loch-na-gar while the stormy mist gathers,
    Winter presides in his cold icy car;
Clouds there encircle the forms of my fathers,
    They dwell 'mid the tempests of dark Loch-na-gar.

Ill-starr'd, though brave, did no vision foreboding
    Tell you that fate had forsaken your cause?
Ah! were ye then destined to die at Culloden,
    Though victory crown'd not your fall with applause?

Still were ye happy in death's earthy slumbers;
    You rest with your clan in the caves of Braemar;
The pibroch resounds to the piper's loud numbers,
    Your deeds to the echoes of wild Loch-na-gar.

Years have roll'd on, Loch-na-gar, since I left you!
    Years must roll on ere I see you again;
Though Nature of verdure and flowers has bereft you,
    Yet still thou art dearer than Albion's plain.
England, thy beauties are tame and domestic
    To one who has rov'd on the mountains afar!
Oh! for the crags that are wild and majestic,
    The steep frowning glories of dark Loch-na-gar!

But grand as these verses are, and worthy of the land that, even more than Switzerland, boasts the happy union of the sublime with the picturesque, they are characteristically more Byronic than Scotch; certainly far removed from the tone of the Scottish patriotic song, of which the lovely and the kindly, not the majestic and the awful, is the habitual key-note. It is notable in this juvenile essay of Byron's lofty fancy, that, though the Scottish pine receives its due honour, neither the graceful birch, nor the blooming heather, nor the yellow broom, nor the fragrant furze, nor the prickly thistle, receives mention; rightly enough, no doubt, for the tone of the poet's mind, but deficient lamentably in the dominant features of the landscape that are dearest to every Scottish heart. Whether it be Andrew Park or Henry Scott Riddell, whether a singer from Paisley fertile in song, or from the Border rich in story, the cloud-cleaving Bens and the sky-sweeping eagles never appear without the blush of the bonnie blooming heather, and the bristling grace of the thistle. From the earliest times, indeed, the sturdy independence of the people, which foiled the ambitious subtlety of the Plantagenets, was fitly symbolised by the prickly plant, which seems to say to every rude invasive hand, in the words of the song :—

> "He's pu'd the rose o' English clowns,
> And broken the harp o' Irish loons,
> But our Scotch thistle will jag his thooms,
> This wee, wee, German Lairdie."

Heraldic tradition asserts that the thistle was borne in the royal achievement of Scotland so early as King Achaius, when he made an alliance with the Emperor Charlemagne; and we are also informed that when Slains Castle in Buchan was attacked by the Danes in 1010, their repulse was owing in no small measure to the reception which their shins met with from the thick array of thistles that bristled in the moat.[1] Certain it is, that in the well-known poem of "The Thistle and the Rose," by William Dunbar, who flourished at the end of the fifteenth century, the thistle is specially lauded as indicative of the instinct of bristling

---

[1] See Mackenzie's Heraldry, p. 98; and Palliser's Historic Devices, p. 328. These notices I owe to G. Seton, Esq., advocate, the highest authority on the subject.

independence, expressed in the national motto, *Nemo me impune lacessit* :—

> "Then called she all flouris that grew on feild,
> Discirning all their fassiones and effeiris;
> Upon the awful thistle she beheld,
> And saw him kepit with a busche of speiris;
> Considering him so able for the weiris,
> A radius crown of rubies she him gaif,
> And said, 'In feild go forth, and fend the laif.'"

In this view Alexander Maclagan, one of the best of our martial song-writers, had good reason to say :—

> "Hurrah for the thistle, the bonnie Scotch thistle!
> The evergreen thistle of Scotland for me;
> Awa' wi' the flowers in your lady-built bowers,
> The strong-bearded, weel-guarded thistle for me."

In the following well-known song, also in the best vein of Scottish patriotism, the traditional significance of the strong-bearded weed is well preserved :—

SCOTLAND YET.[1]

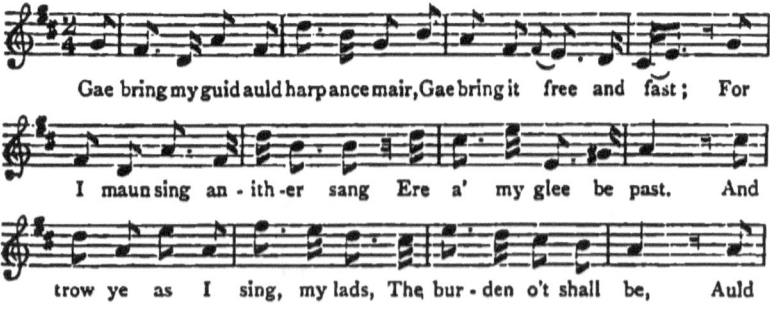

---

[1] Air by kind permission of J. Blockley.

"Scotland yet."

Scotland's howes, and Scotland's knowes, And Scotland's hills for me; I'll drink a cup to Scotland yet, Wi' a' the honours three.

The heath waves wild upon her hills,
    And, foaming frae the fells,
Her fountains sing o' freedom still
    As they dance down the dells.
And weel I lo'e the land, my lads,
    That's girded by the sea;
Then Scotland's dales, and Scotland's vales,
    And Scotland's hills for me;
I'll drink a cup to Scotland yet,
    Wi' a' the honours three.

The thistle wags upon the fields
    Where Wallace bore his blade,
That gave her foemen's dearest bluid
    To dye her auld gray plaid.
And looking to the lift, my lads,
    He sang this doughty glee,
Auld Scotland's right, and Scotland's might,
    And Scotland's hills for me;
I'll drink a cup to Scotland yet,
    Wi' a' the honours three.

They tell o' lands wi' brighter skies,
    Where freedom's voice ne'er rang;
Gi'e me the hills where Ossian dwelt,
    And Coila's minstrel sang;
For I've nae skill o' lands, my lads,
    That ken na to be free.

> Then Scotland's right, and Scotland's might,
> And Scotland's hills for me;
> We'll drink a cup to Scotland yet,
> Wi' a' the honours three.

The title of this excellent song is sadly significant of the change which has been passing over Scotland since the days when Burns and Scott stood before the intellectual world, as at once the most human and the most Scottish of writers. We have now a generation growing up who, subdued by the seductions of London luxury, the glitter of metropolitan and the despotism of official centralisation, are content to sit down as second fiddle and first flunkey to the imperial John Bull—glorying, as St Paul has it, in their shame; so that a national song-writer, feeling all around him the enervating approaches of this insidious foe, is obliged to make *Scotland* YET! the refrain of his song: notwithstanding all this danger and all this degeneracy, Scotland shall still be Scotland, at least in the breast of her native singers, redolent of the blooming heather and the bracing breeze, and not prinkt over with scraps of all sorts of borrowed leaflets from the South. The author of the song, Henry Scott Riddell, like Burns and Hogg, was a shepherd, the son of a shepherd, and amid "the hills of Ettrick wild and lone" grew up in an atmosphere far more favourable to a healthy culture, than a drill in the trick of Latin hexameters and Greek iambics in the fashionable English schools. But, though he could write good poetry without Greek, he could not enter the Church, the top step in the ladder to which every ambitious young Scottish peasant, of intellectual aspirations, naturally points. Born in 1798, on his father's death leaving the cows to some less ambitious cowherd, he went to school at Biggar, and thence to the University of Edinburgh. From this start, in due course, and furnished with laudatory certificates from the professors of Greek and philosophy, he walked into the regular arena of clerical duty in a small manse at Teviothead, under the patronage of the Duke of Buccleuch, with a salary of £50 a-year. Here he performed the duties of his rural episcopacy faithfully and unobtrusively for nine years, till in 1841 he was obliged, from bad health, to remit active work, but was allowed, by the kindness of the Duke of Buccleuch, to remain in the dwelling where he had exercised the ministerial function, and to cultivate his plot of ground, and serve the Border Muses quietly during the rest of his life. He died in 1870, at the ripe age of seventy-two. He was the author of not a few literary works besides songs; and among others, philologers will note with pleasure his translation of the Gospel of St Matthew and the Book of Psalms into Lowland Scotch, made at the request of Lucien Bonaparte.

The patriotic song given above was set to music by Peter M'Leod, and published in a separate form, and the profits of the publication expended upon the erection of a parapet and railing around the monument of our great national poet on the Calton Hill.

It is a commonplace of morality that people never know the full value of the blessings which they enjoy till they are deprived of them; so husbands are found sometimes to write more gracious inscriptions on the tombstones of their dead wives, than their living estimate of them would have led us to expect; and in the same way the natives of any country, whether it be a flat country of dykes and ditches like Holland, or a country of heaven-scaling Bens like Scotland, never know how closely the joys of their human life were bound up with their surroundings, till they are forced to leave them. Scotsmen, it is commonly observed, except, of course, a few featureless souls, who lightly accept a foreign stamp, are more Scotch in London than in Edinburgh; and the Gaelic language, which is the very body and breath of Celtic nationality, is, I am credibly informed, spoken with more purity and preserved with more piety in some Canadian settlements, than in the winding glens and swelling braes of its mountain home. Manfully as the Scotch have on all occasions confronted the necessity of leaving their native hills, and fruitfully as they have cleared the forests and garnered the crops in far lands beyond the seas, there is not one of them, we may safely say, however prosperous in his new abode, who has not sung to himself in moments of pensive thought, or listened to the echo in his heart of Gilfillan's beautiful song—

OH! WHY LEFT I MY HAME?[1]

The palm-tree waveth high,
   And fair the myrtle springs;
And to the Indian maid
   The bulbul sweetly sings.
But I dinna see the broom,
   Wi' its tassels on the lea;
Nor hear the lintie's sang
   O' my ain countrie.

Oh! here no Sabbath bell
   Awakes the Sabbath morn,

---

[1] Air by kind permission of J. Blockley.

Nor song of reapers heard
　Amang the yellow corn;
For the tyrant's voice is here,
　And the wail o' slaverie;
But the sun of freedom shines
　In my ain countrie.

There's a hope for every woe,
　And a balm for every pain;
But the first joys of our heart
　Come never back again.
There's a track upon the deep,
　And a path across the sea;
But for me there's nae return
　To my ain countrie.

The author of this patriotic song was born in Dunfermline, a town dear to the memory of every true Scot, as containing the bones of the royal warrior who founded our nationality at Bannockburn in the glorious June of 1314. Like the majority of our patriotic song-writers, he belonged to the lower classes of society; but after serving as apprentice to a cooper in Leith, he was in due season advanced to the dignity of clerk to an extensive wine merchant, and ended his career in the respectable position of collector of police-rates, in that town. His songs had an extensive circulation, and his name will go far, along with that of Ballantine, to secure to the cold East of Scotland some share of that lyrical reputation which is the special glory of the West. Gilfillan died in 1850, at the early age of fifty-two, and his remains rest in South Leith churchyard, along with those of Home, the well-known author of 'Douglas.'

One other phase of the Scottish patriotic song, more in the humorous style, we may not omit to mention. It was a favourite notion with the London philosopher Mr Buckle, that the character of different races of men depends on the kind of food on which they are nourished; and no doubt there is a certain amount of truth in his view; enough, at all events, to give a hue of philosophic plausibility to Fielding's famous song, in which the eating of roast-beef is accredited with the production of that stout warrior-breed of the seas, each one of whom, Nelson used to say, was equal to three Frenchmen :—

> "When mighty roast-beef was the Englishman's food,
> It ennobled our hearts and enriched our blood,
> Our soldiers were brave, and our courtiers good,—
>   Oh, the roast-beef of Old England,
>   And oh, the Old English roast-beef!"

This song, naturally a great favourite with the substantial feeders of the English army and navy, happened to be played persistently by an English regiment in the granite capital of the north, when stationed there during the time of the American war. The Aberdonians are good Scotsmen, boasting indeed the toughest brains and the broadest skulls of all broad Scotland; they also glory in the birth or in the entertainment of not a few very notable poets, as Barbour, Ross, Beattie, William Thom (above, p. 27), Skinner, Still, Grant, Dr Walter Smith, and not a few others;[1] so it was but natural that the constant echo of this English glorification of beef-eating should rouse a counter-blast in favour of Scottish diet, as it did in the breast of Alexander Watson, a tailor and deacon of the incorporated trades in the city that lies between two rivers. Watson was a man of no literary pretensions, and sang, like many of our best popular song-writers, so to speak, only by accident, and "for fun," as Burns used to say; his pride, so far as he had any, was confined to the fact that he had made Lord Byron's "first pair o' breeks," of which Moore, in his Life of the noble rhymer, failed to make due mention; but his hard-headed fellow-citizens will be prouder of his singing than of his tailoring; and the "Kail Brose of Auld Scotland" will be sung from the Ganges to the Mississippi, on festive occasions, as long as Highland tartan shall not duck before London red-tape, and genuine Highlanders, bred on the hills, shall not be ashamed of showing their brawn:—

[1] See the Bards of Bon Accord from 1375 to 1860, by W. Walker. Aberdeen, 1887.

THE KAIL BROSE OF AULD SCOTLAND.

When our an-cient fore-fa-thers a-greed wi' the laird For a spot o' guid ground for to be a kail-yard, It was to the brose that they paid their re-gard. Oh, the kail brose of auld Scot-land, And oh for the Scot-tish kail brose.

When Fergus, the first of our kings, I suppose,
At the head of his nobles had vanquish'd our foes,
Just before they began they'd been feasting on brose.
    Oh, the kail brose, &c.

Then our sodgers were dress'd in their kilts and short hose,
With bonnet and belt which their dress did compose,
And a bag of oatmeal on their back to make brose.
    Oh, the kail brose, &c.

In our free, early ages, a Scotsman could dine
Without English roast-beef, or famous French wine;
Kail brose, when weel made, he aye thought it divine.
    Oh, the kail brose, &c.

At our annual election of bailies or mayor,
Nae kickshaws of puddings or tarts were seen there,
But a cog of kail brose was the favourite fare.
    Oh, the kail brose, &c.

But now since the thistle is joined to the rose,
And the English nae langer are counted our foes,
We've lost a guid part of our relish for brose.
    Oh, the kail brose, &c.

But each true-hearted Scotsman, by nature jocose,
Can cheerfully dine on a dishful of brose;
And the grace be a wish to get plenty of those.
    Oh, the kail brose, &c.

War-songs, as we remarked, are a species of the genus patriotic. So closely indeed does the enjoyment of our national life hang on the valour with which we defend our country from the invader, that even in peaceful patriotic songs the allusion to the broadsword is never far from the praise of the thistle and the kail brose. In the well-known song, "In the Garb of Old Gaul," of which the music was composed by General Reid, the founder of the Music Chair in the University of Edinburgh, and the words by another gallant soldier, Sir Harry Erskine of Alva, the martial spirit is so decidedly dominant that it may well serve as a transition from the gentle patriotism of peace to the patriotism of sharp warfare, to which we must now proceed:—

In the Garb of Old Gaul.

"In the Garb of Old Gaul."

fought, and they fought not in vain. Such our love of li-ber-ty, our coun-try, and our laws, That like our an-cestors of old, we stand by freedom's cause; We'll bravely fight, like he-roes bright, for honour and ap-plause, And de-fy the French, with all their art, to al-ter our laws.

No effeminate customs our sinews unbrace,
No luxurious tables enervate our race;
Our loud-sounding pipe breathes the true martial strain,
And our hearts still the old Scottish valour retain.
    Such our love, &c.

As a storm in the ocean when Boreas blows,
So are we enraged when we rush on our foes;
We sons of the mountains, tremendous as rocks,
Dash the force of our foes with our thundering strokes.
    Such our love, &c.

We're tall as the oak on the mount of the vale,
Are swift as the roe which the hound doth assail;
As the full moon in autumn our shields do appear,
And Minerva would dread to encounter our spear.
    Such our love, &c.

Quebec and Cape Breton, the pride of old France,
In their troops fondly boasted till we did advance;
But when our claymores they saw us produce,
Their courage did fail and they sued for a truce.
    Such our love, &c.

> In our realm may the fury of faction long cease,
> May our councils be wise, and our commerce increase;
> And in Scotia's cold climate may each of us find
> That our friends still prove true, and our beauties prove kind.
> Then we'll defend our liberty, our country, and our laws,
> And teach our late posterity to fight in freedom's cause;
> That they like our bold ancestors, for honour and applause,
> May defy the French, with all their art, to alter our laws.

As a pendant to this, and sung to the same air, whosoever chooses may sing "The Broadswords of Scotland," by Sir Walter Scott's distinguished son-in-law and biographer, John Gibson Lockhart;[1] but we must pass on.

Of war-songs proper—that is, born out of the bosom, and breathing the atmosphere of hostile movements—we have in the Jacobite ballads, I hesitate not to say, the finest and most complete collection that the popular literature of any country can boast. These ballads have the double advantage of being at once real contemporary history, and real popular poetry of the most classical type; and though in point of political significance and lasting good results they can in no wise bear comparison with the war-songs of the German Liberation war in 1813-14, in point of nobility of sentiment, picturesqueness of situation, and dramatic effect, they are vastly

---

[1] See Rogers's Scottish Minstrel, p. 239, where also will be found the humorously descriptive song, "Captain Paton no mo'e," that originally appeared in 'Blackwood's Magazine.'

superior. In fact, these ballads in their natural historical sequence present to the eye a ready-made national opera of the finest elements and the most effective points, possessing as they do an interesting central figure round which every variety of martial enthusiasm, romantic adventure, broad popular humour, delicate pathos, gathers itself with a natural grace and a completeness of effect which no art could improve. Such rich materials, with all the sweetness of native song and all the strength of native drama, a people like the ancient Greeks, with a complete and well-rounded national culture, would have developed into a trilogy of the most magnificent character and the most potent inspiration; and that it has not done so in Scotland, can be attributed only to the action of that severe and one-sided Calvinism which banished scientific music from the Church, and proclaimed an unnatural divorce between the pulpit and the stage. But, though our Jacobite ballads, within the narrow limits of a year's military action, contain a complete repertory of every scene and situation that the popular song can appropriate and transmute into national poetry, they are naturally not the only expression of the military life of a people whose boast it has been to maintain by steady industry the rights which they gained by gallant achievement. We shall therefore fitly, as a sort of overture to the Jacobite opera, put in the foreground a few of our most popular war-songs, which have either no special historical root, or at least none that distinctly connects them with the rising of the 1745; and here we shall not be surprised that the Celtic element enters largely into the account—for the ardour of attack, and the chivalry of sentiment that make the great soldier, are the peculiar glory of the Celt in all countries, and especially in the Scottish Highlands; as indeed it is quite certain, historically, that the perfervid genius of the Scot, manifested so strongly in our great preachers, flows down to us from the original Celtic element, to which the Saxons and Scandinavians in the south-east and north-west were willing to contribute their ration of less irritable nerve and more sober blood. Broadly, we must say that it is to the Highlanders that Scottish men owe whatever reputation they enjoy for soldiership; as sailors, Nelson did not even own our existence; and, had it not been for the tartan, and the Celtic blood in our veins, we Scotsmen might have gone down to posterity merely as the rivals of Manchester in Titanic industry, and as the great utilisers of the material world by steam-power and bank-notes.

One of the first incidents at the outbreak of a war is the parting of the soldier from his home and from his sweetheart. Sometimes, indeed, the sweetheart may have strength of mind enough to follow her soldier laddie in some capacity to the wars; but still there is a pang, especially to a Highland lassie, who will certainly find the orange-groves of Italy, or the palm-trees of Egypt, a poor exchange for the blaeberries that fringed the woods, the cloudberry that drooped its rich yellow fruit over the upland moor, or the rowan-tree that hung its crimson clusters over the wild and giddy sweep of her native torrents. All this is finely brought out in the following song, not so often sung as it deserves. The words are by Tannahill; the air Gaelic:—

MY DEAR HIGHLAND LADDIE, O.

Blythe was the time when he fee'd wi' my fa-ther, O;
Hap-py were the days when we herd-ed the-gith-er, O;
Sweet were the hours when he row'd me in his plaid-ie, O, And
rall.
vow'd to be mine, my dear High-land lad-die, O.

But, ah, waes me, wi' their sodgering sae gaudy, O,
The laird's wil'd awa' my braw Highland laddie, O;
Misty are the glens, and the dark hills sae cloudy, O,
That aye seem'd sae blythe wi' my dear Highland laddie, O.

The blaeberry banks now are lanesome and dreary, O.
Muddy are the streams that gush'd down sae clearly, O,
Silent are the rocks that echoed sae gladly, O,
The wild melting strains o' my dear Highland laddie, O.

He pu'd me the crawberry, ripe frae the boggy fen,
He pu'd me the strawberry, red frae the foggy glen,
He pu'd me the rowan frae the wild steep sae giddy, O,
Sae loving and kind was my dear Highland laddie, O.

Fareweel my ewes, and fareweel my doggie, O,
Fareweel ye knowes, now sae cheerless and scroggie, O,
Fareweel Glenfeoch, my mammy and my daddie, O,
I will lea' you a' for my dear Highland laddie, O.[1]

A pendant to this is the more sad adieu to the Highland hills, by a soldier going abroad to foreign war—an air familiar to most Scottish ears under the name of "Lochaber no more." The music, of course, is Gaelic, the words by Allan Ramsay, the father of our post-Reformation Scottish poetry, and to whose long literary connection with the capital of his native country the citizens of Edinburgh have erected a becoming tribute in a statue prominently placed in the Gardens of beautiful Princes Street. Ramsay, who was a Lanarkshire man, and died in Edinburgh in the year 1758, the year before Burns was

---

[1] The same sorrowful wrench which war so often gives to love, gives the key-note to the old song, "De'il tak' the Wars," to which Burns wrote the song, "Sleep'st thou, or wak'st thou, fairest creature?" Burns's Works, Philadelphia, 1887, vol. vi. p. 33.

born, as a song-writer has been put out of view by the superior force and fervour of his Ayrshire successor; but he will live for ever by the rural charm of his "Gentle Shepherd," in the bucolic company of Theocritus among the Greeks, and Virgil among the Romans:—

LOCHABER NO MORE.

Though hurricanes rage, and rise ev'ry wind,
They'll ne'er make a tempest like that in my mind;
Though loudest of thunders on louder waves roar,
That's naething like leaving my love on the shore.

To leave thee behind me, my heart is sair pain'd;
But by ease that's inglorious no fame can be gain'd;
And beauty and love's the reward of the brave:
And I maun deserve it before I can crave.

Then glory, my Jeanie, maun plead my excuse;
Since honour commands me, how can I refuse?
Without it, I ne'er can have merit for thee;
And, wanting thy favour, I'd better not be.
I gae then, my lass, to win glory and fame;
And if I should chance to come glorious hame,
I'll bring a heart to thee with love running o'er,
And then I'll leave thee and Lochaber no more.

Next in order follows the gathering of the scattered warriors, their ordering into battalions, the march to the battle-field, and the clash of hostile spears in deadly array; but we shall defer this wisely to its place in the great lyrical drama of the 1745. To the same stage, however, in the general array of Scottish war-songs, belong Scott's "Blue Bonnets over the Border," Maclagan's "We'll hae nane but Highland Bonnets here," and Burns's world-famed pæan over the routed Plantagenet at Bannockburn. Though Scott was not specifically and prominently a song-writer, he had the spirit of song in his soul, a soul rich in the wellspring of all wisdom, the large receptive enjoyment of his surroundings; and so, though locally belonging to Edinburgh, yet with the blood of the Rutherfords and the Scotts in his veins, it was as natural to him to sing the gallantry of a Border foray, as for the mountain streams at the head of Dumfriesshire to flow down into St Mary's Loch :—

BLUE BONNETS OVER THE BORDER.

March, march, Ettrick and Teviotdale, Why, my lads, dinna ye march forward in order? March, march, Eskdale and Liddesdale, All the blue bonnets are over the Border. Many a banner spread flutters above your head, Many a crest that is famous in story; Mount and make ready then, sons of the mountain glen, Fight for your Queen and the old Scottish glory.

Come from the hills where your hirsels are grazing,
  Come from the glen of the buck and the roe;
Come to the crag where the beacon is blazing;
  Come with the buckler, the lance, and the bow.
        March, march, &c.

> Trumpets are sounding, war-steeds are bounding;
> Stand to your arms, and march in good order;
> England shall many a day tell of the bloody fray,
> When the blue bonnets came over the Border.
> March, march, &c.

Alexander Maclagan, whose name will go down to posterity along with the record of the famous charge of our gallant Highlanders on the heights of Alma, was, like most of our noble band of native song-writers, of peasant origin. Born at Brigend, near Perth, in the same year with Thackeray (1811), he left his father's farming business, and earned his livelihood first as a clerk in a jeweller's shop, and then as a journeyman plumber in Edinburgh. But the Muse of Coila, who has always shown a grandly human appreciation of the stuff of which the honest artificer is made, did not in any wise stint her visitations to her chosen military bard, in consideration of the plebeian character of his employment; out of the mouths of shepherds, and plumbers, and ploughmen she hath perfected praise, while she denied her inspiration to the fine gentlemen and nice Greeklings who turned their back on her native charms, and preferred to distinguish themselves by the artificial trickery of dancing on Greek and Latin tight-ropes at Eton and Oxford. Maclagan seized every moment that could be spared from his honest handicraft to add another noble name to the roll of Scottish song-writers; and in this noble endeavour achieved the friendship and patronage of the men of the last generation—Wilson, Glassford Bell, Francis Jeffrey, and Henry Cockburn, whose names at that time made Edinburgh notable as a great centre of literary life. With the true military spirit, so closely allied to the poetic, he in 1860 joined a company of Highland volunteers, having some years previously been honoured with a royal pension. He died in 1879. The song which follows took its key-note from the well-known words of Sir Colin Campbell, when the Guards were pressing on to share the honour of taking the first guns with the Highlanders, "*We'll hae nane but Highland bonnets here*," knowing well, as indeed all the world knows, that whenever anything first-class in the dashing style is to be done in a field of battle, the Highlanders are the men to do it:—

WE'LL HAE NANE BUT HIGHLAND BONNETS HERE.

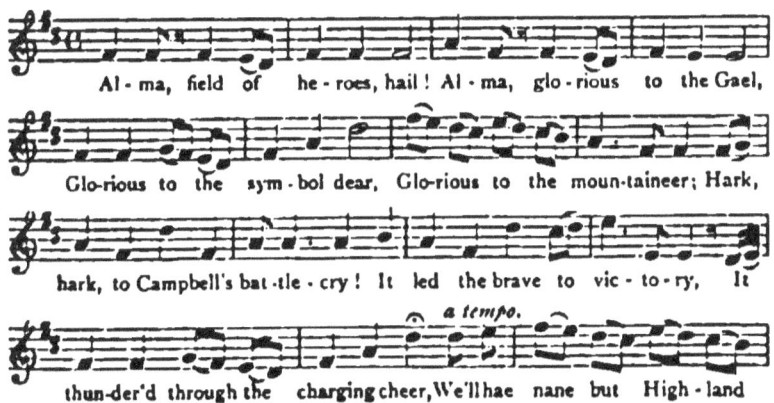

Al-ma, field of he-roes, hail! Al-ma, glo-rious to the Gael,
Glo-rious to the sym-bol dear, Glo-rious to the moun-taineer; Hark,
hark, to Campbell's bat-tle-cry! It led the brave to vic-to-ry, It
thun-der'd through the charging cheer, We'll hae nane but High-land

See, see the heights where fight the brave!
See, see the gallant tartans wave!
How wild the work of Highland steel,
When conquered thousands backward reel.
See, see the warriors of the north,
To death or glory rushing forth!
Hark to their shout from front to rear,
"We'll hae nane but Highland bonnets here!"
    We'll hae nane but Highland bonnets here!
    We'll hae nane but Highland bonnets here!
    Hark to their shout from front to rear,
    We'll hae nane but Highland bonnets here!

Braver field was never won,
Braver deeds were never done;
Braver blood was never shed,
Braver chieftain never led;
Braver swords were never wet
With life's red tide when heroes met!
Braver words ne'er thrilled the ear,
"We'll hae nane but Highland bonnets here!"
    We'll hae nane but Highland bonnets here!
    We'll hae nane but Highland bonnets here!
    Braver words ne'er thrilled the ear,
    We'll hae nane but Highland bonnets here!

Let glory rear her flag of fame,
Brave Scotland cries "This spot I claim!"
Here will Scotland bare her brand,
Here will Scotland's lion stand!
Here will Scotland's banner fly,
Here Scotland's sons will do or die!
Here shout above the "symbol dear,"
"We'll hae nane but Highland bonnets here!"
    We'll hae nane but Highland bonnets here!
    We'll hae nane but Highland bonnets here!
    It thundered through the charging cheer,
    We'll hae nane but Highland bonnets here!

SCOTS, WHA HAE WI' WALLACE BLED.

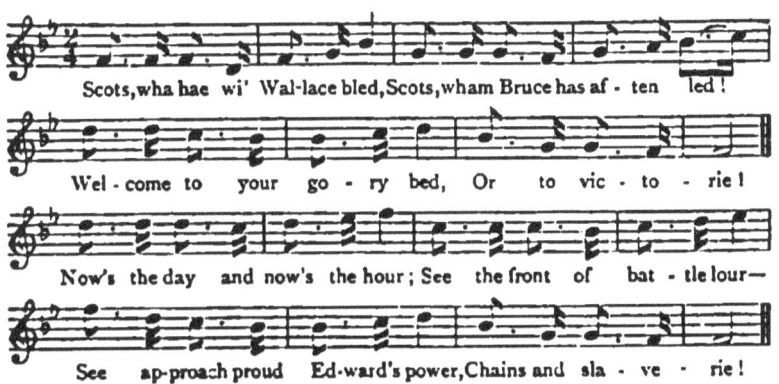

Scots, wha hae wi' Wallace bled, Scots, wham Bruce has aften led!
Welcome to your gory bed, Or to victorie!
Now's the day and now's the hour; See the front of battle lour—
See approach proud Edward's power, Chains and slaverie!

    Wha will be a traitor knave?
    Wha will fill a coward's grave?
    Wha sae base as be a slave?
        Let him turn and flee!
    Wha, for Scotland's king and law,
    Freedom's sword will strongly draw,
    Freeman stand, or freeman fa',
        Let him follow me!

> By oppression's woes and pains,
> By your sons in servile chains,
> We will drain our dearest veins,
>   But they shall be free.
> Lay the proud usurpers low!
> Tyrants fall in every foe!
> Liberty's in every blow!
>   Let us do or dee!

Of course, as every glorious victory on the one side must be accompanied with a tearful defeat on the other, we cannot expect to have our Bannockburn in Scottish history without our Flodden Field, our pæans and odes of triumph without our wails of defeat. James IV. of Scotland, whose name is identified with that bloody business on the English Border, which lopped the heads of our nobility wholesale, as the Borean blast levels the pine-forests, was a man of more genius and gallantry than of wisdom, and more fitted to shine amongst lute-players, and in tournament than in the council chamber of grave statesmanship. So, under the influence of some poetical sensibility, or knightly ideas of honour, he dared to make war on his big father-in-law, the eighth Harry, and paid the penalty of his rashness on the banks of the Till, in a catastrophe which has taken hold of the Scottish Lyrical Muse in a fashion second only to the potent charm of "Scots wha hae." Of the sad mowing down of noble heads on that disastrous field of Flodden in the summer of 1513, we have two musical memorials, composed by two members of that band of accomplished and patriotic ladies who led the society of Scotland in an age when Edinburgh had not yet learned to be ashamed of herself, and to find a shallow satisfaction in aping the manner and adopting the tone of the English metropolis. Miss Jane Elliot, who wrote the oldest and most characteristically Scottish set of "The Flowers of the Forest" (p. 175 *infra*), was a native of Teviotdale, in Roxburghshire, a fair shoot of a noble tree, and the sister of Lord Heathfield, whose defence of Gibraltar against the combined fleets of France and Spain in the last quarter of the last century is familiar to all students of English history, and to most frequenters of print-shops and picture-galleries. Mrs Alison Cockburn, who wrote the other and more current verses to the same air, was by birth Miss Rutherford of Fernielea, situated in that most picturesque stretch of river landscape which lies between Abbotsford and Innerleithen, and where the ruins of the stately old castle, overgrown by (alas! blasted) ivy, are still admired by tourists whom the memory of our great Border-minstrel, or the celebrity of Mr Thomson's vinery at Clovenfords, attracts to that classical region. Between the age of twenty and thirty, when the wisest marriages are made, she became the wife of a Scottish barrister, Patrick Cockburn of Ormiston, and through him transferred her life-stage to Edinburgh, of whose society, in the age immediately before Burns, with her blitheness, brightness, and fresh-heartedness, she soon became a leading ornament. She died in her house, Crichton Street, Edinburgh, at the ripe age of eighty-two, proving thereby, like Joanna Baillie, Lady Ann Barnard, Mrs Grant of Laggan, and not a few other lady-devotees of the Muse of Coila, that the culture of purified passion in song, tends not only to sweeten our lives while we live, but to lengthen our little span for the enjoyment of its sweetness:[1]—

The Flowers of the Forest.

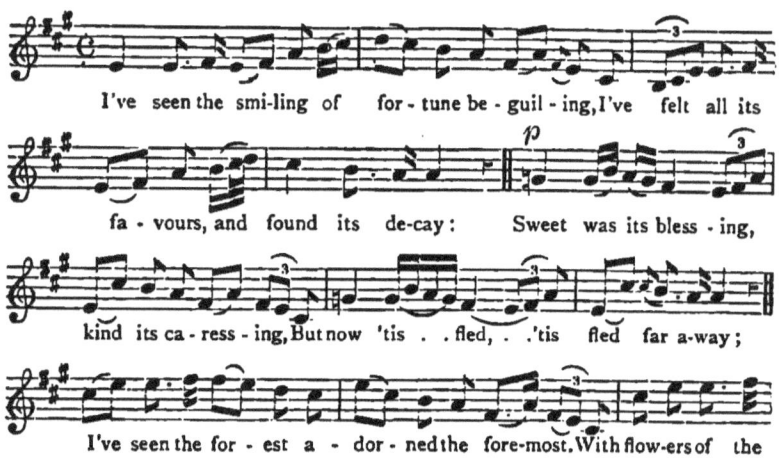

---

[1] The life of Mrs Cockburn in the 'Songstresses of Scotland,' vol. i. p. 52, is full of interesting and instructive material. A full account of the lords of Ormiston, and their worthy achievements—ecclesiastical, judicial, and agricultural—will be found in the Statistical Account, Haddington.

"I've heard the Liltin'."

fair-est, most plea - sant and gay, Sae bon-nie was their blooming, their scent the air per-fum-ing, But now they are wi-ther'd and a' wede a-way.

I've seen the morning with gold the hills adorning,
And the dread tempest roaring before parting day;
    I've seen Tweed's silver streams
    Glitt'ring in the sunny beams,
Grow drumlie and dark as they roll'd on their way.

O fickle fortune! why this cruel sporting?
O why thus perplex us, poor sons of a day?
    Thy frowns cannot fear me,
    Thy smiles cannot cheer me,
For the Flowers of the Forest are a' wede away.

I'VE HEARD THE LILTIN'.

I've heard the lilt-in' at our ewes' milk-in',
Las-ses a-lilt-in' be-fore dawn o' day; But
now there's a moan-in' on ilk-a green loan-in', The
Flowers o' the For-est are a' wede a-way.

At buchts in the mornin', nae blythe lads are scornin',
    Lasses are lanely, and dowie, and wae;
Nae daffin', nae gabbin', but sighin' and sabbin',
    Ilk ane lifts her laiglin and hies her away.

In har'st at the shearin', nae youths now are jeerin',
    The bandsters are runkled, and lyart, and gray;
At fair or at preachin', nae wooin', nae fleechin',—
    The Flowers of the Forest are a' wede away.

At e'en, in the gloamin', nae swankies are roamin'
    'Bout stacks, 'mang the lassies at bogle to play;
But each ane sits dreary, lamentin' her dearie,—
    The Flowers of the Forest are a' wede away.

Dool and wae for the order sent our lads to the Border,
    The English for ance by guile wan the day;
The Flowers of the Forest, that fought aye the foremost,
    The prime o' our land now lie cauld in the clay.

We'll hear nae mair liltin' at our ewe-milkin',
    Women and bairns are dowie and wae;
Sighin' and moanin' on ilka green loanin',—
    The Flowers of the Forest are a' wede away.

We shall now fitly confine ourselves to the special ground of the Jacobite ballads, what we called a ready-made musical drama of war, complete in all its range and perfect in all its parts. And as this grand procession of native Scottish song is a continuous record of notable facts, as well as a consistent unity of lyrical art, we will first sketch the historical root out of which the luxuriant lyrical blossom grew.

The designation by which this rich body of popular poetry is known—Jacobite—carries us back to James II. of England, the last of the ill-starred Stuart dynasty, the restoration of which to their forfeited throne was the object of the two Highland risings of the last century—the first in 1715, and the second in 1745, what the Highlanders call "the year of Charlie." Strictly speaking, however, the birth of the Jacobite ballads is contemporary with the grand struggle for civil liberty carried on against the autocratic and sacerdotal pretensions of Charles II.; and the baptism with which James was honoured in this popular designation was owing simply to the fact that he was the greatest and most prominent fool of the party, and, by the catastrophe which his own persistent stupidity evolved, left that impression on the public mind which the final act of a great dramatic spectacle is calculated to produce. The first ballad in Hogg's collection,[1] "The King shall enjoy his own again," was composed as early as 1643, forty years after the accession of the Stuart dynasty in the person of James I.:—

> "For forty years our royal throne
> Has been his father's, and his own,
> Nor is there any one but he
> With right can there a sharer be.
> For who better may
> Our high sceptre sway

---

[1] The Jacobite Relics of Scotland, by James Hogg (Paisley, Gardiner, 1874); and Jacobite Ballads, by MacQuoy (London, 1888).

>   Than he whose right it is to reign ;
>   Then look for no peace,
>   For the wars will never cease
>   Till the king shall enjoy his own again !"

But the military glory as well as the lyrical excellence of the 1745, so completely eclipsed all previous loyal utterances in favour of the discrowned race, that for purposes of popular recreation and patriotic memory they have mostly died out of the public ear. Some of them are in every way deserving of the oblivion into which they have fallen, being vulgar party abuse, cleverly versified, as in the well-known ditty, with the refrain "Hey then up go we!" charging the friends of liberty and constitutional right with all sorts of irreligion, profanity, tastelessness, and mad revolutionary schemes, as thus :—

>   "We'll break the windows which the whore
>   Of Babylon hath painted;
>   And when the popish saints are down,
>   Then Burges shall be sainted.
>   There's neither cross nor crucifix
>   Shall stand for men to see;
>   Rome's trash and trumpery shall go down,
>   And hey then up go we !
>
>   Whate'er the popish hands have built,
>   Our hammers shall undo;
>   We'll break their pipes, and burn their copes,
>   And burn down churches too.

We'll exercise within the groves,
  And preach beneath the tree;
We'll make a pulpit of a cask,
  And hey then up go we!

We'll down with all the 'Versities,
  Where learning is profest,
Because they practise and maintain
  The language of the Beast.
We'll drive the doctors out of doors
  And parts, whate'er they be;
We'll cry all arts and learning down,
  And hey then up go we!

We'll down with deans and prebends too,
  And I rejoice to tell ye,
How that we will eat pigs at will,
  And capons by the belly.
We'll burn the fathers' learned books,
  And make the schoolmen flee;
We'll down with all that smells of wit,
  And hey then up go we!"[1]

Of the rising in 1715—"a lamentable failure," as Green has it, "from the cowardice and want of conduct in the Earl of Mar"—only two echoes still linger pleasantly in the general ear. The first is a humorous description of the battle of Sheriffmuir, near Dunblane, in November 1715, which may serve as a model for all time of that equivocal style of battle in which both parties gain a partial victory

[1] Hogg, vol. i. p. 15.

and both bear a partial loss; and of which the result is to be sought for, not on the scene of contest, but on the movements which follow. A drawn battle to-day becomes a ruinous defeat to-morrow, when the party whose interests required him to advance, or to maintain his ground, is obliged to retreat. The words that have obtained the largest currency are by Burns; though those who are curious about minute traits of historical verity will no doubt prefer the older version, with which Hogg's second volume takes its start:—

THE BATTLE OF SHERIFFMUIR.

O cam' you here the fight to shun, Or herd the sheep wi' me, man; Or was ye at the Sher-ra-muir, And did the bat-tle see, man? I saw the bat-tle, sair and teuch, And reek-in' red ran mo-ny a sheuch, My heart, for fear, ga'e sough for sough, To hear the thuds, and see the cluds, O' clans frae wuds, in tar-tan duds, Wha glaum'd at kingdoms three, man. Huh! hey dum dir-rum, hey dum dan, Huh! hey dum dir-rum dey dan; Huh! hey dum dir-rum, hey dum dan, Huh! hey dum dir-rum dey dan.

The red-coat lads wi' black cockades,
   To meet them werena slaw, man;
They rush'd, and push'd, and bluid out gush'd,
   And mony a bouk did fa', man.
The great Argyle led on his files,
I wat they glanced twenty miles,
They hough'd the clans like nine-pin kyles;
They hack'd and hash'd, while broadswords clash'd,
And through they dash'd, and hew'd and smash'd,
   Till feymen died awa', man,
      Huh! hey, &c.

But had you seen the philabegs,
   And skyrin' tartan trews, man,
When in the teeth they daur'd our Whigs,
   And Covenant true-blues, man.
In lines extended lang and large,
When bayonets opposed the targe,
And thousands hastened to the charge;
Wi' Highland wrath, they frae the sheath
Drew blades o' death, till out o' breath,
   They fled like frighted doos, man,
      Huh! hey, &c.

O, how de'il, Tam, can that be true?
   The chase gaed frae the north, man;
I saw mysel' they did pursue
   The horsemen back to Forth, man.
And at Dunblane, in my ain sight,
They took the brig wi' a' their might,
And straught to Stirling wing'd their flight,
But, cursed lot, the gates were shut,
And mony a huntit puir red-coat,
   For fear amaist did swarf, man.
      Huh! hey, &c.

My sister Kate cam' up the gate
    Wi' crowdie unto me, man;
She swore she saw some rebels run
    To Perth and to Dundee, man.
Their left-hand general had nae skill,
The Angus lads had nae guid-will
That day their neighbours' bluid to spill;
For fear, by foes, that they should lose
Their cogs o' brose, they scared at blows,
    And hameward fast did flee, man.
        Huh! hey, &c.

They've lost some gallant gentlemen
    Amang the Highland clans, man;
I fear my Lord Panmure is slain,
    Or in his enemies' hands, man.
Now wad ye sing this double fight,
Some fell for wrang, and some for right;
And mony bade the world guid night.
Say pell and mell, wi' musket knell,
How Tories fell, and Whigs to hell
    Flew aff in frighted bands, man.
        Huh! hey, &c.

The next lyrical memorial of that crude adventure, "Kenmure's on an' awa'," takes its present form also from our great ploughman-bard; and has for its hero, William Gordon, Viscount Kenmure, who, while the Earl of Mar was raising the Stuart standard in the North, conceited himself strong enough to make a dash from Galloway into Lancashire, where he paid for his folly by being taken prisoner at Preston, and thence conducted to London, where he suffered the inglorious martyrdom that follows gallantry without policy, by laying his head beneath the axe of the executioner on Tower Hill, in November 1716:—

O KENMURE'S ON AN' AWA', WILLIE.

O Kenmure's on an' a-wa', Wil-lie, O Kenmure's on an' a-wa'; And Kenmure's lord's the brav-est lord That e-ver Gal-loway saw. Suc-cess to Kenmure's band, Wil-lie, Suc-cess to Kenmure's band; There's no' a heart that fears a Whig, That rides by Kenmure's hand.

    Here's Kenmure's health in wine, Willie,
      Here's Kenmure's health in wine;
    There ne'er was a coward o' Kenmure's bluid,
      Nor yet o' Gordon's line.
    O Kenmure's lads are men, Willie,
      O Kenmure's lads are men;
    Their hearts and swords are metal true,
      And that their faes shall ken.

    They'll live or die wi' fame, Willie,
      They'll live or die wi' fame;
    But soon wi' sounding victory
      May Kenmure's lord come hame.

> Here's him that's far awa,' Willie,
>   Here's him that's far awa';
> And here's the flow'r that I lo'e best,
>   The rose that's like the snaw.[1]

We shall now cast a hasty glance over the remarkable series of events in the rising of the '45, of which the Jacobite ballads are the lyrical commentary; but, before doing this, we must give a distinct recognition to one of the most popular of those ballads, which stands in the anomalous position of being associated in the popular ear with "the year of Charlie," but without any historical warrant for such fellowship. We allude to "The Bonnie House o' Airlie," a ballad which describes an attack made by the Campbells from the West country, stout adherents of Scottish Liberalism in Church and State, against the Ogilvies in the East, equally noted for their loyalty to the Stuarts; an attack, however, of which no trace is found in the familiar record of the '45. We are therefore forced to recognise here one of the common tricks of the traditional memory of the common people, in virtue of which, historical events of a kindred hue and drift are massed round some central figure that happens to stand most prominent in the cycle of events to which it belongs. In this way, as Hogg informs us, an attack made by the Marquis of Argyll against the castle of Airlie in the year 1640, at the instance

[1] See the song "The Snow-white Rose." J. Muir Wood, Glasgow.

of the Estates of the Scottish Parliament, in order to punish Lord Ogilvie for refusing to subscribe to the Covenant, was by the popular imagination uprooted from its native soil, and made to form part of a cognate drama that happened a hundred and five years afterwards; possibly on no more profound suggestion than the easy rhyme that the familiar name of the Prince formed with the old castle of the Ogilvies. Of this beautiful ballad, distinguished even among the distinguished company to which it belongs, by its dramatic picturesqueness, and the alternation of vigour and pathos which it presents, there exists, as was to have been expected from its equivocal birth, a variety of versions; but the best for singing purposes is, I think, that given in 'The Lyric Gems of Scotland,' and which follows here:—

THE BONNIE HOUSE O' AIRLIE.

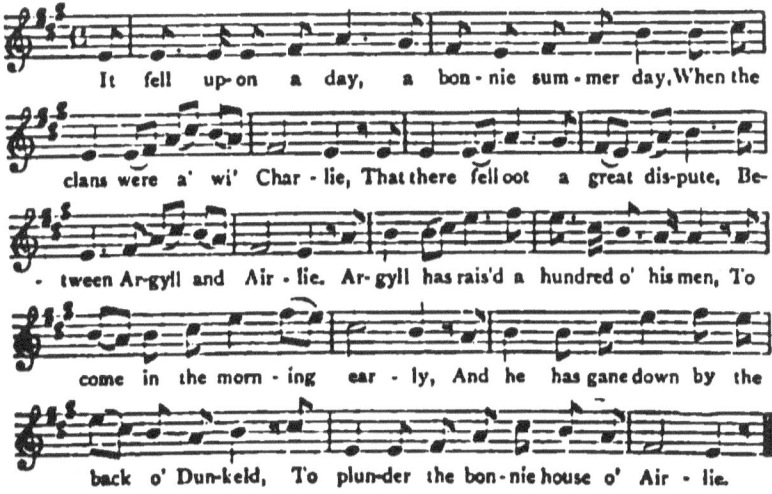

Lady Ogilvie look'd frae her high castle wa',
  And O but she sighed sairly,
To see Argyll and a' his men
  Come to plunder the bonnie house o' Airlie.
"Come doon, come doon, Lady Ogilvie," he cried,
  "Come doon and kiss me fairly,
Or ere the morning daylight dawn
  I'll no' leave a standing stane in Airlie."

"I wadna come doon, proud Argyll," she cried,
  "I wadna kiss thee fairly;
I wadna come doon, thou false lord," she cried,
  "Tho' ye leave na a standing stane in Airlie.
But were my ain gude lord at hame,
  As this night he's wi' Charlie,
It's nae Argyll nor a' his men
  Durst plant a foot within the ha' o' Airlie.

O I hae born him seven bonnie sons,
  The last ne'er saw his daddie,
But gin I had as mony o'er again
  They su'd a' gang and serve Prince Charlie."
Argyll in a rage attacked the bonnie ha',
  And his men to the plundering fairly,
And tears tho' he saw like dew-draps fa',
  In a lowe he set the bonnie house o' Airlie.

"What lowe is yon?" quo' the gude Lochiel,
  "That rises this morning sae early;"
"By the God o' my kin," cried the young Ogilvie,
  "It's my ain bonnie house o' Airlie.
It's no' my bonnie house, nor my lands a' reft,
  That grieves my heart sae sairly,
It's for my winsome wife, and the sweet babes I left,
  They'll be smor'd in the dark reek o' Airlie."

The Rising of the 1745.

"Draw your dirks, draw your dirks," cried the brave Lochiel,
 "Unsheath your swords," cried Charlie,
"And we'll kindle sic a lowe round the false Argyll,
 And licht it wi' a spark out o' Airlie."

The motive forces which gave rise to the rebellion of the '45 lie on the surface. Nothing comes more easily to human beings than, while they fret against the discomforts of the present, to feed on the glories of the past real or imaginary, and to revel in the prospect of a more congenial future. To this, in the case of a dethroned dynasty, must be added the reverential affection of a dissentient party, which will always exist, and which, while it exists, will serve as a convenient nucleus round which less noble elements of dissatisfaction may cluster. In this way it was natural that the Highlanders, who had never felt strongly the pressure of the Stuart despotism, and who, moreover, from the inspiration of the clan system, were royalists and legitimists, while magnifying the stupidities and vexations of the Hanoverian Government, should forget the blessings that came in with the dethronement of James, and promise to themselves a sort of political millennium with the restoration of the exiled race. Not a few of them also were Catholics; and the man who honestly believes in ecclesiastical absolutism, is always sure to prefer the divine right of kings to any governmental arrangement that savours of a social contract. Not a few Episcopalians also, as claiming cousinship with the Bishop of Rome, and disowning all alliance with priestless Presbyterianism, whatever their political principles might be, could not but secretly wish for the success of a despotism which used its divine right to exalt their party and to humiliate the adverse. These considerations, no doubt, weighed with various persons and classes in the Lowlands, as well as far north among the granite Bens; but the rising in favour of Charlie was nevertheless, both in soul and body, a Highland movement, and could not have advanced a single step out of its cradle had it been started in any other quarter. The men of the Pentlands, the Merse, and the straths of the South Highlands, and the moors of the West, had smarted too recently under the scourge of a graceless king, an unpatriotic court, and an unfeeling soldiery, to dream, even for a moment, of displacing the dull Hanoverian Government by a recall of the tiger fierceness and fox-like subtlety of the Stuarts. A few gallant cavaliers, fond of dashing adventure, and inspired by a traditional loyalty to a native race of kings, might picture it as a very brave business to recall an exiled prince and restore a disowned Government; but the vague sentiment of loyalty to kingship and Stuarts, which set the Celtic fancy in a blaze, was in the Lowlands transformed into a firm conviction that it was better to have no kingship at all, than such kings as Scotland had sent to England only to betray her trust and to trample on her independence. The Lowlanders had the living image before them of four kings of Scottish descent who, full of lofty conceit to acclimatise the oriental idea of absolute monarchy on European soil, had paid the penalty of their folly by decapitation and deportation: James I., a bookish pedant and a timid trickster, a man without any kingly quality, striving to undermine secretly the national faith which he had not the courage openly to attack; Charles I., a dignified gentleman and a good Christian, but with all his virtues persistent in his devout adherence to the dogma of a foolish father, and his stout blindness to the rights of a manly people; Charles II., the most easy-going, unprincipled of sensualists whose worthless souls ever died enswathed in Episcopacy and embalmed in Popery; and James II., the most narrow-minded religionist, the most intense stony-hearted bigot, and the most pig-headed blunderer that ever sat on a throne, —these were portraits of kingship that stood stark in all their staring lineaments in the picture-gallery of Lowland memories, when, in the spring of 1745, the young grandson of this same blundering James conceived the idea of making a descent on his ancestral home, and a dash on the British crown. Of course, in the face of such memories, strong not in Presbyterian Scotland only, but generally in Episcopal England, he could not succeed. Even with the whole Highlands at his back—had he been able to get that instead of the section which actually adhered to him—success was impossible; and we may safely assert that no military expedition was ever more false in principle, more ill-advised in policy, and more ruinous in its results than the Stuart rising of 1745. And yet none was ever more brilliant, more picturesque, more poetical in its progress, or more permanently popular in its lyrical expression. No national songs ever were so pervasive, so dramatic, so pathetic at once and so humorous, as the Jacobite ballads; none ever so rich and so exuberant; the lyrical growth which grew directly out of the events having been succeeded by a rich after-growth of cognate inspiration for at least two generations. How was this? For two reasons: first because their inspiration, though going in the teeth of all sound judgment and all probable calculation, was in the highest degree noble, chivalrous, devoted, and self-sacrificing. No doubt we should have felt a more deep-rooted satisfaction in singing these songs, if, as at Bannockburn in 1314, and at Leipzig in 1813, the cause had been as good as the venture was noble; but, in one view, the want of wisdom in the policy only sets in a stronger light the unselfishness and the loyalty of the persons who, in a cause which seemed to them so sacred, were forward to hope against hope, and to believe that political, like religious faith, on great occasions may prevail to remove mountains, and who flung their lives into the scale with a grand confidence in the feeling that, as Burns has it—

> "The heart's aye
> The part aye
> That makes us richt or wrang."

Few things, indeed, are more difficult to reconcile on slippery occasions than sentiment and policy; and so it may come to pass that, while sound policy, as in the case of Queen Elizabeth, may be so utterly destitute of any noble element as to create a certain moral revulsion rather than the admiration which it claims, nobility of sentiment and gallantry of conduct will be readily accepted as a sufficient compensation for the worthlessness of the cause in which they have been enlisted, and the fatal consequences which they have entailed. Certain in this case it is, that the good of the inspiring principle remains to all ages, while the evil of the accidental misapplication is forgotten or condoned; and thus the breeze of loyalty, which blows with such exuberant freshness in the Jacobite ballads, will continue to fan the best sentiments of public life in the British breast long after the blindness that caused them or the blood that followed them shall have been forgotten. And another reason that has given the lyrical memorials of the '45 so striking a dramatic effect, so well-rounded a dramatic completeness, and such an undisputed sway over the hearts of all lovers of national song, is that they naturally disposed themselves round a central figure in the highest degree attractive by his person, by his station, by his conduct, by the memory of past misfortune and the hope of imminent success. Without such a central figure no career of military achievement, however glorious, can shape for itself an enduring place in the poetical literature of its country. Such a figure to the English in our naval warfare was Nelson, to the French Napoleon, to the Germans in the Liberation war Blücher, to the Italians Garibaldi; but none of these typical men of the people, though superior in not a few other respects, were, from an æsthetical point of view, so well equipped as Prince Charlie, with all the trappings that belong to a grand cycle of patriotic song and military adventure.

Prince Charlie landed at Arisaig on the 25th July 1745, with a handful of adventurous adherents. He had touched at Eriskay, one of the southmost Hebrides, some days before; but found Clanranald there too well girt with the wisdom of caution to risk his life and the fate of the Highlands on such a miscalculated throw. At Arisaig he had a meeting with Lochiel, the head of the Cameron clan, mighty in those parts; and here, in the face of wise advice to the contrary, he threw himself dramatically on the fidelity of his loyal Highlanders, and sentiment carried the day over policy. It required no divination, indeed, with a cool head, to see from the start that there was no hope of success in the business. One-half of the Highlands planted against nine-tenths of the Lowlands, and ninety-nine out of every hundred in England, was a game which might start with a brilliant dash of surprise, but could not end otherwise than with dire discomfiture and defeat. A very slight infusion of prudence might have taught the gallant young aspirant to a forfeited throne, that it was madness to attempt an expedition from the far north against the English throne without a combined movement from the east and south on the part of France. And, in fact, the sound instinct of the people had already sung—

"When France had her assistance lent,
A royal prince to Scotland sent,
Welcome, Royal Charlie!"

But it remained only a verse in a song; and the assistance, whether promised or not, never came. The only bit of calculation, or what looked like calculation, in the matter, was the fact that, when the Prince effected his landing on the extreme west nook of Scotland, the English army was engaged on the Continent in the entanglement of the Austrian succession war, caused by the death of the Emperor Charles VI. without male issue. But this was an advantage that could serve the young adventurer only at the start: the Duke of Cumberland, commander of the English army, who had been wounded at Dettingen, and fought with distinguished valour at Fontenoy about two months before the rising, could "come o'er the water" as well as Charlie; and so he did in due season. Meanwhile, however, all England was in alarm; and Sir John Cope was sent up with what soldiers he could command, to meet the kilted insurgents in the north. But they were too many for him; and besides, they were on their own ground, of which they were fully master. Sir John, finding the way blocked to Fort Augustus, turned off by a side route to Inverness; and from Inverness, where he found himself little more comfortable, turned back by sea to Dunbar! Thus the way south was clear for Charlie; and accordingly, marching through Atholl to Perth, he appeared at Doune on the Teith about the middle of September, and thence proceeded through Linlithgow to Edinburgh, entered Holyrood in triumph, and in a few days showed himself to admiring crowds of his countrymen on the top casement of the south-west tower of Holyrood Palace. Never first blow of a gallant insurrection was struck more brilliantly, or apparently with better promise of success;

but, as we have said, it was only a brilliant surprise and a sentimental show: the movement, as it started, so it remained, a Highland, not a Scotch business. Many were pleased to stare at the procession of red-lion banners and white-rose badges which rode gallantly down the Canongate, but who were too shrewd and too far-sighted, and, as true Scots, too cautious, to take any active part in an insurrection which, like the blaze of furze on fire in a hot summer day, rises with a sounding whiz, but soon crackles into ashes. However, Highlanders could not rise without giving the Saxons a very tangible token of the stuff of which they were made. Sir John Cope, acting unwisely on the defensive, found his men bowled down like ninepins before the sweep of the Gaelic claymore. Prestonpans proved that Highlanders could fight as well as sing, and were more than a match for the English redcoats even on their own low grounds. But brilliant as this stroke was, it was coincident with the first warning of the coming failure. The kilted host, so forward to strike a single effective blow, for a prolonged campaign wanted equipment, training, and perseverance. Prestonpans testified loudly to the mettle of Highland soldiers; but Edinburgh Castle was not taken. After the battle Charles remained six weeks in Edinburgh, by an enforced delay no doubt, but not the less fatal. As the Duke of Wellington said, "time is everything in war;" and the benefit of a surprise is lost when the surprised party has time to recover and take a sober view of the situation. It was soon apparent that the flashing suddenness of the start had left it without basis or bones. The young Chevalier, leaving Edinburgh in the hands of the Government, marched in three divisions—by Peebles, Hawick, and Kelso—to Carlisle, and entered that city, with the blast of pipers and the flash of claymores, in a fashion which made it more conspicuous than glorious in the annals of the Border. His victorious foot was now on English ground; and the road to London through Lancashire, where the Catholic party was strong, to the fervid imagination of the princely adventurer seemed straight as an arrow. But the unsubstantial dreaminess of the assumption on which the insurrection had proceeded, now appeared in all the nakedness of fact. The march through Manchester by a sergeant, a drummer, and "a bonnie lassie," produced only the meagre result of 180 recruits, followed by an enforced show of tallow candles, called an illumination. From Manchester the route went straight to Derby; but here they stopped. They had reached the limit where daring self-confidence must give place to wise deliberation. They had hastily thrust themselves into the midst of an ordered array of legitimate force, gathering surely around them, and were in a position where their only safety lay in retreat—and retreat in such circumstances meant defeat. Only the impetus of a continued advance could be strong enough to overcome resistance in a cause which had law, and habit, and sober-mindedness, and established force in its favour. The retreat was commenced forthwith, and Carlisle revisited under very different auspices, and with very different omens, from those which had accompanied its submission to the hundred pipers a few weeks before. Planting themselves on the high ground above Falkirk, the Prince's army made a stand, which his partial adherents at the moment might call a victory; but a battle only half gained by one party, and only half lost by the other party, when followed by the retreat of the victorious party, as we had occasion to remark above, is virtually a defeat: the battle was not for a few acres of ground in the neighbourhood of Falkirk, but for a permanent position to the claimant of the British crown, south of the Forth; and the going north to Inverness which soon followed, was certainly not the way to strike for a crown in London and to drive "the wee German lairdie" back to his Hanoverian kail-yard. Culloden followed; and what with superiority of numbers on the part of the Government, the power of artillery, the buffeting of the weather, and the want of a substantial breakfast, the Celtic claymore yielded to the

Saxon bayonet. What remains is a scene of mingled sorrow and horror—sorrow which only song can beautify, and horror from which even prose revolts. Hounded from glen to glen and from isle to isle by the victorious royalists, inspired with all the fierceness which a civil strife so naturally engenders, the fugitive Prince owed his escape and his life to the fidelity and the honour so nobly rooted in the breast of the Highlander; while of those who had most distinguished themselves in aiding and abetting his revolt, three notable persons—Lords Balmerino and Kilmarnock, and Fraser of Lovat—paid the penalty of their daring under the executioner's axe on Tower Hill. The baffled Prince retired to France whence he came: there he found ample leisure to indulge no very pleasant meditations on the vanity of his own juvenile dream, and the ruin which his hasty romance had brought on his countrymen. Poets of strongly pronounced Jacobite tendencies have composed, and even in this nineteenth century may here and there compose, sympathetic ballads on his woful precipitation from so lofty a platform; but Clio, the Muse of history, records her verdict with impartial pen—he hath reaped as he sowed. Pity in such case is human; but Justice is divine. While the moral nobility and the lyrical virtue of his daring adventure remain with his followers, the shame and the penalty of his juvenile folly remain with himself.

So much for the historical sequence of facts, alongside of which the lyrical accompaniment arranges itself naturally in five divisions, thus,—(1) songs of expectation, invitation, and preparation; (2) songs of welcome and gathering of the clans; (3) songs of the different points of the military progress; (4) songs of lamentation and wail for the sad issue of the rising; (5) songs of the bloody sequel. We shall give specimens of each division in their order.

One of the best specimens of the first class, both for words and air, announces its character by its title, "When the King comes owre the Water." It was written by Lady Keith, the mother of the famous Marshal Keith, or by some one in her name. She was a Drummond, daughter of the Earl of Perth, and a Roman Catholic. Her son George, the elder brother of the Field-Marshal, was attainted for the share he took in the rebellion of 1715, with whose attainder she lost her social status and dignity. No lady of the time had a better hereditary right to feel warmly in the cause of the old royal blood of Scotland; for both her father's family and that of her husband traced their ancestral honours and their patriotic character back to the glorious field of Bannockburn. This very justifiable pride of ancestry shines clearly forth in the song:—

When the King comes owre the Water.

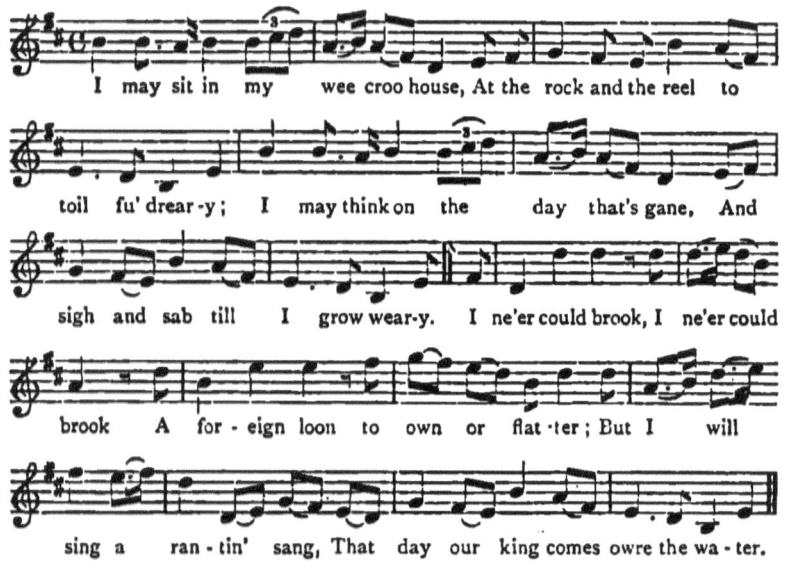

I may sit in my wee croo house, At the rock and the reel to toil fu' drear-y; I may think on the day that's gane, And sigh and sab till I grow wear-y. I ne'er could brook, I ne'er could brook A for-eign loon to own or flat-ter; But I will sing a ran-tin' sang, That day our king comes owre the wa-ter.

O gin I live to see the day,
    That I hae begg'd, and begg'd frae heaven,
I'll fling my rock and reel away,
    And dance and sing frae morn till even:
For there is ane I winna name,
    That comes the reigning bike to scatter;
And I'll put on my bridal gown,
    That day our king comes owre the water.

I hae seen the gude auld day,
    The day o' clans and chieftain glory,
When royal Stuarts bore the sway,
    And ne'er heard tell o' Whig nor Tory.
Though lyart be my locks and grey,
    And eild has crook'd me down—what matter?
I'll dance and sing some ither day,
    That day our king comes owre the water.

> A curse on dull and drawling Whig,
>   The whining, ranting, low deceiver,
> Wi' heart sae black, and look sae big,
>   And canting tongue o' clishmaclaver!
> My father was a good lord's son,
>   My mother was an earl's daughter,
> And I'll be Lady Keith again,
>   That day our king comes owre the water.

In connection with this song, a remark may be made which applies generally to the whole sentiment of the time and of the songs—viz., that the fair sex makes itself particularly prominent. In the lament, for instance, for Lord Maxwell, who rose in the '15, and was enabled to make his escape from the Tower by the craft of his wife Lady Nithsdale, we find the lines—

> "O merry was the lilting amang our ladies a',
>   They danced i' the parlour, and sang in the ha'—
> O Charlie he's come o'er, and he'll put the Whigs awa'!"[1]

And when the head of the Clan M'Intosh refused to join the rising, we find that the lady of Moy herself came boldly forth at the head of two hundred gallant adherents. In the same chivalrous style, when the Prince made his procession down the High Street, Lady Murray of Broughton, Peeblesshire, appeared on horseback profusely bedizened with white ribbons.[2] But the great female protagonist of the

---

[1] Hogg, vol. ii. p. 14.   [2] Chambers, vol. i. p. 121.

drama was a member of the gallant Clan Cameron, bearing the good Scotch Christian name of Jenny. This lady, when her nephew, a youth and a lad of small capacity, refused to follow the call of the chief, without a moment's hesitation took the cause into her own hand, and appeared in the headquarters of the Prince at the head of 250 well-armed men. She was dressed in a sea-green riding-habit, with a scarlet lapel trimmed with gold, her hair tied behind in loose buckles, with a velvet cap and scarlet feather; she rode on a bay gelding decked with green furniture which was trimmed with gold; and instead of a whip she carried a naked sword in her hand. The Prince, of course, received her with all courtesy, and she accompanied his army till their march into England; joined it again at Annandale on their return from Derby; and being at the battle of Falkirk, she was taken prisoner there and committed to prison, from which, however, by some kindly personal intervention, aided by the grace of her virgin chivalry, she got free, and lived quietly on her nephew's estate till her death.[1] It thus appears pretty plainly that the ladies were, from a Government point of view, the ringleaders of the Rebellion, and from a lyrical point of view, the breeze that blew up the flame of the patriotic rising.[2] And the ladies had three

[1] Hogg, vol. ii. p. 351.
[2] Ibid., p. 290, Song xxxviii.

good reasons, or at least fair pleas, for the part which they took in that notable exploit. For Charlie, in the first place, was, by universal testimony and by witness of well-known portraits, a handsome young man, described thus in one of the Gaelic songs :—

> "As he stood in the glen that brave young fellow,
> While streamed o'er his neck his locks so yellow,
> Like the call of the cuckoo in May month early
> Was the voice to me of bonnie Prince Charlie.
>
> Sweet was thy kiss like French wine glowing,
> Thy cheeks like bright berry on mountain growing,
> Thy full blue eye with eyebrows arched rarely :
> Who could behold and not follow Prince Charlie?"[1]

Again, Charlie was not only a handsome young man, but a handsome young prince; and carried about with that addition a fascination, a mingled charm of love and loyalty, to which the best specimens of the fair sex would be the first to yield. He was also an unfortunate prince, the son of an exiled father, born and bred in the land of exile. But noble as this divine madness—θεία μανία—for the handsome prince certainly was, and admirable rather than blamable in the emotional breasts from which it proceeded, it was not to be expected that the sound-hearted, soberminded, thoughtful, sagacious Presbyterians besouth the

---

[1] Popular Songs of the Scottish Highlanders—in Macmillan's Magazine for August 1885—by J. S. B.

Forth should allow themselves to be juggled out of their self-possession by a flash of Celtic fire of this description however brilliant. The women would go out, and wear the cockade, and see the show, and shout for the old Scottish throne; but the "douce gudeman" sat at his fireside crooning to himself his neglected warnings, to the following tune :—

THE WOMEN ARE A' GANE WUD.

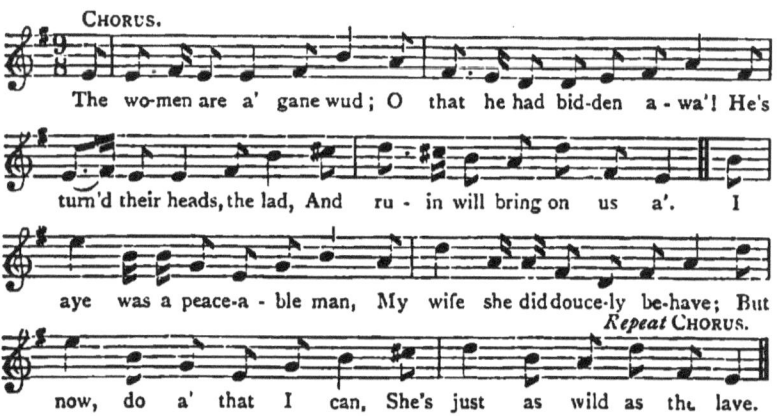

The wo-men are a' gane wud; O that he had bid-den a-wa'! He's turn'd their heads, the lad, And ru-in will bring on us a'. I aye was a peace-a-ble man, My wife she did douce-ly be-have; But now, do a' that I can, She's just as wild as the lave.

Repeat CHORUS.

My wife she wears the cockade,
    Though she kens it's the thing that I hate;
There's ane too prinn'd on her maid,
    And baith will tak' the gate.
        The women are, &c.

I've lived a' my days in the strath;
    Now Tories infest me at hame;
An' though I tak' nae part at a',
    Baith sides do gie me the blame.
        The women are, &c.

> The senseless creatures ne'er think
>   What ill the lad will bring back;
> We'll hae the Pope an' the de'il,
>   An' a' the rest o' the pack.
>   The women are, &c.
>
> The wild Highland lads they did pass,
>   The yetts wide open they flee;
> They ate the very house bare,
>   An' ne'er speir'd leave o' me.
>   The women are, &c.
>
> But when the red-coats gaed by,
>   D'ye think they'd let them alane?
> They a' the louder did cry—
>   Prince Charlie will soon get his ain.
>   The women are, &c.

But if the loyal sentiment, of which women are the best exponents, must be set down as the great positive force that set the rising in motion, we must not omit to emphasise the impulse given to this force by the want of any strong counteracting force from the side of the Government. As representative leaders of a great people, proud of the achievements of a noble ancestry, the Hanoverians were a complete failure. There was nothing kingly about them; nothing to attract the popular eye or to stir the popular heart. They were men sitting on a high seat called a throne, and nothing more. Hear how Green, in his great History, describes them:—

"Both were honest and straightforward men, who frankly accepted the irksome position of Constitutional Kings. But neither had any qualities which could make their honesty attractive to the people at large. The temper of George the First was that of a Gentleman Usher, and his one care was to get money for himself and his favourites. The temper of George the Second was that of a drill-sergeant, who believed himself master of his realm, while he repeated the lessons he had learned from his wife, and his wife had learned from the minister. Their Court is familiar enough in the witty Memoirs of the time, but as political figures the two Georges are almost absent from our history."[1]

And of the contempt felt by the Highlanders, accustomed as they were to follow the leading of men of real manhood and mettle, no better testimony can be given than we have in the popular humorous song of—

THE WEE, WEE GERMAN LAIRDIE.

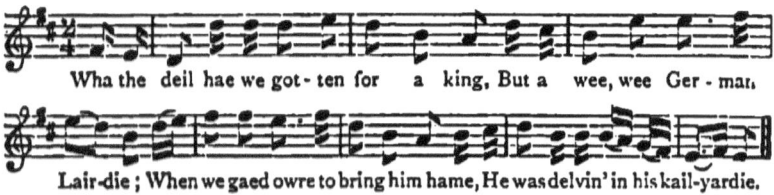

Wha the deil hae we gotten for a king, But a wee, wee German Lairdie; When we gaed owre to bring him hame, He was delvin' in his kail-yardie.

---

[1] Green, vol. iv. p. 123.

He was sheughing kail, and lay-ing leeks, With-out the hose, and but the breeks, And up his beggar duds he cleeks, This wee, wee German Lair-die.

  And he's clappit down in our gudeman's chair,
   The wee, wee German Lairdie;
  And he's brought fouth o' his foreign trash,
   And dibbled them in our yardie.
  He's pu'd the rose o' English clowns,
   And broken the harp o' Irish loons;
  But our Scotch thistle will jag his thooms,
   This wee, wee German Lairdie.

  Come up amang our Hieland hills,
   Thou wee, wee German Lairdie,
  And see the Stuart's lang-kail thrive,
   They hae dibbled in our kail-yardie.
  But if a stock ye daur to pu',
   Or haud the yokin' o' a plough,
  We'll break your sceptre owre your mou',
   Ye feckless German Lairdie.

  Auld Scotland, thou'rt owre cauld a hole,
   For nursin' siccan vermin;
  But the very dogs in England's Court,
   They bark and howl in German.
  Then keep thy dibble in thy ain hand,
   And on their ain legs stoutly stand;
  For wha the deil now claims your land,
   But a wee, wee German Lairdie.

The soil being thus richly prepared by sour discontent on

the negative side, and sweet hope on the positive, the invitation to the Prince to cross the water naturally comes next; and some are so eager to see the Prince that they will not wait his coming, but will give the ferryman another halfpenny to "ferry them over to Charlie." Of the note of invitation two of the most popular specimens may suffice :—

OWRE THE WATER TO CHARLIE.

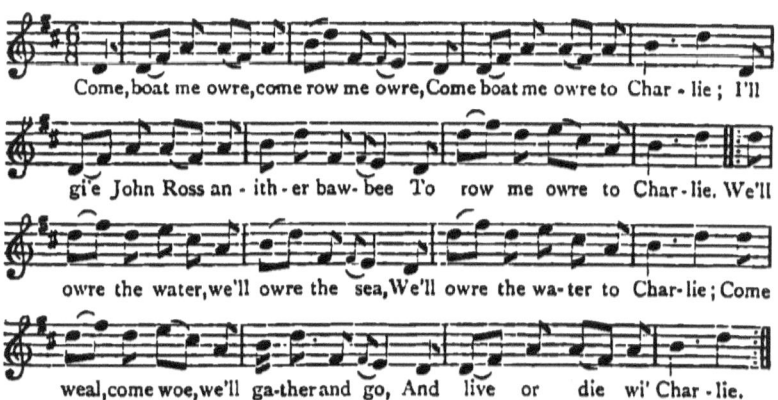

Come, boat me owre, come row me owre, Come boat me owre to Char-lie; I'll gi'e John Ross an-ith-er baw-bee To row me owre to Char-lie. We'll owre the water, we'll owre the sea, We'll owre the wa-ter to Char-lie; Come weal, come woe, we'll ga-ther and go, And live or die wi' Char-lie.

> It's weel I lo'e my Charlie's name,
>   Though some there be abhor him;
> But, oh! to see Auld Nick gaun hame,
>   And Charlie's faes before him.
>   We'll owre the water, &c.
>
> I swear by moon and stars sae bright,
>   And the sun that glances early;
> If I had twenty thousand lives,
>   I'd gie them a' for Charlie.
>   We'll owre the water, &c.

I ance had sons, I now hae nane—
I bred them, toiling sairly;
But I would bear them a' again,
And lose them a' for Charlie.
   We'll owre the water, &c.

The next is that commonly called "MacLean's Welcome," though, strictly speaking, it is not a welcome to the Prince on landing, but an invitation to him to come where he will be sure of receiving a hearty welcome. The words are by Hogg—a free rendering, as he says, from the Gaelic. Hogg, like Scott, had a strong element in him of what we may call poetical Toryism, and the boon companions with whom he associated at Ambrose's Hotel and Tibbie Shiel's were all Tories of the same pleasant description; and like Professor Aytoun, who followed on the same stage afterwards, it was the humour of these gentlemen to throw a loyal glamour over the stupidities, pedantries, and brutalities of the Stuarts, and represent them as alone worthy of every praise to which the healthy instincts of the country could give utterance :—

COME O'ER THE STREAM, CHARLIE.

Come o'er the stream, Charlie, dear Charlie, brave Charlie, Come o'er the stream, Charlie, and dine wi' Mac-Lean; And though you be weary, we'll

And you shall drink freely the dews of Glen Sheerly,
    That stream in the starlight, when kings dinna ken;
And deep be your meed of the wine that is red,
    To drink to your sire and his friend the MacLean.
                    Come o'er the stream, &c.

If aught will invite you, or more will delight you,
    'Tis ready—a troop of our bold Highlandmen
Shall range on the heather, with bonnet and feather,
    Strong arms and broad claymores, three hundred and ten.
                    Come o'er the stream, &c.

We now come to the real hand-to-hand welcome. Charlie stands on Celtic ground at Arisaig, and the chorus of applausive reception leaps vigorously from rock to rock and from creek to creek, as follows:—

WELCOME, ROYAL CHARLIE.

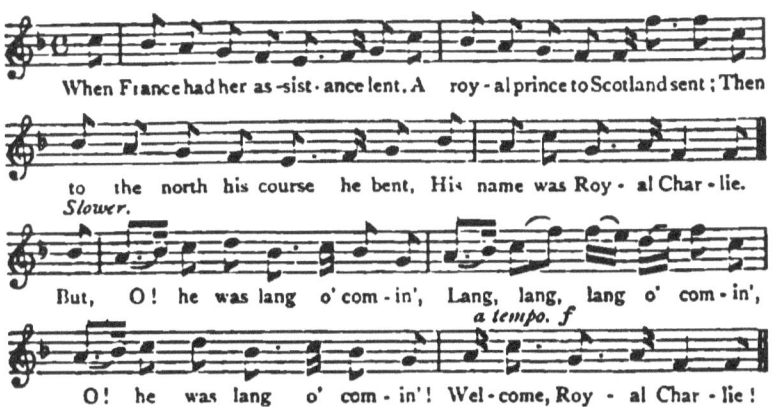

When he on Moidart's shore did stand,
The friends he had within the land
Came down and shook him by the hand,
    And welcomed Royal Charlie.
        An' O! ye've been lang o' comin',
        Lang, lang, lang o' comin';
        O! he was lang o' comin',
            Welcome, Royal Charlie!

The dress that our Prince Charlie had,
Was bonnet blue and tartan plaid;
And O he was a handsome lad,
    A true king's son was Charlie.
        But O! he was lang o' comin',
        Lang, lang, lang, o' comin',
        Oh! he was lang o' comin',
            Welcome, Royal Charlie!

These verses—for there are many words to the same tune, and in the same dramatic attitude—are particularly interesting, as showing in the very first line the false notion from which the insurrection started, that there was to be a combined movement of the Highlanders and the French; and, in the last stanza, the impression of princely dignity and manly beauty made by the Prince. The same charm of personal appearance, and its effect on the loyal young ladies wherever he showed himself, is effectively expressed in a song of very amphibious parentage:[1]—

CHARLIE IS MY DARLING.

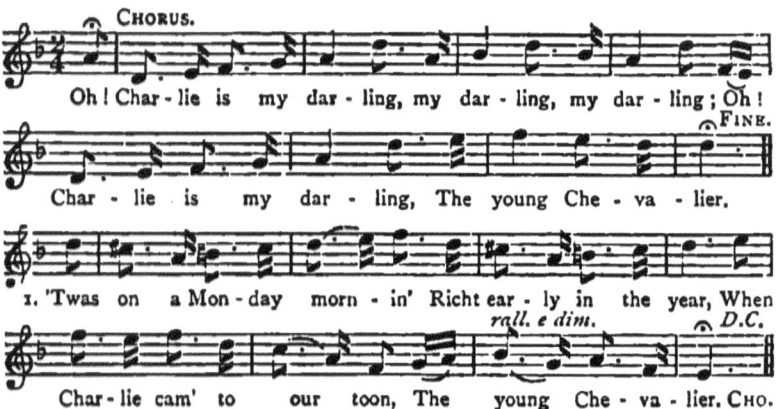

As he cam' marchin' up the street,
The pipes played lood an' clear,
An' a' the folk cam' rinnin' oot
  To meet the Chevalier.
    Oh! Charlie is my darling, &c.

---

[1] Balmoral Scottish Songs, p. 221.

Wi' Hieland bonnets on their heads,
An' claymores bricht an' clear,
They cam' to fecht for Scotland's richt,
   An' the young Chevalier.
     Oh! Charlie is my darling, &c.

They've left their bonnie Hieland hills,
Their wives an' bairnies dear,
To draw the sword for Scotland's lord,
   The young Chevalier.
     Oh! Charlie is my darling, &c.

Oh! there were mony beatin' hearts,
An' mony hopes an' fears;
An' mony were the prayers put up
   For the young Chevalier.
     Oh! Charlie is my darling, &c.

The enthusiasm with which the war-cry was raised, the fervid soul of loyalty which would have secured victory against great odds, had victory been possible, comes strongly out in the two following ballads, the first from Buchan, a district of Aberdeenshire long famed for its Episcopal proclivities and Episcopal genius:[1]—

WHA WADNA FIGHT FOR CHARLIE?

Wha wad-na fight for Char-lie? Wha wad-na draw the sword?
Wha wad-na up and ral-ly At the roy-al prin-ce's word?

---

[1] See Bards of Bon Accord, by Walker, 1887, p. 184.

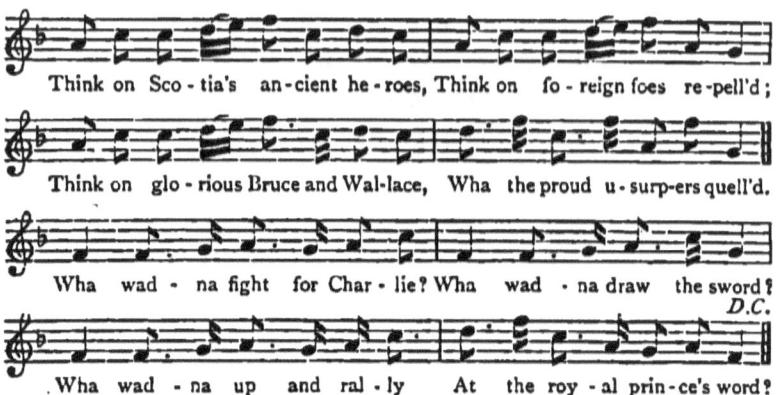

Rouse, rouse, ye kilted warriors!
   Rouse, ye heroes of the north!
Rouse, and join your chieftain's banners,—
   'Tis your prince that leads you forth.
Shall we basely crouch to tyrants?
   Shall we own a foreign sway?
Shall a royal Stuart be banish'd,
   While a stranger rules the day?
      Wha wadna fight, &c.

See the northern clans advancing,
   See Glengarry and Lochiel;
See the brandish'd broadswords glancing,
   Highland hearts are true as steel.
Now our prince has raised his banner,
   Now triumphant is our cause;
Now the Scottish lion rallies—
   Let us strike for prince and laws.
      Wha wadna fight, &c.

WHA'LL BE KING BUT CHARLIE?

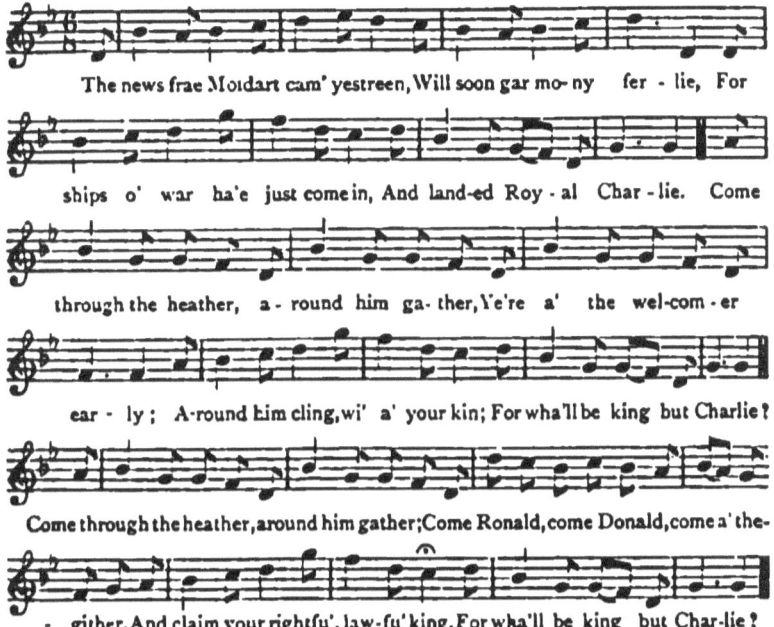

The Highland clans wi' sword in hand,
    Frae John o' Groat's to Airly,
Hae to a man declared to stand
    Or fa' wi' Royal Charlie.
        Come through the heather, &c.

The Lowlands a', baith great an' sma',
    Wi' mony a lord an' laird, hae
Declared for Scotia's king an' law,
    An' speir ye wha, but Charlie?
        Come through the heather, &c.

There's ne'er a lass in a' the land,
But vows baith late an' early,

> To man she'll ne'er gie heart or han'
> Wha wadna fecht for Charlie.
> Come through the heather, &c.
>
> Then here's a health to Charlie's cause,
> An' be't complete an' early;
> His very name our heart's blood warms,
> To arms for Royal Charlie.
> Come through the heather, &c.

Perhaps the best specimen of the gathering-song proper is that of the "M'Donald's Gathering," in Hogg, vol. ii. p. 84, containing the verse—

> "Gather, gather, gather!
> From Loch Morar to Argyle.
> Come from Castle Tuirim,
> Come from Moidart and the Isles."

But as that has not obtained any general hold of the popular ear, we shall let it pass. In the 'Songs of the North,' dedicated to her Majesty Queen Victoria, and put forth under the editorship of Harold Boulton and a daughter of the late Dr Norman Macleod, and the musical direction of Malcolm Lawson, there is a very brisk and lively song of the rising, giving to the Macdonalds of Glencoe the prominent place which their traditions assigned them in the ranks of Highland loyalty. The Gaelic title of this song, "*Gabhaidh Sinn an Rathad Mor*," has been almost literally preserved in the English version, "We will take the Good Old Way." The English rendering of the song is from the hand of the Rev. Dr Alexander Stewart of Nether Lochaber, a gentleman well known in the literary circles of the North, not more for his remarkable wealth of popular tradition, than for his nice observation of nature and the ways of beasts and birds in the picturesque regions where he exercises his Presbyterian episcopate:—

GABHAIDH SINN AN RATHAD MOR.[1]

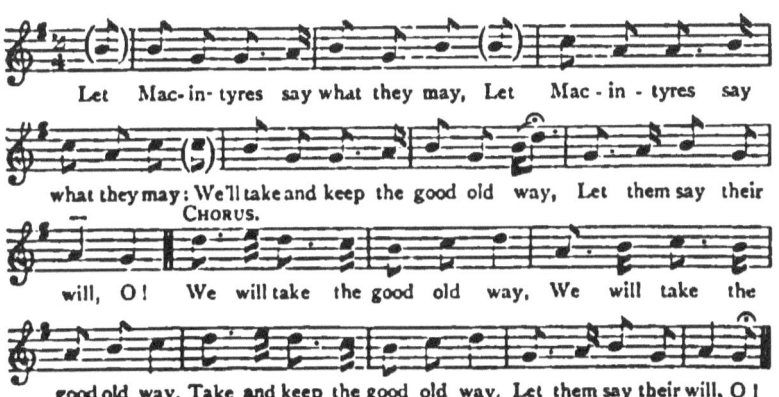

Up the steep and heathery Ben,
Down the bonnie winding glen,
We march a band of loyal men,
Let them say their will, O!
    We will take, &c.

---

[1] Air inserted here by kind permission of Field & Tuer, Leadenhall Street, London.

We will march adown Glencoe,
We will march adown Glencoe,
By the ferry we will go,
Let them say their will, O !
    We will take, &c.

To Glengarry and Lochiel,
Loyal hearts with arms of steel,
These will back you in the field,
Let them say their will, O !
    We will take, &c.

Cluny will come down the brae,
Keppoch bold will lead the way,
Toss thine antlers Cabar Feidh,[1]
Let them say their will, O !
    We will take, &c.

Forward, sons of bold Rob Roy !
Stewarts—conflict is your joy ;
We'll stand together *pour le Roy*,
Let them say their will, O !
    We will take, &c.

But certainly the most popular and the most widely sung of the gathering-songs is that which belongs to the Athole district, and to the Murrays, who took a leading part in the insurrection. Lord George Murray, indeed, the direct ancestor of the present Duke of Athole, was Lieutenant-General of the Prince's army, and approved himself through the

---

[1] The Mackenzies designated here, from the stag's head on their scutcheon. *Cabar*, a rafter or antler ; and *feidh*, a deer.

campaign as admirably qualified for such a responsible post. The song "Cam' ye by Athol?" owes great part of its popularity, no doubt, to the combination of musical and poetical genius from which it drew its birth. Like not a few others of the best-known Jacobite songs, though its inspiration came from the Highlands, its cradle was in the Lowlands; the contagion of that right chivalrous loyalty having acted so powerfully on the Scottish mind, that for more than one generation after the date of the dashing adventure, the patriotic pulse was strong enough to shape forth not a few songful utterances, not less genuine and not less vivid than the sparks which were shot directly from the glowing furnace of the collision. The musical artist who allied himself with the Ettrick Shepherd to give immortality to the chivalrous loyalty of the lords of Athole, was himself a Perthshire man, being the youngest son of Neil Gow, the distinguished violinist, contemporary of Burns, and of whom our great master of song makes honourable mention in his Highland tour:—

CAM' YE BY ATHOL?

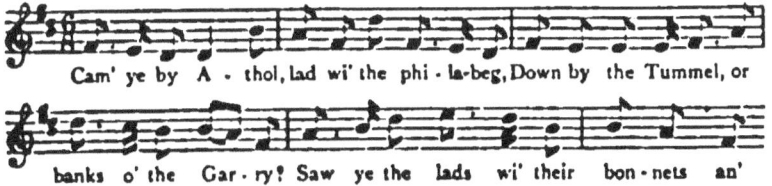

I hae but ae son, my gallant young Donald;
  But if I had ten they should follow Glengarry;
Health to Macdonald and gallant Clanronald,
  For these are the men that will die for their Charlie.
    Follow thee, follow thee, &c.

I'll to Lochiel and Appin, and kneel to them;
  Down by Lord Murray and Roy of Kildarlie;
Brave Mackintosh, he shall fly to the field wi' them;
  These are the lads I can trust wi' my Charlie.
    Follow thee, follow thee, &c.

Down through the Lowlands, down wi' the Whigamore,
  Loyal true Highlanders, down wi' them rarely;
Ronald and Donald drive on wi' the braid claymore,
  Over the necks of the foes of Prince Charlie.
    Follow thee, follow thee, &c.

As an interesting pendant to these gathering-songs we may place here the popular song written by a Banffshire Roman Catholic, Bishop Alexander Geddes, contemporary of Burns:—

O SEND LEWIE GORDON HAME.

Oh! to see his tartan trews,
Bonnet blue, and laigh-heel'd shoes,
Philabeg aboon his knee,
That's the lad that I'll gang wi',
   Ohon! my Highlandman, &c.

Princely youth, of whom I sing,
Thou wert born to be a king;
On thy breast a royal star
Shines on Highland hearts afar.
   Ohon! my Highlandman, &c.

Oh! to see the princely one
Seated on a royal throne;
Disasters a' would disappear,
Then begins the jubilee year.
   Ohon! my Highlandman, &c.

The person thus eagerly invited to join the great rising was a younger brother of the then Duke of Gordon, and had been bred to the sea; but on the breaking out of the rebellion, he left the naval service, joined the Prince's standard, fought at Culloden, and surviving that tragic business, retired to France, where he died not long after.

We now come to the serious part of the business—to hard blows and bloody battles; but, though every step in the military progress is faithfully recorded in the ballads of the day, we must not expect to find here the same rich material for popular singing as in the events that precede and follow the great battles. It is for military history to deal with the strategic movements that bring on a great battle, and with the tactical movements which decide it; but it is in the incidents that rise out of a war, strongly marked by personal character and dramatic situation, that the popular song finds its themes ready-made. We shall not, therefore, be surprised to find that the first great stroke of success in Charlie's progress, the battle of Prestonpans, fell more naturally into the hands of the jocund Thalia, and the mocking Momus of popular humour, than of any more dignified Muse. That the trained troops of a great power like England should have been blown about like straw before the apparition of a yellow-haired laddie of no experience in warfare, a hasty rush of kilted mountaineers, and a savage blast of screeching bagpipes, could afford material for nothing but a burst of broad popular humour; and such it accordingly received. Sir John Cope might have been a very respectable man, and a good soldier for common occasions; but the popular Muse judges of character, as schoolmasters are paid under the existing Code, by results; and the result here was destined simply to be that the king's champion, after much preparation, marching and countermarching, found himself planted face to face with his insurrectionary antagonist, only to run away. On the morning of the 18th September, three days before the battle, Cope was at Dunbar, on the coast, nearly thirty miles east from Edinburgh; and from this point the popular song introduces him as sending a challenge to the Prince, who was stationed at Prestonpans, a small town on the Firth of Forth, about ten miles east of Edinburgh. The allusion in the refrain is to the coal-mines at Tranent, in the neighbourhood of Prestonpans; and the author of the song, Adam Skirving, a farmer in the district, humorously supposes one of the miners of the neighbourhood being in a greater hurry to go to his daily underground task, than the king's general was to leave his bed and do his military duty. Here follows the song :—

JOHNNIE COPE.

Cope sent a let-ter frae Dun-bar, Say-ing, Char-lie, meet me gin ye daur, And I'll show you the art o' war, If you'll

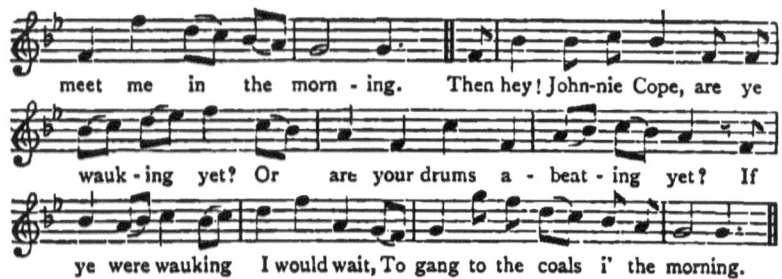

meet me in the morning. Then hey! Johnnie Cope, are ye wauking yet? Or are your drums a-beating yet? If ye were wauking I would wait, To gang to the coals i' the morning.

When Charlie look'd the letter upon,
He drew his sword the scabbard from;
"Come, follow me, my merry, merry men,
   And we'll meet Johnnie Cope i' the morning."
      Hey! Johnnie Cope, &c.

When Johnnie Cope he heard o' this,
He thought it wadna be amiss
To hae a horse in readiness,
   To flee awa' i' the morning.
      Hey! Johnnie Cope, &c.

Fy, Johnnie! now get up and rin,
The bagpipes mak' an unco din;
It's best to sleep in a hale skin,
   For 'twill be a bluidy morning.
      Hey! Johnnie Cope, &c.

When Johnnie Cope to Dunbar came,
They speir'd at him, where's a' your men?
"The de'il confound me gin I ken,
   For I left them a' i' the morning."
      Hey! Johnnie Cope, &c.

"Now, Johnnie, troth ye werena blate,
To come wi' the news o' your ain defeat,

> And leave your men in sic a strait,
> 　Sae early i' the morning."
> 　　Hey! Johnnie Cope, &c.
>
> "I' faith," quo' Johnnie, " I got a fleg,
> Wi' their lang claymores and philabegs;
> If I face them again, de'il break my legs,
> 　Sae I wish you a guid morning."
> 　　Hey! Johnnie Cope, are ye wauking yet?
> 　　Or are your drums a-beating yet?
> 　　If ye were wauking I would wait,
> 　　　To gang to the coals i' the morning.

The next stage in the progress is Carlisle, where, however, after a short show of resistance, the white flag was displayed, the gates opened, and the castle surrendered, and the mayor, like Sir John Cope, dishonourably immortalised in the popular ballad:—

> "O Pattison, ohone! ohone!
> 　Thou wonder of a mayor!
> Thou blest thy lot thou wert no Scot,
> 　And bluster'd like a player.
> What hast thou done with sword or gun
> 　To baffle the Pretender?
> Of mouldy cheese and bacon grease
> 　Thou much more fit defender."[1]

But the real lyrical gem of this stage of the progress is the favourite song of—

[1] Hogg, vol. ii. p. 135.

THE HUNDRED PIPERS.[1]

Oh! our sodger lads look'd braw, look'd braw,
Wi' their tartans, kilt, an' a', an' a',
Wi' their bonnets an' feathers, an' glitterin' gear,
An' pibrochs sounding loud and clear.
Will they a' return to their ain dear glen?
Will they a' return, our Highland men?
Second-sighted Sandy look'd fu' wae,
And mithers grat when they march'd away.
   Wi' a hundred pipers, &c.

---

[1] This and the other airs of the songs of Lady Nairne in this volume inserted by the kind permission of Roy Paterson, Esq., musical publisher, Edinburgh.

Oh! wha is foremost o' a', o' a'?
Oh! wha is foremost o' a', o' a'?
Bonnie Charlie, the king o' us a', hurrah!
Wi' his hundred pipers, an' a', an' a'.
His bonnet an' feather he's wavin' high,
His prancing steed maist seems to fly;
The nor' wind plays wi' his curly hair,
While the pipers blaw wi' an unco flare!
   Wi' a hundred pipers, &c.

The Esk was swollen, sae red an' sae deep;
But shouther to shouther the brave lads keep;
Twa thousand swam ower to fell English ground,
And danced themselves dry to the pibroch's sound.
Dumfounder'd, the English saw, they saw,
Dumfounder'd, they heard the blaw, the blaw;
Dumfounder'd, they a' ran awa', awa',
Frae the hundred pipers, an' a', an' a'.
   Wi' a hundred pipers, &c.

The authoress of this song was a noble lady whom we have already had occasion to mention (p. 91), and whose appearance, in that case as here, invites particular notice to the fact that our notable Scottish lady-lyrists were no less distinguished for the delicate humour than for the tender pathos of their genius. Caroline Oliphant was born in the old mansion of Gask, in the county of Perth, in the year 1766, seven years later than Robert Burns. Her family were devoted Jacobites; and, after taking part in the rising of the '45, her father and grandfather spent ten years in exile, before they found it safe to return to their native land, where they remained in no wise better affected to the dynasty of "the wee German lairdie" than they had departed. In her youth she was so notable for her personal charms that she was known in popular language as the Flower of Strathearn; and the beauty of her mind, manifested in an early occupation with music and lyrical poetry, was not inferior to the fascination of her person. She lived single till she was forty years of age, and then married Captain William Murray Nairne, a military gentleman of noble descent, whose duties as inspector-general of barracks in Scotland forced him to reside in Edinburgh. The house which she occupied, still recognised by the visitor in the letters C. N. above the portal, is pleasantly situated beneath the shadow of the lofty Arthur's Seat, looking eastward towards Portobello and the Forth. In this abode Lady Nairne dwelt for about thirty years, performing her part gracefully in the literary society of the Modern Athens, and at the same time, as a Christian woman, signalising herself, in her own modest way, by contributing munificently towards the support of the popular charities, then rising into notice under the intelligent apostleship of Dr Chalmers. Her husband, Major Nairne, after being restored to his rank in the peerage, died in 1830; and her only son, Lord Nairne, who seems to have been of a delicate constitution, died not many years afterwards. This double bereavement naturally lay heavily on the soul of the good lady; and from that time she resided principally on the Continent. She died at Gask, in the old mansion, at the advanced age of seventy-nine; affording another proof to the many already brought forward in these pages, of the fact that the occupation of the lyrical poet, so far, as is sometimes said, from shortening the span of human life, rather tends, by harmonising the whole emotional soul with the nervous machinery of emotional expression, to prevent those frets and jerks and plunges of disorderly passion, which, like a rough road, cause the car to break down before the natural termination of the journey. It is not song, but unsanctified, unregulated, and overstrained energy of all kinds, that ruins the health, which only a wise balance and a harmonious moderation can preserve.

We have run to the end of our triumphs; and our song, so far as it follows the sequence of decisive military strokes, naturally ceases. For, though the Highlanders have a lyrical record of the whole campaign — it being not in their habit to write prose, but to sing songs as in the Homeric age—this complete record did not pass into the general currency of the popular ear, partly on account of the melancholy nature of the subject, partly on account of the concentration of poetic interest on the person of the misfortuned hero of the adventure after the crowning catastrophe of Culloden. After the retreat from Derby, the first notable halt was made at Carlisle; and we can have little doubt that to this retreat of female camp-attendants the favourite song of "The bonnie, bonnie Braes o' Loch Lomond" (No. III. in the 'Songs of the North') must refer. The battle of Falkirk Muir which followed, like Prestonpans, gave occasion to the Comic Muse to disport herself; but the sort of panic which dispersed the whole army in the one case, seized only a wing in the other, and the victory which in the first affair was followed by an important advance, in the second served only to cover an ill-omened retreat with a boastful semblance of success. So the song was sung in vain:—

> "Says brave Lochiel, pray have we won?
> I see no troop, I hear no gun.
> Says Drummond, faith, the battle's done,
> I know not how nor why, man.
> But, my good lords, this thing I crave,
> Have we defeat these heroes brave?
> Says Murray, I believe we have;
> If not, we're here to try, man!
>
> But tried they up, or tried they doun,
> There was nae foe in Falkirk toun,
> Nor yet in a' the country roun',
> To break a sword at a', man."

And equally vain was the satirical skit against the commander-in-chief of the royal army, made to the refrain of an old song—" Up and war them a', Willie " :—

> " Up and rin awa', Hawley!
> Up and rin awa', Hawley!
> The philabegs are coming doun
> To gi'e your lugs a claw, Hawley.
> Young Charlie's face at Dunipace
> Has gi'en your mou' a thraw, Hawley;
> A blasting sight for bastard wight,
> The warst that e'er he saw, Hawley." [1]

Alas, poor Charlie! neither at Dunipace nor elsewhere since he retraced his steps from central England, did his face show either terror to his foes or encouragement to his friends. His game lay in a surprise; and the surprise had failed. In the council of war held at Derby, the delusive show of success at Falkirk, and the fatal eclipse of all hope at Culloden, lay in embryo, and its pulse was felt boding disaster in the bosom of the ill-starred adventurer. The disastrous overthrow of all Stuart hopes on that fatal field received from native and from sympathetic Lowland singers its lyrical celebration; but, for the reasons already mentioned, and also because the Highlands are only a part of Scotland, it never received such a classical place in the temple of Scottish historical song as its fellow in disaster on the banks of the Till. Quite recently the genius of Malcolm

[1] Hogg, vol. ii. pp. 136-138.

Lawson has buckled itself to the task of giving musical expression to Shairp's admirable verses on this tragic theme, in a composition which well deserves to become popular; in the meantime we content ourselves with the words, referring the singer to the well-known work for the music:[1]—

CULLODEN MUIR.

The moorland, wide, and waste, and brown,
Heaves far and near, and up and down,
Few trenches green the desert crown,
And these are the graves of Culloden!

Alas! what mournful thoughts they yield,
Those scars of sorrow yet unhealed,
On Scotland's last and saddest field!
O! the desolate moor of Culloden!

Ah me! what carnage vain was there!
What reckless fury, mad despair,
On this wide moor such odds to dare!
O! the wasted lives of Culloden!

For them laid there, the brave and young,
How many a mother's heart was wrung,
How many a coronach sad was sung!
O! the green, green graves of Culloden!

Here Camerons clove the red line through,
There Stewarts dared what men could do,
Charged lads of Athol, staunch and true,
To the cannon-mouths on Culloden.

---

[1] Songs of the North, "Culloden Muir," p. 94.

What boots it now to point and tell—
Here the Clan Chattan bore them well
Shame-maddened, yonder, Keppoch fell,
Lavish of life at Culloden?

In vain the wild onset, in vain
Claymores cleft English skulls in twain,
The cannon-fire poured in like rain,
Mowing down the clans on Culloden?

Through all the glens, from shore to shore,
What wailing went! But that is o'er;
Hearts now are cold that once were sore
For the loved ones lost on Culloden.

Now strangers come to pry and peep,
Above the mounds where clansmen sleep;
But what do we, their kinsmen, reap
For our sires' blood shed on Culloden?

Our small farms turned to deserts dumb,
Where smoke no homes, no people come,
Save English hunters,—that's the sum
Of what we have reaped for Culloden.

This too will pass—the hunter's deer,
The drover's sheep will disappear;
But when another race will ye rear
Like the men that died at Culloden?

The civil strife, so far as the public interest was concerned, being thus concluded, the Muse of Coila, willing to find a close to her great lyrical drama, not unworthy of its brilliant start, drew her inspiration exclusively from the personal adventures of the unfortunate Prince. And here, as all the world knows, she found not only a hero—for a prince in misfortune is always a hero—but a heroine, worthy of her most pathetic strains. Perhaps the most touching of these sorrowful memorials, these heartrending wails from wives harshly bereft of loving husbands, and mothers of hopeful sons, is the lament of Christiana Fergusson over her husband, who fell at Culloden. This most pathetic utterance of chaste and reverential sorrow is found, so far as I know, only in the Gaelic, from which I transfer it here, along with the short note of the editor of the collection.[1]

"Christiana Fergusson was a native of the parish of Contin, Ross-shire, where her father was a blacksmith, chiefly employed in making dirks and other implements of war. She was married to a brave man of the name of Chisholm, a native of Strathglass (a near kinsman of the chief of that name). On the memorable day of Culloden, William was flag-bearer or banner-man of the clan, and the task of preserving the *bratach choimheach* from the disgrace of being struck down could not have fallen into better hands. He fought long and manfully; and even after

---

[1] 'Sar Obair nan Bard Gaidheil,' by John Mackenzie; 5th edition, Edinburgh, 1882, p. 373. A monument to Mackenzie stands on the roadside near Gairloch inn, in the north-west Highlands. The translation was printed in my article in 'Macmillan,' above, p. 203.

the rout became general, he rallied and led his clansmen again and again to the charge, but in vain. A body of the Chisholms ultimately sought shelter in a barn, which was soon surrounded by hundreds of the red-coats, who panted for blood. At this awful conjuncture William literally cut his way through the Government forces. He then stood in the barn-door, and with his trusty blade high raised, and in proud defiance, guarded the place. In vain did their spears and bayonets aim their thrusts at his fearless heart; he hewed down all who came within reach of his sword, and kept a semicircle of eight feet clear for himself in the teeth of his desperate enemies. At length he was shot by some Englishmen who climbed up to the top of the barn from behind, where he fell as a hero would wish to fall, with seven bullets lodged in his body. His wife forthwith composed the following beautiful and heart-touching lament, which is altogether worthy of a high-hearted and affectionate woman:—

> "O Charlie, brave young Stuart,
> From thee came my heart's sore bleeding!
> All my best, my all I gave thee
> In the battle for thy speeding.
> Not for sheep, and not for cattle,
> Now I give my tears not sparely;
> Who was all the world to me,
> Him I gave to die for Charlie.

Who will draw the sword for Charlie?
Who will fill his chair to-morrow?
Little cares me now to ask,
Pining here in widowed sorrow.
And yet, and yet, I may not blame thee;
Though by thee I'm ruined fairly,
Though by thee my lord lies bleeding,
Thou art still my king, my Charlie!

Oh, but thou wert tall and comely,
From top to toe equipped completely;
Never swan more stately fair;
Never honey flowed more sweetly
Than thy kisses; with thy brown locks
Down thy neck so richly flowing,
Thou didst draw all eyes, the honour
Of thy manly beauty showing.

Broad thy shoulders; and thy waist
Nicely shaped for supple beauty;
Not a prentice hand was his
Who did for thee the tailor's duty.
Who for thee would trim the trews,
He must cut the cloth not scanty;
No light work to fit short hose,
To thy stout legs with step so jaunty.

Thou didst lay the finny people
Glancing on the river's border;
Lightly, lightly on the heather
Trod thy foot with gun in order.
When the deer were on the hill,
No man rated thy delaying;
Sweetest music to my ears
Were thy hounds when they were baying.

When the social cup was circling
Thou wert ever stout and able;
Thou didst stand and pay thy scot
When all weak brains were 'neath the table;
Never o'er the foaming ale
Didst thou teach thy wits to maunder,
Never gave thy foot loose rein
From thy faithful wife to wander.

O waly, waly woe, my sorrow,
Would the truth might be a lie now!
Far from me be mirth and joy
When thou in death dost lowly lie now!
Who will show another like thee,
Brain and brawn well joined together?
No red blood from veins more loyal
At Culloden stained the heather.

Many a silken-vested lady,
Titled dames, and dainty misses,
Envied me the right to claim,
As a wife may claim, thy kisses.
All the wealth of Guinea mines
Might not make me to disclaim thee;
I'd sooner break all God's commands
Than say amen to who should blame thee!

Woe's me! woe that I must drag
Days and nights in groans and moaning;
Weary, weary, wakeful nights,
With no hope for thy returning!
Never more shall fife or fiddle
Rouse my love where he is sleeping,
Never more his dear voice whisper
Kindly words to stay my weeping.

When he left me I was hoping—
Hoping nightly, hoping daily—
He would come back from the battle
With his banner floating gaily.
But the time is past for hoping;
I shall see thee never, never;
'Neath the turf my hopes I bury
With my dear heart's love for ever.

There's many a widow weeping sore
From Trotternish to Sleat in Skye now;
But never widow wept a lord
So worthy of hot tears as I now.
When he was here, how bright my life!
How dim, how dark, with him departed!
No sorriest wight would envy me
In Skye this day so dreary-hearted!"

The loyal devotion of Flora Macdonald, and her gallant achievement of guiding the unfortunate Prince to ultimate safety, through the roaring dangers of the sea, and the bristling environment of his eager pursuers, has gained for her a place in the romance of history second only to that enjoyed by the familiar figures in Greek and Roman story, who had the good fortune to find a Homer and a Virgil to immortalise their praises. She was the daughter of Macdonald of Milton, in the island of South Uist, and a person of such goodly presence, sound sense, sprightly manner, and brave purpose, as the Lyrical Muse delights to find in the deliverer of a misfortuned prince. For the details of her character and conduct we refer to Chambers, and more especially to the valuable volume of Mr Jolly;[1] for our purpose it is enough to present her lyrically in two pictures, one of which, the English version written by Hogg, has long enjoyed a large popularity, and the other in the fair way to enjoy a similar wide recognition through the 'Songs of the North,' a book specially patronised by the Royal Lady of Balmoral, which we have already laid under tribute. We shall take it first; the words by Mr Lawson's accomplished co-operator, Mr Harold Boulton; the music by kind permission of the publishers:—

SKYE BOAT-SONG.

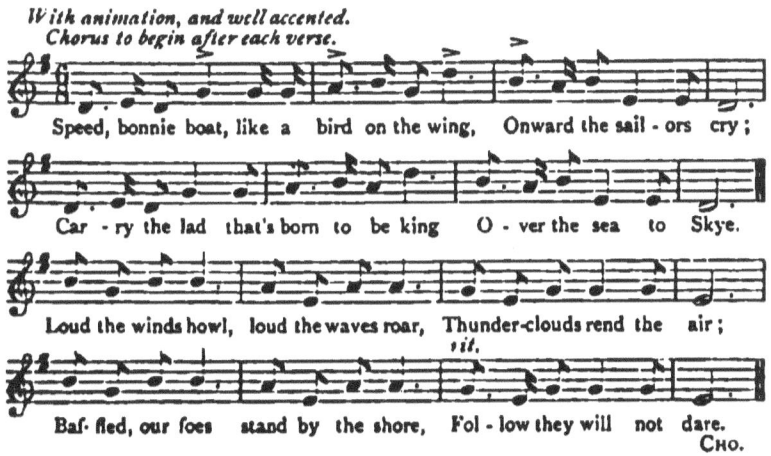

---

[1] *Flora Macdonald in Uist: A Story of the Heroine in her Native Surroundings.* By William Jolly, H.M.I.S. Perth, 1886.

Though the waves leap, soft shall ye sleep;
  Ocean's a royal bed.
Rocked in the deep, Flora will keep
  Watch by your weary head.
      Speed, bonnie boat, &c.

Many's the lad fought on that day,
  Well the claymore could wield,
When the night came silently lay
  Dead on Culloden's field.
      Speed, bonnie boat, &c.

Burned are our homes, exile and death
  Scatter the loyal men;
Yet ere the sword cool in the sheath,
  Charlie will come again.
      Speed, bonnie boat, &c.

The other song represents the heroine—her royal charge being now safely beyond the reach of his pursuers—as sitting lonely on the lonely shore of Skye, thrown back on those sorrowful meditations of hopeless bereavement, from which the excitement of the sea voyage and the gallant rescue had for a short interval delivered her:—

Flora Macdonald's Lament.

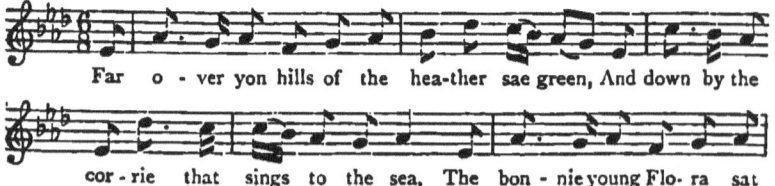

Far o-ver yon hills of the hea-ther sae green, And down by the cor-rie that sings to the sea, The bon-nie young Flo-ra sat

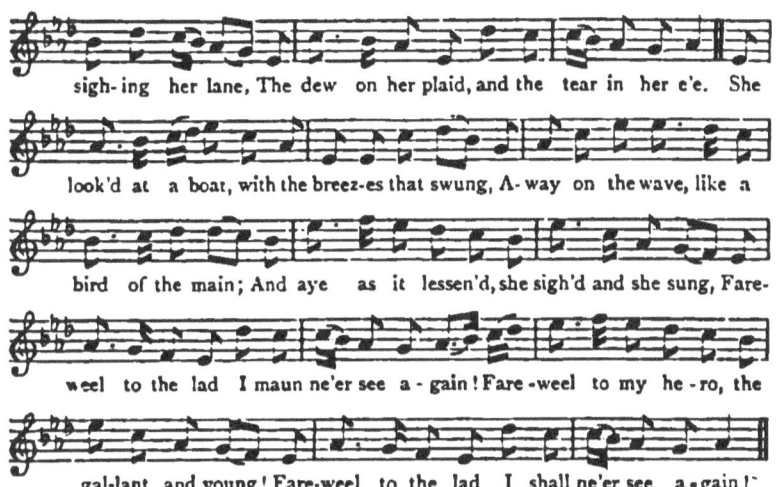

sigh-ing her lane, The dew on her plaid, and the tear in her e'e. She look'd at a boat, with the breez-es that swung, A-way on the wave, like a bird of the main; And aye as it lessen'd, she sigh'd and she sung, Fare-weel to the lad I maun ne'er see a-gain! Fare-weel to my he-ro, the gal-lant and young! Fare-weel to the lad I shall ne'er see a-gain!

> The moorcock that craws on the brow of Ben Connal,
>   He kens o' his bed in a sweet mossy hame;
> The eagle that soars on the cliffs of Clanronald,
>   Unawed and unhunted, his eyrie can claim;
> The solan can sleep on his shelve of the shore,
>   The cormorant roost on his rock of the sea;
> But oh! there is one whose hard fate I deplore,
>   Nor house, ha', nor hame in this country has he.
> The conflict is past, and our name is no more:
>   There's naught left but sorrow for Scotland and me.

A lament of a similar nature, though in every respect inferior, we find in Burns.[1] It wants both the scenery and the atmosphere of the '45; and seems, in fact, to have been rather cooked up for Edinburgh purposes, than to have grown vigorously out of the genius of the poet; and, if it

---

[1] Paterson, vol. ii. p. 150. Set to music by Mackenzie. Roy Paterson, Edinburgh, 1888,—by whose kind permission it appears here.

ever should have the good luck to supplant Hogg's, it will owe it to the genius of the great composer who has wedded it to sweet sounds, more than to its own merit :—

THE CHEVALIER'S LAMENT.

The small birds re-joice in the green leaves re-turn-ing, The mur-mur-ing stream-let winds clear thro' the vale; The prim-ros-es blow in the dews of the morn-ing, And wild scat-ter'd cow-slips be-deck the green dale. But what can give pleasure, or what can seem fair, When the lin-ger-ing mo-ments are num-ber'd by care? No birds sweetly singing, nor flow'rs gai-ly spring-ing, Can soothe the sad bo-som of joy-less des-pair, Can soothe the sad bo-som of joy-less des-pair.

The deed that I dar'd, could it merit such malice,
A king and a father to place on his throne?
His right are these hills, and his right are these valleys,
Where wild beasts find shelter, but I can find none.
But 'tis not my sufferings, thus wretched, forlorn,
My brave gallant friends, 'tis your ruin I mourn;
Your faith proved so loyal in hot bloody trial,
Alas! can I make it no sweeter return?

The hopelessness so justly felt and so finely expressed

by the lady in Hogg's poem, was not, of course, shared by all who had taken part in that ill-starred enterprise. A loyal movement from the heart of a loyal people, that had half succeeded under unfavourable circumstances, might succeed altogether on some not far-distant day, when the continued unpopularity of the Georges should combine with changes in European policy to render the restoration of the exiled dynasty as much a matter of politic desire to the mass of the British people, as it was a chivalrous passion in the breast of the Highlander. France and Ireland were always at hand to give a riskful jog to the unsteady basement of the Hanoverian throne. Such imaginations, not altogether fanciful, and fondly cherished by persons in whom it was a necessity, for the moment, to hope against hope, and to believe in the improbable, gave birth to the popular song—

WILL YOU NO' COME BACK AGAIN?

Mony a traitor 'mang the isles
  Brak' the band o' nature's law;
Mony a traitor, wi' his wiles,
  Sought to wear his life awa'.
    Will he no' come back again? &c.

The hills he trod were a' his ain,
  And bed beneath the birken tree;
The bush that hid him on the plain,
  There's none on earth can claim but he.
    Will he no' come back again? &c.

Whene'er I hear the blackbird sing,
  Unto the e'ening sinking down,
Or merle that makes the woods to ring,
  To me they hae nae ither soun',
    Than, will he no' come back again? &c.

Mony a gallant sodger fought,
  Mony a gallant chief did fa';
Death itself was dearly bought,
  A' for Scotland's king and law.
    Will he no' come back again? &c.

Sweet the lav'rock's note and lang,
  Lilting wildly up the glen;
And aye the o'ercome o' the sang
  Is, "Will he no' come back again?"
    Will he no' come back again? &c.

In singing this song we recommend that the second verse be omitted — as the fidelity of the clans was as true to fact as to poetry; and anything deserving the name of treachery belonged to an exceptional individual, not to the class. Perhaps the writer of the song had in his eye the chiefs of the Western Isles who refused from the beginning to take part in the rising; but to call this treachery were an abuse of language which not even in an impassioned Celtic Pindar can be excused.

We conclude our strains of lamentation and exile with one which has always appeared to the present writer as the most perfect in the whole series of these so admirable ballads; a song which is as widely appreciated as it is finely conceived, and which addresses itself with equal power to the cultivated taste of the most fashionable audience, as to the untrained susceptibilities of a poor Highland cottar. This charm it owes to that combination of picturesque scenery, dramatic attitude, and genuine natural pathos, which gives the stamp of classicality to so many Scottish songs :—

A WEE BIRD CAM' TO OUR HA' DOOR.

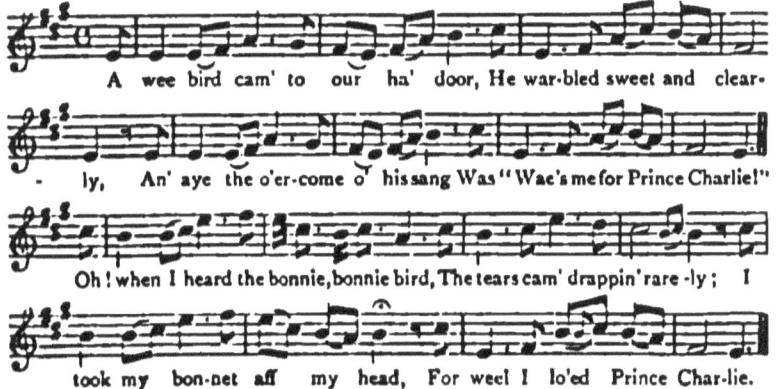

A wee bird cam' to our ha' door, He war-bled sweet and clear-ly, An' aye the o'er-come o' his sang Was "Wae's me for Prince Charlie!" Oh! when I heard the bonnie, bonnie bird, The tears cam' drappin' rare-ly; I took my bon-net aff my head, For weel I lo'ed Prince Char-lie.

Quoth I, "My bird, my bonnie, bonnie bird,
    Is that a sang ye borrow?
Are these some words ye've learnt by heart,
    Or a lilt o' dool and sorrow?"
"Oh! no, no, no," the wee bird sang,
    "I've flown sin' morning early,
But sic a day o' wind an' rain—
    Oh! wae's me for Prince Charlie!

"On hills that are by right his ain,
    He roams a lonely stranger,
On ilka hand he's press'd by want,
    On ilka side by danger:
Yestreen I met him in a glen,
    My heart maist burstit fairly;
For sairly changed indeed was he—
    Oh! wae's me for Prince Charlie!

"Dark night cam' on, the tempest roar'd
    Cold o'er the hills and valleys;
An' whaur was't that your prince lay down,
    Whase hame should been a palace?
He row'd him in a Highland plaid,
    Which cover'd him but sparely,
An' slept beneath a bush o' broom—
    Oh! wae's me for Prince Charlie!"

But now the bird saw some red-coats,
    An' he shook his wings wi' anger;
"Oh! this is no' a land for me;
    I'll tarry here nae langer."
A while he hover'd on the wing,
    Ere he departed fairly,
But weel I mind the fareweel strain
    Was, "Wae's me for Prince Charlie!"

The writer of this gem was William Glen, one of that notable troop of singers whose names, as we have had frequent occasion to mention, so characteristically illustrate the western districts of Scotland. His family appears with observation in the history of Renfrewshire; while himself was born in Glasgow, where his father was a merchant in the Russian trade. After a short essay of the military life, his Glasgow connection brought him back to take part in the West India trade; and, engaged in this branch of the mercantile profession, he resided for some time in one of the West Indian islands. Makers of verses, however, are seldom makers of money; so we find him, after a few years' vain attempt to do battle in economic fields, living in retirement near Aberfoyle, where he died of consumption in 1826, like Burns and Byron, at the early age of thirty-seven. His principal poems will be found in Rogers's 'Minstrel,' and in Wilson's 'Poets of Scotland,' from which these notes are taken.

CHAPTER IV.

SONGS OF CHARACTER AND INCIDENT IN DAILY LIFE.

"Poetry is the blossom of any sort of experience, rooted in truth and growing up into beauty."—LEIGH HUNT.

WE now pass to a diverse chapter, the pictures and incidents of peace as celebrated in popular song, a chapter no doubt more pleasing to a great number of singers; for, though war stirs more powerful passions and spurs the Muse to loftier strains, there is always an undercurrent of sadness connected with it which music may veil pleasantly but cannot altogether conceal. Peace, on the contrary, or peaceful work as the common pace of the cosmic movement, has no horrors to hide; like the breath of a bright summer day, it is satisfied with its own fragrance, and fears no poison beneath its blossom. Of course the love-songs with which we started are specially songs of peace; but what we have elected for this chapter are such healthy scenes and striking incidents of daily life as, like the pictures on the walls of a parlour, entertain the eye pleasantly without tempting the spectator to rise from his easy-chair. Under this rubric we can commence with nothing more fitly than—

My Ain Fireside.

O, I ha'e seen great anes, an' sat in great ha's, 'Mang lords an' 'mang la-dies, a' cov-er'd wi' braws; But a sight sae de-light-fu' I trow I ne'er spied, As the bon-nie blythe blink o' my ain fire-side. My ain fire-side, my ain fire-side, As the bon-nie blythe blink o' my ain fire-side.

Ance mair, heaven be praised! round my ain heartsome
    ingle,
Wi' the friends o' my youth I cordially mingle;
Nae forms to compel me to seem wae or glad,
I may laugh when I'm merry, and sigh when I'm sad.
    My ain fireside, my ain fireside,
      O there's nought to compare wi' ane's ain fireside.

Nae falsehood to dread, and nae malice to fear,
But truth to delight me, and kindness to cheer;

> O' a' roads to pleasure that ever were tried,
> There's nane half sae sure as ane's ain fireside.
> My ain fireside, my ain fireside,
> O sweet is the blink o' my ain fireside.[1]

The writer of this song was Mrs Elizabeth Hamilton, the author of a well-known popular novel, 'The Cottagers of Glenburnie,' that still commands readers, and of a work on education, which was notable enough in its day to command public commendation from Professor Dugald Stewart, during the first quarter of the present century, the great Edinburgh authority on all matters of social philosophy. Elizabeth Hamilton was a lady who had the great advantage of combining Scottish descent with Irish nurture; a mixture which naturally tends to give to the Irish element that stability which is so necessary in the root, and to the Scottish element that sprightliness which is so attractive in the blossom, of human character. Though born in Belfast in 1758, she was brought up with her aunt in the neighbourhood of Stirling, where she had the best of all possible educations for a Scotch literary lady, amid the historical traditions of castle and river and crag in which that picturesque old town is embosomed, and with the grand outlook to the green Ochills and the purple Grampians which the situation commands. She was a young

---

[1] See a third verse in 'Songstresses of Scotland.'

woman, essentially healthy-minded, sensible, cheerful, and practical, and brought up in the middle condition of life, where her intellectual tendencies were neither dissipated by indulgence nor depressed by poverty. Unfortunate in her first early attachment, she lived single through life, first at Bath with her sister, where she enjoyed the society of Lucy Aikin, Joanna Baillie, Madame d'Arblay, Horace Walpole's favourite Mary Berry, and other literary notables of the time. In the year 1803, like a true Scot she yielded to a long-suppressed instinct of home-sickness, and passing through the English Lake district, took up her residence in Edinburgh, where her house soon became a familiar haunt to Stewart, Playfair, Alison, and other Academic notabilities, and among persons of her own sex, chiefly to the celebrated Mrs Grant of Laggan. Shortly after her settlement in Edinburgh, her health began to decline; "but," says her biographer, "amid fast-failing strength, she was engaged in every intellectual, charitable, and truly religious enterprise of old Edinburgh."[1] She died at Harrogate in 1816, in her fifty-eighth year.

The author of the next song, also a Hamilton, but of the stronger sex, was an Edinburgh man, who had by no means a position in the literary world entitling him to rank with this accomplished lady; nevertheless the Muse,

[1] Songstresses of Scotland, vol. i. p. 320.

who is no respecter of persons, inspired him with an effusion of the most characteristically Scotch type, both in scenery and sentiment, that in these latter times has laid a firm hold of the popular ear. John Hamilton was a music-seller and music-teacher in Edinburgh. He died there in the year before the battle of Waterloo, at the early age of fifty-three. The air seems to have been originally English :[1]—

Up in the Morning Early.

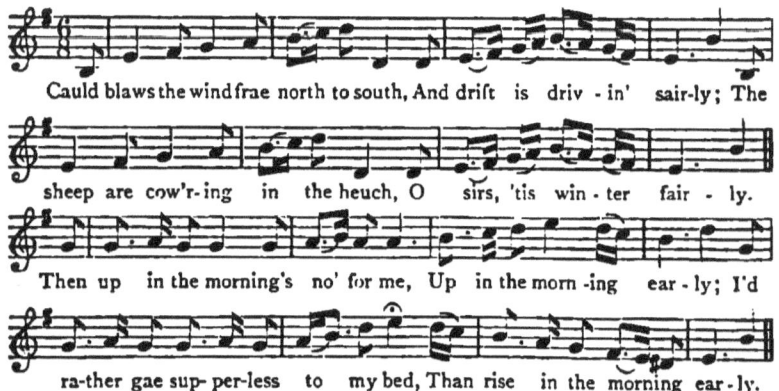

Cauld blaws the wind frae north to south, And drift is driv-in' sair-ly; The sheep are cow'r-ing in the heuch, O sirs, 'tis win-ter fair-ly. Then up in the morning's no' for me, Up in the morn-ing ear-ly; I'd ra-ther gae sup-per-less to my bed, Than rise in the morning ear-ly.

> Loud roars the blast among the woods,
>   And tirls the branches barely;
> On hill and house hear how it thuds!
>   The frost is nippling sairly.
> Now up in the morning's no' for me,
>   Up in the morning early;
> To sit a' nicht wad better agree,
>   Than rise in the morning early.

---

[1] See the Balmoral edition of Scottish Songs, full of excellent historical notes. J. Muir Wood & Co., Buchanan Street, Glasgow.

The sun peeps owre yon southland hills
    Like ony timorous carlie,
Just blinks a wee then sinks again,
    And that we find severely.
Now up in the morning's no' for me,
    Up in the morning early;
When snaw blaws in at the chimley-cheek,
    Wha'd rise in the morning early?

Nae linties lilt on hedge or bush:
    Poor things, they suffer sairly;
In cauldrife quarters a' the nicht;
    A' day they feed but sparely.
Now up in the morning's no' for me,
    Up in the morning early;
A pennyless purse I wad rather dree,
    Than rise in the morning early.

A cosie house and cantie wife
    Aye keep a body cheerly;
And pantries stowed wi' meat and drink,
    They answer unco rarely.
But up in the morning—na, na, na!
    Up in the morning early;
The gowans maun glent on bank and brae,
    When I rise in the morning early.

In countries which, like Italy and Greece, can count upon a long continuity of bright days and clear mornings, such a song would be the freak of an individual or the exceptional utterance of an ill-conditioned nervous system; but in Scotland, where, as an American expressed it, we have no climate but only weather, and where the weather

254 *Songs of Character and Incident in Daily Life.*

is as unsteady as the character of the people is the reverse, such a song is as full of native expression as the heather on the brae or the blaeberry in the wood.

The next two songs are by a noble lady whom we have already had more than once on our stage—the Baroness Nairne, a songstress whose lyrical sympathies were more broad and various than her other fair competitors in the service of the Lyrical Muse, most of whom maintain their popularity only by the virtue of a single song:—

THE ROWAN TREE.[1]

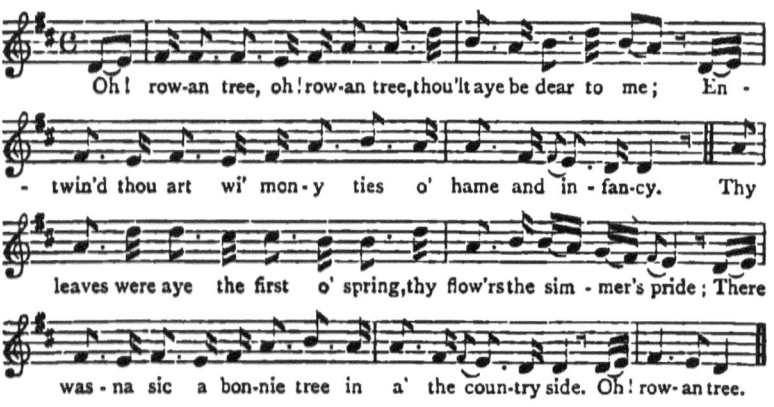

Oh! row-an tree, oh! row-an tree, thou'lt aye be dear to me; En-twin'd thou art wi' mon-y ties o' hame and in-fan-cy. Thy leaves were aye the first o' spring, thy flow'rs the sim-mer's pride; There was-na sic a bon-nie tree in a' the coun-try side. Oh! row-an tree.

How fair wert thou in simmer time, wi' a' thy clusters white!
How rich and gay thy autumn dress, wi' berries red and bright!
On thy fair stem were many names, which now nae mair I see,
But they're engraven on my heart, forgot they ne'er can be,
      Oh! rowan tree.

---

[1] Air of this and the following song by kind permission of Paterson & Sons.

"The Auld House."

We sat aneath thy spreading shade, the bairnies round thee ran,
They pu'd thy bonnie berries red, and necklaces they strang;
My mither, oh! I see her still, she smiled our sports to see,
Wi' little Jeanie on her lap, and Jamie at her knee.
         Oh! rowan tree.

Oh! there arose my father's prayer in holy evening's calm,
How sweet was then my mother's voice, in the martyr's psalm!
Now a' are gane! we meet nae mair aneath the rowan tree,
But hallowed thoughts around thee turn o' hame and infancy.
         Oh! rowan tree.

THE AULD HOUSE.

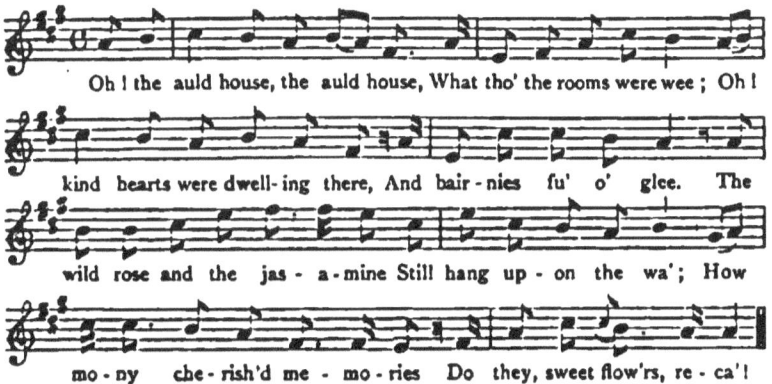

Oh! the auld house, the auld house, What tho' the rooms were wee; Oh! kind hearts were dwelling there, And bairnies fu' o' glee. The wild rose and the jas-a-mine Still hang upon the wa'; How mony cherish'd memories Do they, sweet flow'rs, re-ca'!

  Oh! the auld laird, the auld laird,
   Sae canty, kind, and crouse;
  How mony did he welcome
   To his ain wee dear auld house!
  And the leddy too, sae genty,
   There shelter'd Scotland's heir,

And clipt a lock wi' her ain hand
   Frae his lang yellow hair.

The mavis still doth sweetly sing,
   The blue-bells sweetly blaw;
The bonnie Earn's clear winding still,
   But the auld house is awa'.
The auld house, the auld house,
   Deserted though you be,
There ne'er can be a new house
   Will seem sae fair to me.

Still flourishing the auld pear-tree
   The bairnies liked to see;
And oh! how aften did they speir
   When ripe they a' wad be?
The voices sweet, the wee bit feet,
   Aye rinnin' here and there;
The merry shout—oh! whiles we greet
   To think we'll hear nae mair.

For they are a' wide scatter'd now,
   Some to the Indies gane;
And ane, alas! to her lang hame,
   Not here we'll meet again.
The kirkyard, the kirkyard,
   Wi' flow'rs o' every hue;
Shelter'd by the holly's shade,
   And the dark sombre yew.

The setting sun, the setting sun,
   How glorious it gaed down!
The cloudy splendour raised our hearts
   To cloudless skies aboon.

> The auld dial, the auld dial,
>   It tauld how time did pass;
> The wintry winds hae dang it down,
>   Now hid 'mang weeds and grass.[1]

This is a song that, with a large interpretation of its significance and a liberal recall of its associations—for the lairds of the auld house of Gask were all arch-Jacobites—may well be called the poetry of Toryism, as Burns's "A Man's a Man for a' that" is the best lyrical expression of all that is best in Liberalism. It is the glory of the popular song to belong to no party; and to make "Whig and Tory a' agree" is the great harmony of the national heart.

But, though there is a poetry of Toryism and a poetry of Liberalism, there is a poetry of something wider than either—a poetry, in fact, which includes both, and by its gracious influences harmonises for the moment, even with the most narrow-minded, the jars and discords that are apt to arise out of the antagonistic stirrings by which the social machine is worked,—the poetry of humanity and of catholic social sympathy. The popular song that does not perform this blessed harmonising function, is like a stimulant drug that stirs only one limb of the body social to excited action,

---

[1] The copyright of these and other songs of this noble lady belongs to Roy Paterson, musical publisher, Edinburgh, by whose kind permission they appear here.

while the general heart beats feebly, and the veins swell faintly with pulses of watery blood. No Scottish songwriter acknowledged more powerfully than the author of "Tullochgorum" this harmonising and humanising function of song; and in the particular song with which his name is popularly associated, he has, with a happy instinct, wedded the lyrical expression of his catholic humanity to the national Scottish dance—a reel. The Greeks, with that fine æsthetical sensibility which was their special gift, knew to unite piety, poetry, and philosophy with the dance, which of all arts is the most universal expression of that fulness of exuberant vitality in which, so to speak, the power of the divine creativeness revels in its own energy. In Scotland, where the severe aspect of religion has been abnormally accentuated, this so natural union of divinity with dancing has been disowned, to such a degree indeed in some districts, as to have dancing and card-playing, theatrical representations, and every graceful sportiveness of healthy nature, relegated into the region of sin and profanity. But this awful sort of piety never extended beyond the pale of the extreme Presbyterian party, of whose Calvinism it was the natural outcome; while the Episcopalians, to which body the bard of "Tullochgorum" belonged, whatever sacerdotal pedantries they might fondle, never committed the great mistake of proclaiming a formal divorce between sacred reverence and social sport. Here follows the song :—

TULLOCHGORUM.

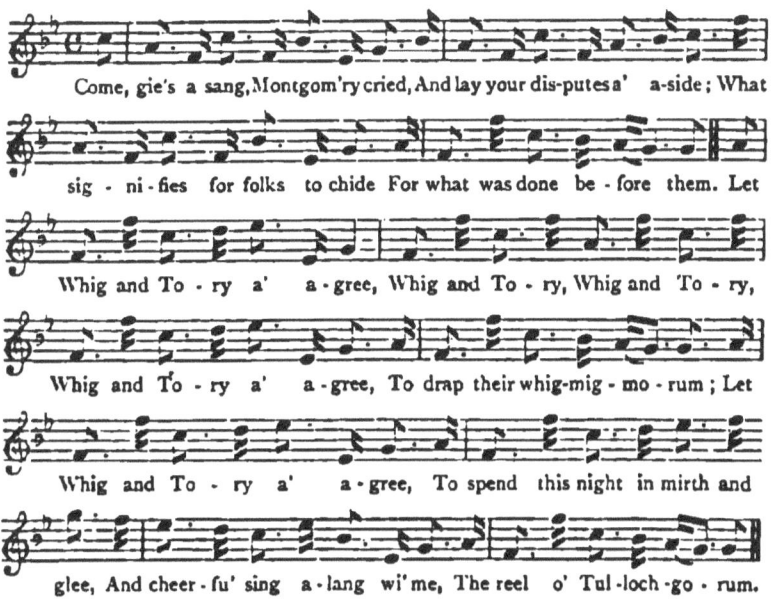

Come, gie's a sang, Montgom'ry cried, And lay your disputes a' a-side; What signifies for folks to chide For what was done before them. Let Whig and Tory a' agree, Whig and Tory, Whig and Tory, Whig and Tory a' agree, To drap their whig-mig-mo-rum; Let Whig and Tory a' agree, To spend this night in mirth and glee, And cheerfu' sing a-lang wi' me, The reel o' Tulloch-go-rum.

O, Tullochgorum's my delight,
It gars us a' in ane unite,
And ony sumph that keeps up spite,
   In conscience I abhor him.
Blythe and merry we'll be a',
Blythe and merry, blythe and merry,
Blythe and merry we'll be a',
   An' mak' a cheerfu' quorum.
For blythe and merry we'll be a'
As lang as we hae breath to draw,
And dance till we be like to fa',
   The reel o' Tullochgorum.

What need's there be sae great a fraise,
Wi' dringin', dull Italian lays;
I wadna gie our ain strathspeys
   For half-a-hunder score o' them.
They're dowf and dowie at the best,
Dowf and dowie, dowf and dowie,
Dowf and dowie at the best,
   Wi' a' their variorum.
They're dowf and dowie at the best;
Their *allegros* and a' the rest,
They canna please a Scottish taste
   Compared wi' Tullochgorum.

Let worldly worms their minds oppress
Wi' fears o' wants and double cess,
And sullen sots themsel's distress
   Wi' keeping up decorum.
Shall we sae sour and sulky sit?
Sour and sulky, sour and sulky,
Sour and sulky shall we sit,
   Like auld philosophorum?
Shall we sae sour and sulky sit,
Wi' neither sense, nor mirth, nor wit,
Nor ever rise to shake a fit
   To the reel o' Tullochgorum?

May choicest blessings aye attend
Each honest, open-hearted friend,
And calm and quiet be his end,
   And a' that's guid watch o'er him.
May peace and plenty be his lot,
Peace and plenty, peace and plenty,
Peace and plenty be his lot,
   And dainties a great store o' them:

May peace and plenty be his lot,
Unstained by ony vicious spot,
And may he never want a groat
 That's fond o' Tullochgorum.

But for the discontented fool,
Wha wants to be oppression's tool,
May envy gnaw his rotten soul,
 And discontent devour him.
May dool and sorrow be his chance,
Dool and sorrow, dool and sorrow;
Dool and sorrow be his chance,
 And nane say, "Wae's me, for him!"
May dool and sorrow be his chance,
And a' the ills that come frae France,
Whae'er he be that winna dance
 The reel o' Tullochgorum.

The author of this song, which Burns declared to be one of the best in our rich lyrical roll, was a man of whom, independently of his contributions to the song-literature of his country, Scotland has every reason to be proud; a man from whose healthiness of mind, large human sympathies, rare moral courage, and great-hearted cheerfulness, displayed on a humble and remote stage, those who are willing to learn may learn more of the wisdom of life than from many a loudly trumpeted and widely belauded actor in the great events of the time. The Rev. John Skinner was the son of an Aberdeen man, who performed the onerous but too often ill-rewarded duties of a parochial schoolmaster for more than fifty years, first at Birse, where our singer was born in the year 1721, and then down in the low part of the county at Echt, not far from that. He enjoyed the advantages which every lad of fair talent at the period was sure to have within his power at a good parish school, and at the early age of thirteen was so far advanced in his Latin studies as to gain a bursary, which enabled him to pass through the four years of the University curriculum of Marischal College with all the honour and all the profit that belonged to young Academicians in the granite metropolis of the North. To a lad so precociously equipped with bookish lore, the Church presented itself as the natural field of his life-work. He had been brought up a Presbyterian; but, while residing at Monymusk, a beautiful country district on Donside, where he acted for a short time as assistant schoolmaster, with a mind ever open to new impressions, he saw reason to change his views, and join himself to the Episcopalian Church, a body at that time so low in social estimation that nothing but the purest and most disinterested motives could have led any young man a born Presbyterian to court its communion. A short course of theological study was sufficient to prepare so proved a Latinist for the sacred ministry; and in 1742 we find him settled in what St Paul would have called the overseership of the parish of Longside, passing rich on £40 a-year, not many years before the time when not a few persons thought Robert Burns very scurvily served by getting £70 a-year as an exciseman. How wisely and how sweetly he spent his long life in the unobtrusive routine of parochial work here — far from human dwellings, and in a district as remarkable for the prose of its landscape as the upper part of the same county is for its poetry—the following autobiographical sketch in verse, as a model of evangelical contentment to all underpaid curates and country parsons, though more indeed of a sermon than a song, deserves a place here :—

THE STIPENDLESS PARSON.

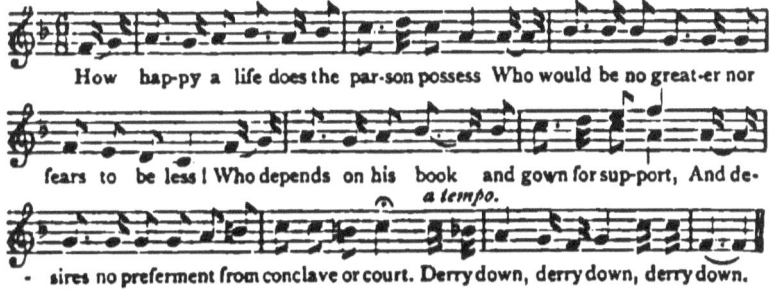

How happy a life does the parson possess Who would be no greater nor fears to be less! Who depends on his book and gown for support, And desires no preferment from conclave or court. Derry down, derry down, derry down.

  Without glebe or manse settl'd on him by law,
  No stipend to sue for, nor vic'rage to draw ;
  In discharge of his office he holds him content,
  With a croft and a garden, for which he pays rent.
      Derry down, &c.

  With a neat little cottage and furniture plain,
  And a spare room to welcome a friend now and then ;

With a good-humour'd wife in his fortune to share,
And ease him at all times of family care.
     Derry down, &c.

With a few of the fathers, the oldest and best,
And some modern extracts pick'd out from the rest;
With a Bible in Latin, and Hebrew, and Greek,
To afford him instruction each day of the week.
     Derry down, &c.

With a pony to carry him when he has need,
And a cow to provide him some milk to his bread;
With a mug of brown ale when he feels himself for't,
And a glass of good whisky in place of red port.
     Derry down, &c.

What children he has, if any are given,
He thankfully trusts to the kindness of Heaven;
To religion and virtue he trains them while young,
And with such a provision he does them no wrong.
     Derry down, &c.

With labour below, and with help from above,
He cares for his *flock*, and is blest with their love;
Though his living perhaps in the main may be scant,
He is sure, while *they* have, that he'll ne'er be in want.
     Derry down, &c.

With no worldly projects nor hurries perplext,
He sits in his closet and studies his text;
And while he converses with Moses or Paul,
He envies not bishop, nor dean in his stall.
     Derry down, &c.

Not proud to the poor, nor a slave to the great,
Neither factious in Church, nor pragmatic in State,
He keeps himself quiet within his own sphere,
And finds work sufficient in preaching and pray'r.
    Derry down, &c.

In what little dealings he's forc'd to transact,
He determines with plainness and candour to act;
And the great point on which his ambition is set,
Is to leave at the last neither riches nor debt.
    Derry down, &c.

Thus calmly he steps through the valley of life,
Unencumber'd with wealth, and a stranger to strife;
On the bustlings around him unmov'd he can look,
And at home always pleas'd with his wife and his book.
    Derry down, &c.

And when in old age he drops into the grave,
This humble remembrance he wishes to have:
"By good men respected, by evil oft tried,
Contented he liv'd, and lamented he died!"
    Derry down, &c.

In the year 1753 this most excellent man had the honour of suffering imprisonment for six months, as a violator of one of those monstrous laws of intolerant malignity which characterised the Hanoverian Government in that course of brutal revenge which followed on the catastrophe of Culloden. As a considerable number, perhaps the majority, of those who took part in the chivalrous rising of the '45 were either Roman Catholics or Episcopalians, the Government, after the battle had drenched the field with the warm blood of the gallant clansmen, proceeded in cold blood, or in a fit of nervous tremor unworthy of a manly Government, to pass an Act that no person of the Episcopal persuasion should be allowed to minister in sacred things to any assembly consisting of more than four persons besides the members of the household. Against this most inhuman and most unchristian enactment the kindly-hearted singer of "Tullochgorum" had been led to offend, and was in consequence surprised one morning by an order from the sheriff-substitute of Aberdeen, in virtue of which he was confined in prison for six months.

Connected with this period of shameful restriction on the freedom of preaching, is an anecdote which may stand here as containing an interesting lesson to young preachers. In both Churches, but especially in the Episcopalian, there has been allowed to grow up the lazy or timorous habit of reading from dead paper, instead of speaking from living heart to heart with a direct manly appeal; a habit that, after being followed for a period of years, is only too apt to generate in the mind of our pulpit-prelectors the notion that to speak freely, as a Greek or Roman would have done, without paper, is a feat impossible to the modern occupier of the sacred rostrum. The effect of the laborious course of education which the candidates for the sacred ministry in our country undergo, results too frequently, not in a greater command of language, or a ready power of utterance, when occasion may demand, but simply in being dumb, or in reading from a paper in circumstances when to read, if the instincts of nature are to be regarded, is as much out of place as it would be to make love to a fair damsel by the recitation of a formal epistolary composition, instead of looking in her face and holding her hand. The Episcopal presbyter of Longside had, like his fellow-orators in big cathedrals at the present day, been bred to the slavishness of this artificial style of addressing his fellow-sinners, and would have gone on to his last sermon preaching in the same style of respectable tameness had not the following little incident occurred. No chapel being tolerated to men of his persuasion, and it being forbidden to admit more than four persons into his dwelling for ministerial purposes, he fell upon the device of preaching from an open window to the people assembled on the outside in the open air. One Sunday, shortly after the sermon commenced, a hen, which had somehow or other got into the house, set up a cackling which both annoyed the speaker and disturbed the hearers; on this, one of the most sensible of the auditors contrived so dexterously to plant himself inside the room where the gallinaceous concert was being enacted, that he left no means of escape to the cackling intruder but right over the shoulder of the preacher, in performing which evolution with an unceremonious haste justified to the gallinaceous mind by the strange and critical nature of the situation, the winged fugitive with a tremendous flap of both wings scattered the unstitched pages of the sermon to a wanton distance all around. An effort was made by some of the pious congregation to collect them; but "Never mind them!" cried the preacher; "a fowl shall not shut my mouth again;" and so, trusting to nature, he was redeemed henceforth from the slavery of the paper, and preached with much extempore power to the end of his life, using as much natural intonation and gesture as any Red Indian in the Transatlantic West, or a fervid prophetess in the early Christian Church.

Born nearly forty years before Burns, the author of "Tullochgorum" survived our great national singer eleven years, and died, as he had lived, at Longside, on the 16th June 1807.[1]

But we must not take leave of this admirable man without introducing, to those who have the misfortune not to know it, the other most popular song of the reverend minstrel, "The Ewie wi' the Crookit Horn," which here fol-

---

[1] Songs and Poems by the Rev. John Skinner, with a Sketch of his Life by H. S. Reid. Peterhead, 1859.

lows—a composition in which the tender kindliness and broad catholic sensibility of the singer stand out as characteristically and as favourably as the well-known verses of Burns to the Daisy and the Field-mouse. It is indeed, as is well remarked by a pious student of the great peasant-singer,[1] in this fine perception of the idealism that underlies the commonest things that the magic craft of the great poet resides. Any ambitious young man with a gift of lyrical utterance may be moved to strain after things great and lofty, which cannot escape the notice even of the vulgar spectator; but it is the special privilege of genius, as it is the greatest grace of a truly evangelical temper, to "mind not high things, but to condescend to men of low estate;" and so a poor sheep with a crooked horn comes in for a poetical glorification, on the same principle that Lazarus, whose sores the dogs licked, gets into Paradise before the rich man :—

THE EWIE WI' THE CROOKIT HORN.[2]

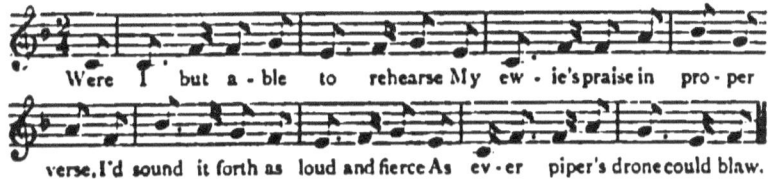

Were I but a-ble to rehearse My ew-ie's praise in pro-per verse, I'd sound it forth as loud and fierce As ev-er piper's drone could blaw.

---

[1] Burns in Mossgiel, by W. Jolly. Paisley, 1881.

[2] The vulgar notion that this is merely an allegory of "A Whisky Still," a notion that would utterly destroy the poetry of the conception, is distinctly disproved by the author of the Life above quoted.

I never needed tar nor keil,
To mark her upo' hip or heel;
Her crookit hornie did as weel,
　　To ken her by amang them a'.

She never threaten'd scab nor rot,
But keepit aye her ain jog-trot;
Baith to the fauld and to the cot,
　　Was never sweirt to lead nor ca'.

Cauld nor hunger never dang her,
Wind nor weet could never wrang her;
Ance she lay an ouk and langer
　　Furth aneath a wreath o' snaw.

Whan ither ewies lap the dyke,
And ate the kail for a' the tyke,
My ewie never play'd the like,
　　But tyc'd about the barn wa'.

A better or a thriftier beast
Nae honest man could weel hae wist;
For, silly thing, she never misst
　　To hae, ilk year, a lamb or twa.

The first she had I ga'e to Jock,
To be to him a kind o' stock;
And now the laddie has a flock
　　O' mair nor thirty head ava.

I lookit aye at even for her,
Lest mishanter should come o'er her,
Or the foumart might devour her,
   Gin the beastie bade awa'.

My ewie wi' the crookit horn,
Weel deserv'd baith gerse and corn;
Sic a ewe was never born,
   Hereabout, or far awa'.

Yet, last ouk, for a' my keeping,
(Wha can speak it without greeting?)
A villain cam' when I was sleeping,
   Sta' my ewie, horn and a'.

I sought her sair upo' the morn;
And down aneath a buss o' thorn,
I got my ewie's crookit horn,
   But my ewie was awa'.

O! gin I had the loon that did it,
Sworn I have, as weel as said it,
Though a' the warld should forbid it,
   I wad gi'e his neck a thraw.

O! a' ye bards benorth Kinghorn,
Call your Muses up and mourn
Our ewie wi' the crookit horn
   Stown frae's, and fell'd an' a'!

Next comes a no less valuable lyric gem from the pen of that versatile songstress, whom we have once and again laid under tribute, the Baroness Caroline Nairne; a song which is inferior to none, whether we regard the vivid picturesqueness of its expression, the aptness of its musical accompaniment, or its power of touching the general heart of the people. In "Caller Herrin'" the noble authoress has interpreted, for all times, the poetic significance of a costume as characteristic of the streets of Edinburgh as the grey plaid is of the Lowland shepherd, and the tartan kilt of the Highland soldier. The music, dramatically expressing the mingled harmony of the bells in St Andrew's Church, and the clear, mellow, prolonged cry of the fishwives as they pace, heavy-laden with the creel, the cold pavement of the Modern Athens, was composed by Nathaniel, the son of the celebrated Neil Gow, the genial violinist of Strathbran in Perthshire: [1]—

CALLER HERRIN'.[2]

Wha'll buy my cal-ler herr - in'? They're bon-nie fish and hale-some far- in';
Buy my cal-ler herr - in', New drawn frae the Forth. When ye were sleep-ing
on your pillows, Dreamt ye aught o' our puir fellows, Darkling as they faced the billows,

---

[1] There is a similar song celebrating "Caller Oysters" (Edinburgh, Paterson), which the student of street music will not wisely neglect, offering, as it does, such a mellow qualification to the harshness of the east wind, which blows with such an unkindly sweep through the long-drawn streets of Dunedin.

[2] By permission from Paterson & Sons.

"Caller Herrin'."

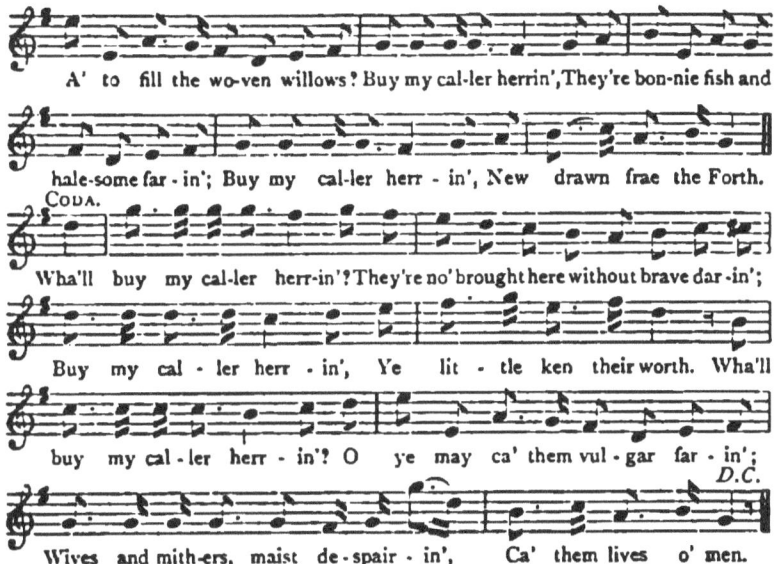

But when the creel o' herrin' passes,
Ladies clad in silks and laces,
Gather in their braw pelisses,
Cast their heads and screw their faces.
    Wha'll buy my caller herrin'? &c.

Caller herrin's no' got lichtlie,
Ye can trip the spring fu' tightlie,
Spite o' tauntin', flauntin,' flingin',
Gow has set you a' a-singin'.
    Wha'll buy my caller herrin'? &c.

Noo neebour wives come tent my tellin',
When the bonnie fish you're sellin',
At ae word aye be your dealin',
Truth will stand when a' things failin'.
    Wha'll buy my caller herrin'? &c.[1]

---

[1] Verses 2, 3, and 4 begin at *.
The coda is sung after each verse, or after the last verse only, *ad lib*.

Our next song is one of which Edinburgh has every reason to be proud; for, though Lady Nairne drew her blood from Perthshire, and sojourned only in the romantic town for a season, Sir Douglas Maclagan is a man in every way identified with Edinburgh, and has the honour of composing a song that, not only for lyrical excellence, but for legal and political significance, has no superior in the whole range of our national song. If any class of men deserve to be specially immortalised in the songs of the Scottish people, it is the Highland crofters, who from their humble cabins have sent forth so many stout-hearted workers to furnish our great towns with preachers and teachers, and our battle-fields with the most gallant soldiers and the most daring captains. But great as these services were, and proud as the men of Great Britain naturally were of them in the hour of victory, in times of peace they are too readily forgotten by a people engrossed with schemes of industrial enterprise, and a nobility, by the unequal terms of the Union of 1707, and other superinduced influences, withdrawn more and more from living connection with their faithful dependants, whom it is their special function in the social system to cherish, to cultivate, and to guide. Favoured by laws which, instead of protecting the weak against the strong—the first object of all wise legislation—had a direct tendency to make the strong stronger, and the great greater, and acting under no check of a healthy public opinion, these gentlemen proceeded, in the self-indulgence of an unpatriotic lordship, to such a pitch of insolence as to block up all the natural lines of communication betwixt glen and glen in the Highlands, and to claim the whole range of the mountain-land as an exclusive possession for game and gamekeepers, and mighty hunters before the Lord; and not only did they do this for their personal indulgence in a favourite sport, as if holding land for themselves, and not as members of a social system, but they sold their interest in the soil on purely mercantile principles to Lowland farmers in hot haste to be rich by gigantic sheep-farms, or to English plutocrats and American millionaires willing to pay any amount of money for a free range over the haunts of artificially accumulated deer. Nor was this all; as if willing to show that they cared as little for the interests of science as for the welfare of the human beings committed to their charge, they passed a practical interdict against all botanists and geologists presuming to study the ways and works of the Creator in regions which they had consecrated to the service of wild beasts. This stretch of insolence brought their monstrous pretensions directly under the public eye; an Edinburgh professor of botany, heading a party of students, was not a person to be stopped in his scientific pedestrianism without observation; and so it chanced that in the month of August 1847, the then guide of the professional students under his charge, Professor Balfour, was stopped in the old Glen Tilt road from Braemar to Blair-Atholl, by the venatorial Duke. This event, which soon after led to a law plea, in which the Duke was worsted, was one, from its dramatic incidents as well as its social significance, peculiarly calculated to stir the humorous vein of which Sir Douglas Maclagan is so great a master; and so "The Battle o' Glen Tilt" appeared, a song first-class of its kind, and which will continue to give healthy amusement to social gatherings, and a great lesson to political thinkers, so long as Scotland remains Scotland. The air, very appropriately, is the same as that sung to "The Battle of Sheriffmuir," above, p. 180:—

The Battle o' Glen Tilt.

"O cam' ye here to hear a lilt,
  Or hae a crack wi' me, man;
Or was ye at the Glen o' Tilt,
  An' did the shindy see, man?"
"I saw the shindy sair an' teugh,
The flytin' there was loud an' rough;
    The Duke cam' o'er,
    Wi' gillies four,
    To mak' a stour
    An' drive Balfour
Frae 'yont the Hielan' hills, man.

"The Sassenach chap they ca' Balfour,
　　Wi' ither five or sax, man,
Frae 'yont the braes o' Mar cam' o'er,
　　Wi' boxes on their backs, man.
Some thocht he was a chapman chiel—
Some thocht they cam' the deer to steal ;
　　　　But nae ane saw
　　　　Them, after a',
　　　　Do ocht ava
　　　　Against the law,
Amang the Hielan' hills, man.

"Some folk 'll tak' a heap o' fash
　　For unco little en', man ;
An' meikle time an' meikle cash
　　For nocht ava they'll spen', man.
Thae chaps had come a hunder mile
For what was hardly worth their while :
　　　　'Twas a' to poo
　　　　Some gerse that grew
　　　　On Ben M'Dhu,
　　　　That ne'er a coo
Would care to pit her mouth till.

"The gerse was poo't, the boxes fill't,
　　An' syne the hail clamjamfrie
Would tak' the road by Glen o' Tilt,
　　Awa' to whar' they cam' frae.
The Duke at this put up his birse ;
He vowed, in English an' in Erse,
　　　　That Saxon fit
　　　　Sud never get
　　　　Ae single bit
　　　　Throughout his yett,
Amang the Hielan' hills, man.

"Balfour he had a mind as weel
   As ony Duke could hae, man;
Quo' he, 'There's ne'er a kilted chiel
   Shall drive us back this day, man.
It's justice an' it's public richt;
We'll pass Glen Tilt afore the nicht.
        For Dukes shall we
        Care ae bawbee?
        The road's as free
        To you an' me
As to his Grace himsel', man.'

"The Duke was at an unco loss
   To manage in a hurry,
Sae he sent roun' the fiery cross,
   To ca' the clan o' Murray.
His men cam' doon frae glen an' hill—
Four gillies an' a writer chiel—
        In kilts and hose,
        A' to oppose
        Their Saxon foes,
        An' gie them blows,
An' drive them frae the hills, man.

"When Hielan' chiefs, in days o' yore,
   Gaed oot to fecht the foe, man,
The piper he gaed on afore,
   The line o' march to show, man.
But noo they've ta'en anither plan—
They hae a pipe for ilka man:
        Nae chanter guid
        Blaws pibroch loud,
        But a' the crowd
        Noo blaw a cloud
Frae cutty pipes o' clay, man.

"Balfour he wadna fled frae fire,
　Frae smoke he wadna flee, man;
The Saxons had but ae desire—
　It was the foe to see, man.
Quo' he to them—'My bonny men,
Tak' tent when ye gang doon the glen;
　　　Keep calm an' douce,
　　　An' quiet as puss,—
　　　For what's the use
　　　To mak' a fuss
Amang the Hielan' hills, men?'

"To keep them cool aboot the head
　The Sassenachs did atten', man;
The Duke himsel' was cool indeed,
　But at the ither en', man;
For win' an' rain blew up Glen Tilt,
An' roun' his houghs an' through his kilt,
　　　Baith loud an' lang,
　　　An' cauld an' strang,
　　　Wi' mony a bang,
　　　It soughed alang
Amang the Hielan' hills, man.

"The Sassenachs they cam' doon to Blair,
　An' marched as bauld as brass, man;
The glen was closed when they got there,
　And out they couldna pass, man:
The Duke he glower'd in through the yett,
An' said that out they sudna get;
　　　'Twas trespass clear
　　　Their comin' here,
　　　For they wad fear
　　　Awa' his deer,
Amang the Hielan' hills, man.

"Balfour he said it was absurd;
　　The Duke was in a rage, man;
He said he wadna hear a word,
　　Although they spak' an age, man.
The mair they fleeched, the mair they spoke,
The mair the Duke blew out his smoke.
　　　　　He said, (guid lack!)
　　　　　Balfour micht tak'
　　　　　An' carry back
　　　　　His Saxon pack
Ayont the Hielan' hills, man.

"The gangin' back was easier said
　　Than it was dune, by far, man;
The nearest place to rest their head
　　Was up ayont Braemar, man:
'Twas best to seek Blair-Atholl Inn,
For they were drookit to the skin:
　　　　　Sae syne they a'
　　　　　Lap o'er a wa',
　　　　　An' ran awa',
　　　　　Wi' a guffaw,
An' left the Hielan' hills, man.

"The battle it was ended then,
　　Afore 'twas focht ava, man;
An' noo some ither chaps are gaen
　　To tak' the Duke to law, man.
Ochon! your Grace, my bonny man,
An' ye had sense as ye hae lan',
　　　　　Ye'd been this hour
　　　　　Ayont the poor
　　　　　O' lawyers dour,
　　　　　An' let Balfour
Gang through your Hielan' hills, man."[1]

---

[1] Nugæ Canoræ Medicæ: Edinburgh, Douglas, 1873. The Glen

We give now a lyrical effusion, of which the sufferings of the Highland crofters are the theme, from the pen of a reverend gentleman who has done much in various publications to purify the moral atmosphere of his native country by that combination of piety, poetry, and good sense, which makes piety enjoyable, and poetry salubrious, and gives common-sense wings; we mean the Rev. Dr Walter Smith. The crofter question, of which we hear so much every winter, like other questions, has two sides. While the misery of some parts of the Highlands is justly attributed to the rage for large farms, and the depopulation of large tracts of country consequent on that phase of agricultural economy, other districts have suffered not less from over-population, produced by the lack of foresight in the crofters, and the want of wise and firm superintendence on the part of resident landlords; the indulgence of good fathers of the people being sometimes the cause of as great evils as the severity of absentee lords, who devolve their local duties on land agents. Anyhow, the feelings of the expatriated cottars, so vividly expressed in the following lines, will meet with no stinted measure of righteous sympathy from all Christian people who have their hearts exercised in the

Tilt song refers exclusively to the count of deer-stalking; the rage for large farms has found a lyrical memorial in my song called "Bonnie Strathnaver"—Edinburgh: Paterson & Sons.

habitual response to the grand apostolic text, *Rejoice with those who rejoice, and weep with those who weep:—*

KENNETH'S SONG.

There is no fire of the crackling boughs
    On the hearth of our fathers;
There is no lowing of brown-eyed cows
    On the green meadows,
Nor do the maidens whisper vows
    In the still gloaming,
        Glenaradale.

There is no bleating of sheep on the hill,
    Where the mists linger;
There is no sound of the low hand-mill
    Ground by the women;
And the smith's hammer is lying still,
    By the brown anvil,
        Glenaradale.

Ah! we must leave thee, and go away
    Far from Ben Luibh;
Far from the graves where we hoped to lay
    Our bones with our fathers;
Far from the kirk where we used to pray
    Lowly together,
        Glenaradale.

We are not going for hunger of wealth,
    For the gold and silver;
We are not going to seek for health
    On the flat prairies;

Nor yet for the lack of fruitful tilth,
  On thy green pastures,
    Glenaradale.

Content with the croft and the hill were we,
  As all our fathers;
Content with the fish in the lake to be
  Carefully netted,
And garments spun of the wool from thee,
  O black-faced wether
    Of Glenaradale.

No father here but would give a son
  For the old country,
And his mother the sword would have girded on
  To fight her battles;
Many's the battle that has been won
  By the brave tartans,
    Glenaradale.

But the big-horned stag and his hinds, we know,
  In the high corries,
And the salmon that swirls the pool below
  Where the stream rushes,
Are more than the hearts of men, and so
  We leave thy green valley,
    Glenaradale.[1]

Any attempt to give the general public a notion of the social significance of Scottish song would be extremely imperfect that did not give prominence to the part the

[1] Kildrostan: A Dramatic Poem. By the author of 'Olrig Grange.' Glasgow: Maclehose, 1884.

members of the Bar have played in enlarging and enriching our lyrical repertory. No doubt law, in its strictly legal manifestation, has nothing to do with poetry; as the most severe and formal, it is certainly the least emotional and the least humorous of the professions; and no man looks among the gentlemen of the long robe for the full flow of sentiment and that furnace-glow of passion which makes a Burns or a Byron. Nevertheless, though it is perhaps as impossible a thing for a great lawyer to be a great poet as it is for an elephant to be an eagle, there are fields in the wide domain of lyrical exercitation which the distinguished members of that most intellectual profession have ever been forward to claim as specially their own. We mean, of course, the field of the humorous and the characteristic; as indeed any one may see when present at a jury trial, that in this form of eliminating right the wall of partition is broken down that separates the severe and often artificial formalism of strict law from the genial humanities of common life. At the Scottish bar specially, it was always a boast that barristers in the largest practice were not seldom those who possessed an amount of various literary culture which redeemed their social intercourse from the pedantry of what is familiarly called *shop*. Sir Walter Scott, as everybody knows, was not only a lawyer, but a very sound-headed county judge; and some of our most popular songs, with a broadly humorous brush, proceeded from the genial touch of Sir Alexander Boswell of Auchinleck, son of the biographer of Johnson. But perhaps the most distinguished of our legal humorists, and one who exercised his wit with great success on strictly legal themes, was George Outram, a native, like so many other singers, of the Celtic west, born at the Clyde Ironworks, near Glasgow, in the year 1805.[1] Like many young men of marked intellectuality, though without any special genius for law, he became a member of the Faculty of Advocates, Edinburgh. Here, after pacing the boards of the Parliament House for a few years, and refreshing with his rich flow of kindly humour the socialities of his brethren of the wig and gown, he found his literary leanings too strong to allow him to hope for advancement in that most engrossing of all severely intellectual professions; so he accepted an invitation to Glasgow, to act as editor of the leading western newspaper, the 'Glasgow Herald,' a function which he performed with a gentlemanly moderation and a wise discrimination that did honour to the Conservative party, of which he was a member. He died at Rosemore, on the Holy Loch, in the fifty-second year of his age.

Of his songs, not a few are too legal in their allusions

---

[1] Of Lord Neaves we shall have occasion to speak afterwards, under another head.

and in their vocabulary to be fit for being received into the general body of popular song. Some, however, are either quite human, or free enough from any legal formalism, to be relished by the general public. Of these, "The Annuity," describing the misfortuned plight of a speculator who had sold an annuity to an old lady, apparently not far distant from the churchyard, but who lived to the age of ninety-four, and not even then had any thought of dying, is one of the most comical, certainly the most cunningly rhymed of any song in the language:—

> "The Bible says the age o' man
>   Threescore an' ten perchance may be;
> She's ninety-four;—let them wha can
>   Explain the incongruity.
> She should hae lived afore the Flood—
> She's come o' Patriarchal blood—
> She's some auld Pagan, mummified
>   Alive for her annuity."

But as a lay of the law, and yet with a distinct human intelligibility, we prefer to give here at length his famous song on a process for division of commonty, called in the technical language of Scottish Law—

SOUMIN AN' ROUMIN.

My Grannie!—she was a worthy auld woman; She keep-it three geese an' a cow on a common. Puir body!—she sune made her fu' purse a

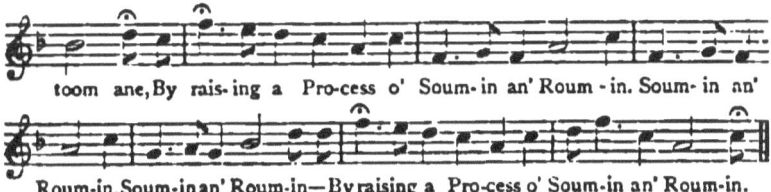

toom ane, By rais-ing a Pro-cess o' Soum-in an' Roum-in. Soum-in an' Roum-in, Soum-in an' Roum-in—By raising a Pro-cess o' Soum-in an' Roum-in.

A young writer lad put it into her head;
He gied himsel' out for a dab at the trade—
For guidin' a plea, or a proof, quite uncommon,
And a terrible fellow at Soumin an' Roumin.
     Soumin an' Roumin, &c.

He took her three geese to get it begun,
And he needit her cow to carry it on,
Syne she gied him her band for the cost that was comin',
And on went the Process o' Soumin an' Roumin.
     Soumin an' Roumin, &c.

My Grannie she grieved, and my Grannie she graned,
As she paid awa' ilk honest groat she had hained;
She sat in her elbow-chair, glow'rin' and gloomin'—
Speakin' o' naething but Soumin an' Roumin.
     Soumin an' Roumin, &c.

She caredna for meat, and she caredna for drink—
By night or by day she could ne'er sleep a wink;
"O Lord, pity me, for a wicked auld woman!
It's a sair dispensation this Soumin an' Roumin."
     Soumin an' Roumin, &c.

In vain did the writer lad promise success—
Speak of Interim Decrees, and final redress;
In vain did he tell her that judgment was comin'—
"It's a judgment already this Soumin an' Roumin!"
     Soumin an' Roumin, &c.

The Doctor was sent for—but what could he say?
He allowed the complaint to be out o' his way;
The Priest spak' o' Job—said to suffer was human—
But she said "Job kent naething o' Soumin' an' Roumin."
    Soumin an' Roumin, &c.

The Priest tried to read, and the Priest tried to pray,
But she wadna attend to ae word that he'd say;
She made a bad end for sae guid an auld woman—
Her death-rattle sounded like "Soumin an' Roumin."
    Soumin an' Roumin, &c.

I'm Executor—heir-male—o' line—an' provision,—
An' the writer lad says that he'll manage the seisin;
But of a' the Estate, there's naething forthcomin',
But a guid-gangin' Process o' Soumin an' Roumin.
    Soumin an' Roumin, &c.[1]

Perhaps the most delicately touched sketch of character in the whole range of Scottish poetry, is "The Lament of Captain Paton," by John Gibson Lockhart, the distinguished son-in-law and biographer of Sir Walter Scott. Though not specially a song-writer, Mr Lockhart's classical translations from the Spanish ballads display an amount of lyrical talent which, had he lived some centuries earlier in the days of the minstrels, instead of in the age of Quarterly Reviews, would have given him a high place in the fellowship of

---

[1] Legal and other Lyrics. By George Outram. Edited by J. H. Stoddart, LL.D. With Life by Henry Glassford Bell. Edinburgh, 1888.

Thomas the Rhymer, and the royal author of "Peblis to the Play:"—

CAPTAIN PATON NO MO'E![1]

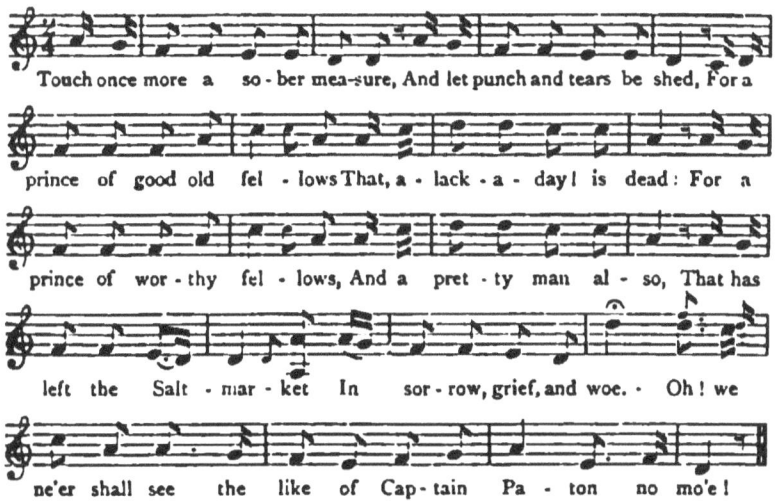

Touch once more a sober measure, And let punch and tears be shed, For a prince of good old fellows That, a-lack-a-day! is dead: For a prince of worthy fellows, And a pretty man also, That has left the Salt-market In sorrow, grief, and woe. Oh! we ne'er shall see the like of Captain Paton no mo'e!

His waistcoat, coat, and breeches,
 Were all cut off the same web,
Of a beautiful snuff colour,
 Or a modest genty drab.
The blue stripe in his stocking,
 Round his neat slim leg did go;
And his ruffles of the cambric fine,
 They were whiter than the snow.
  Oh! &c.

His hair was curl'd in order,
 At the rising of the sun,
In comely rows and buckles smart,
 That about his ears did run.

---

[1] By kind permission of J. Muir Wood, Buchanan Street, Glasgow, from the Balmoral Edition of Scottish Songs, Glasgow, 1887, p. 374.

And before there was a toupee
  That some inches up did go;
And behind there was a long queue,
  That did o'er his shoulders flow.
           Oh! &c.

And whenever we forgather'd,
  He took off his wee three-cockit,
And he proffer'd you his snuff-box,
  Which he drew from his side pocket;
And on Burdett or Bonaparte
  He would make a remark or so,
And then along the plainstanes
  Like a provost he would go.
           Oh! &c.

In dirty days he picked well
  His footsteps with his rattan;
Oh! you ne'er could see the least speck
  On the shoes of Captain Paton!
And on entering the coffee-room
  About *two*, all men did know
They would see him with his 'Courier'
  In the middle of the row.
           Oh! &c.

Now and then upon a Sunday,
  He invited me to dine
On a herring and a mutton-chop,
  Which his maid dress'd very fine.
There was also a little Malmsey
  And a bottle of Bordeaux,
Which between me and the Captain
  Passed nimbly to and fro.
           Oh! &c.

Or if a bowl was mention'd,
  The Captain he would ring,
And bid Nelly to the West-Port,
  And a stoup of water bring.
Then would he mix the genuine stuff,
  As they made it long ago,
With limes that on his property
  In Trinidad did grow.
            Oh ! &c.

And then all the time he would discourse
  So sensible and courteous,
Perhaps talking of the last sermon
  He had heard from Dr Porteous ;
Or some little bit of scandal
  Of Mrs So-and-so,
Which he scarce could credit, having heard
  The *con*, but not the *pro*.
            Oh ! &c.

Or when the candles were brought forth,
  And the night was (fairly) setting in,
He would tell some fine old stories
  About Minden-field or Dettingen ;
How he fought with a French major,
  And despatched him at a blow,
While his blood ran out like water
  On the soft grass below.
            Oh ! &c.

But at last the Captain sicken'd,
  And grew worse from day to day,
And all miss'd him in the coffee-room,
  From which now he stay'd away.

On Sabbaths, too, the Wynd Kirk
 Made a melancholy show,
All for wanting of the presence
 Of our venerable beau.
             Oh! &c.

And in spite of all that Cleghorn
 And Corkindale could do,
It was plain, from twenty symptoms,
 That death was in his view.
So the Captain made his testament,
 And submitted to his foe,
And we laid him by the Ram's-horn Kirk;
 'Tis the way we all must go.
             Oh! &c.

Join all in chorus, jolly boys,
 And let punch and tears be shed,
For this prince of good old fellows,
 That, alack-a-day! is dead:
For this prince of worthy fellows,
 And a pretty man also,
That has left the Saltmarket
 In sorrow, grief, and woe!
             Oh! &c.

We conclude this chapter with a song born of that delight in field-sports in which, from the days of Nimrod downwards, all well-constituted and vigorous peoples have rejoiced. In Scotland it is notable that we have no hunting-songs; how this comes to pass let the gentlemen who follow the bushy-tailed marauder of the farmyard and the hen-house explain.[1] But to compensate for this we have angling-songs of classical excellence, and among these specially "The Muckle May-Flee" of Ballantine, and "The Taking of the Salmon," by Thomas Tod Stoddart, one of that genial company of large human-hearted gentlemen who for so many years enlivened with their flashes of honest mirth and skits of unconventional wisdom the Ambrosian nights of Blackwood's supper-parties, and the pastoral joviality of St Mary's Loch. Mr Stoddart was an Edinburgh man, who, with a decided poetical talent, like Outram joined the society of advocates, as an honourable brotherhood, without having any serious intention of following out the profession in actual practice; and, after a few years' formal display of the gown and wig, and saturation with the gossip of the Parliament House, having a small independence and no ambition for what is called rising in the world in any hot-spurred career of severe brain-labour, he settled in the picturesque Border town of Kelso, and from that as head-quarters followed the profession of an angler through all the wimpling brooks and rolling rivers of auld Scotland, from Tweed to Spey, with a dexterity and a persistency which

---

[1] Though not strictly a hunting-song, "The Place where the Old Horse died," by the late distinguished novelist, Major Whyte Melville, deserves a place in all repertories of the venatorial Muse.

rendered him at once the highest authority in the prose, as he was the best exponent of the poetry, of the craft. Here follows one of the most dramatically descriptive, perhaps as an angler's song the best, in the language :—

THE TAKING OF THE SALMON.[1]

A birr! a whirr! a salmon's on,
　A goodly fish! a thumper!
Bring up, bring up, the ready gaff,
And if we land him we shall quaff
　　Another glorious bumper!
　Hark! 'tis the music of the reel,
　　The strong, the quick, the steady;
　The line darts from the active wheel,
　　Have all things right and ready.

A birr! a whirr! the salmon's out,
　Far on the rushing river;
Onward he holds with sudden leap,
Or plunges through the whirlpool deep,
　　A desperate endeavour!
　Hark to the music of the reel!
　　The fitful and the grating;
　It pants along the breathless wheel,
　　Now hurried—now abating.

A birr! a whirr! the salmon's off!—
　No, no, we still have got him;
The wily fish is sullen grown,
And, like a bright imbedded stone,
　　Lies gleaming at the bottom.

---

[1] Songs and Poems, by Thomas Tod Stoddart, author of the "Death Wake," "Scottish Angler," &c.　Edinburgh : Blackwood, 1879.

"The Taking of the Salmon."

Hark to the music of the reel!
  'Tis hush'd, it hath forsaken;
With care we'll guard the magic wheel,
  Until its notes rewaken.

A birr! a whirr! the salmon's up—
  Give line, give line and measure;
But now he turns! keep down ahead,
And lead him as a child is led,
  And land him at your leisure.
  Hark to the music of the reel!
    'Tis welcome, it is glorious;
  It wanders through the winding wheel,
    Returning and victorious.

A birr! a whirr! the salmon's in,
  Upon the bank extended;
The princely fish is gasping slow,
His brilliant colours come and go,
  All beautifully blended.
  Hark to the music of the reel!
    It murmurs and it closes;
  Silence is on the conquering wheel,
    Its wearied line reposes.

No birr! no whirr! the salmon's ours,
  The noble fish—the thumper!
Strike through his gill the ready gaff,
And bending homewards, we shall quaff
  Another glorious bumper!
  Hark to the music of the reel!
    We listen with devotion;
  There's something in that circling wheel
    That wakes the heart's emotion!

CHAPTER V.

DRINKING-SONGS, CONVIVIAL SONGS.

Χρὴ δ'ἐν συμποσίῳ, κυλίκων περινισσομενάων
Ἡδέα κωτίλλοντα καθήμενον οἰνοποτάζειν.
—PHOCYLIDES.

"EATING," says a great German thinker, "is an accentuated life:" if so, drinking, as it were a superlative degree of the same affection, may aptly be called a potentiated life. The instinct of all peoples and the utterance of all literatures assert in every variety the inherent superiority of the liquid to the solid element, in the nutrimental forces that go to build up the complex vitality of that physico-moral wonder of the universe—a human being. The Greeks, whose imaginative theology was always nicely in harmony with Nature, felt this strongly; and so, while they gave all due prominence to the god of drinking, they kept Ceres in the background, in the corn-field and the corn-yard, not at the dinner-table; and, when they met together to enjoy a social meal, they did not call it συσσίτιον—*eating together*—the word used for the common meal of the Spartans; but συμπόσιον—*drinking together*. Alcinous in the 'Odyssey' (vi. 309) sits drinking, not eating, "like an immortal god." The natural reason of this distinction is manifest. When a man is faint, food, even the most choice, can have only one result, to give strength to the weak; but wine, which is the best form of the liquid element, not only strengthens but quickens and elevates. Eating puts a man on his legs, so that, if prostrate, he is normally himself again; drinking gives a man wings, and teaches him to fly for a season, in a state of exaltation above his normal level. And, even when he does not exactly fly, a glass of good wine gives a pleasant spur to his nervous system, making his utterance rise from the dull ditch of utilitarian prose to the bickering flow of animated conversation. Among the Greeks, not only Anacreon, who was specifically an Epicurean, spreading himself out luxuriantly on a bank of tender myrtle or grassy clover, could sing—

> Ἐπὶ μυρσίναις τερείναις
> Ἐπὶ λωτίναις τε ποίαις
> Στορέσας θέλω προπίνειν—

but the wise old Phocylides, a didactic poet, after the manner of Theognis, and a sort of Milesian Solomon in his day, says emphatically—

Χρὴ δ' ἐν συμποσίῳ, κυλίκων περινισσομενάων
Ἡδέα κωτίλλοντα καθήμενον οἰνοποτάζειν—

a stanza familiarly known from its standing as a motto to the 'Noctes Ambrosianæ' of 'Blackwood's Magazine,' where it had the good fortune to be honoured with the very clever version from the pen of glorious John Wilson, or perhaps the fine and delicate touch of John Gibson Lockhart:—

> " This is a distich by wise old Phocylides,
> An ancient who wrote crabbed Greek in no silly days;
> Meaning, ''Tis right for good wine-bibbing people,
> Not to let the jug pace round the board like a cripple;
> But gaily to chat while discussing their tipple.'
> An excellent rule of the hearty old cock 'tis—
> And a very fit motto to put to our *Noctes*."

But not only the Greeks, with whom it was a matter not only of healthy human enjoyment, but a religious duty in honour of Dionysus, to drink wine, gave forth these rhythmical expressions of its praise; but the Hebrews, whose religion in some aspects savoured more of the fear of a jealous God than of sympathy with a genial God, again and again bear pious witness to the virtues of the kindly stimulating potation. In the Book of Judges (ix. 9), in one of those significant parables which are the gems of Biblical literature, to an invitation made to the vine to be elected king of the trees and reign over the forest, the sacred tree of Dionysus replies, "Shall I leave my wine which cheereth God and man, and go to be promoted over the trees?" wisely preaching this doctrine, which ambitious souls are apt to forget, that, though power is pleasant when pleasantly seasoned, pleasantness without power is better than power without pleasantness. And King David, or whoever it was that put together that harmonious outflow of grateful piety which we read in the 104th Psalm, after celebrating His goodness who makes the grass to grow for the cattle and herbs for the service of man, does not forget, with that zest for vital enjoyment which belongs to every healthy creature, to praise the divine gift of wine, which maketh glad the heart of man, and goes hand in hand with the oil which makes his face to shine. But not only in the lyric poetry of the Hebrews, but, as with the Greeks, in the severe didactic form, the virtues of the juice of the grape are not forgotten. In the notable concluding chapter of the Book of Proverbs, where a wise mother gives her most urgent advices to a wise king, while she warns him in the strongest terms against the indulgence of strong passions and the imbibing of strong liquors in the persons of those who are expounding law and decreeing justice to the people, she at the same time does not omit to make the significant addition, "Give strong drink unto him that is ready to perish, and wine unto those that be heavy of heart. Let them drink, and forget their poverty, and remember their misery no more!"—displaying in this a catholic wisdom of sentiment, standing in instructive contrast to the hasty logic of not a few in these times who cannot see a good thing abused without rushing to the conclusion that it is a bad thing, and relegating it wholesale into the realms of devildom. In the New Testament we find an equal freedom from all one-sided denunciations of good things because they are sometimes badly used. When alluding in his parables to dancing and wedding parties, and personally turning dull water into spirit-stirring wine, our blessed Lord showed no tincture of Pharisaic sourness or Essenic asceticism; and though, no doubt, His apostles had frequent occasion to denounce the offence of being drunk with wine, wherein is excess (Ephes. v. 18), yet the fear of this excess, which was the besetting sin both of the Greeks to whom he wrote, and of the age in which he lived, did not prevent him from saying to the most eminent of his young coadjutors, "Take a little wine for your stomach's sake, and for your many infirmities." And if the merry Greeks and the stern Hebrews were equally averse from indulging in the one-sided denunciation of one of the best gifts of God, we shall not be slow to find that the stout Romans, who were hard-hitting soldiers and strong-brained lawyers, showed an equal sympathy with the sparkling wine-cup, as the natural accompaniment of all great demonstrations of social joy. Quinctilian (i. 10) tells us that from the old Roman banquets the lyre and the flute were never absent; and Horace sings—

> "Nunc est bibendum; nunc pede libero
> Pulsanda tellus, nunc Saliaribus,
> Ornare pulvinar Deorum
> Tempus erat dapibus sodales!"[1]

Of course the Asiatics of the far East, with whom any kind of asceticism, or gymnosophistry, was only an exceptional reaction from their general luxuriousness, could not be behind their Western neighbours in any Bacchabund tripudiations of this sort; and so in Goethe's "West-Eastern Divan," so thoroughly oriental in its spirit, there is one speaker who even dares to say—

> "Did the Korán exist for ever?
> I really do not care to know.
> Was the Korán a created thing?
> I know not, but it may be so;
> That 'tis the best of all books that be,
> This is a dutiful creed with me.
> But that wine from eternity was,
> This as God's truth I receive;
> Or, if created, created before
> The angels were, I can well believe.
> Anyhow, he who drinks most cheerly,
> Looks God in the face, and sees more clearly."[2]

---
[1] See Seneca, De Tranquillitate Animi, xv. 14.
[2] West-östlicher Divan: Saki-Nameh—Das Schenkenbuch.

This sounds bold enough, almost profane to a Presbyterian sour, or a severe Calvinist, or one of that class of pious persons not uncommon in the religious world, who know not that in all moral utterances, of which the New Testament is full, the letter killeth and the spirit maketh alive. Goethe himself, though a person of infinitely more self-command than Robert Burns, was in his rollicking zest of life in no whit inferior to our great song-writer, and in one of his "Gesellige Lieder" goes so far as to make a formal confession of the besetting sin of having on various occasions abstained from plashing in the pool of festive enjoyment with as genial a joviality as a healthy human being ought to do. Here it is:—

General Confession.

(A Convivial Song.)

Listen to a good advice,
    When 'tis not denied you;
Boldly, ere it be too late,
    For the right decide you.
For your faults yet to be mended,
Much begun and little ended,
    Soundly must I chide you.

Penance must we do at least,
    Once before we die all;
Let us, then, confess our sins,
    With an honest sigh all;

"General Confession."

To forsake what most besets us,
Care that vexes, freak that frets us,
   Let us nobly vie all.

Yes, we have, confess we must,
   Waking oft been dreaming,
Emptied not the friendly cup,
   When the wine was gleaming;
Many a roving hour have watched not,
Many a waiting kiss have snatched not,
   As was well beseeming.

Often have we sat and gaped,
   Silent when we should not;
Pratings of the pedant crew,
   When we could, eschewed not;
Listened to their prosy comments
On a poet's happy moments,
   That they understood not.

Wilt thou absolution give,
   Of all good things Giver,
From thy faithful precepts swerve,
   Will thy servants never;
And each sorry half-work leaving,
To the good, the lovely, cleaving,
   Resolute live ever.

Pedants, while we sit at ease,
   To a smile may move us;
Bumpers waiting to be quaffed,
   Shall no more reprove us;
Not with empty phrase harangue we,
But with faithful passion hang we,
   On the lips that love us.

In England, from the time of Henry II. downwards, and further back, no doubt, to those who care to make curious inquiry, we have distinct evidence of the popularity of the drinking-song. In the reign of this sagacious and energetic Norman, when the churchmen played a prominent part in public life, and the Latin language was as familiar in their mouth as Greek was to Cicero, there came out of Wales, or one of the conterminous counties, one of those adventurous students, who, in a military age, knew to combine rare learning with administrative genius, and in virtue of their intellectual and moral superiority rose to the highest offices in Church and State. This was Walter de Mapes, the contemporary of the celebrated Giraldus Cambrensis, who, after serving a worthy apprenticeship in the household of Thomas à Becket, was raised by the discerning patronage of the sovereign to various judicial, ecclesiastical, and academical offices, and employed as a trustworthy negotiator in several foreign missions of importance. But as often happens with men engaged in the conduct of affairs, while his public virtues are now known only to a few students of special history, his memory is preserved in one of those spirts of lyrical good-humour with which the gravest men do chiefly affect to season the severity of an earnest life. The drinking-song from his sportive vein which follows, "*Mihi est propositum in taberna mori*," was no doubt originally intended as a satire against the very free-and-easy style of comfortable living in which many members of the religious orders in those days largely indulged; but taken out of its dramatic connection, and holding, as it does, a prominent place in the German *Commerslieder* and other song-books, it may stand as a very fair specimen of the drinking-songs in the century before the French Revolution, so largely spread in all popular song-books both at home and abroad; and in so far as, like the purring of the cat at the fireside, these drinking-songs serve only to express the genial comfort of the physical man in the accentuated vitality of eating and drinking, there can be no harm in them:—

CANTILENA POTATORIA.[1]

Mihi est propositum in taberna mori;
Vinum sit appositum morientis ori:
Ut dicant, cum venerint, angelorum chori:
" Deus sit propitius huic potatori!"

Poculis accenditur animi lucerna,
Cor imbutum nectare volat ad superna.
Mihi sapit dulcius vinum in taberna,
Quam quod aqua miscuit præsulis pincerna.

---

[1] Allgemeines Lieder- und Commersbuch. Von A. Methfessel. 4te Auflage. Hamburg und Itzehoe, 1831.

> Suum cuique proprium dat natura munus,
> Ego nunquam potui scribere jejunus;
> Me jejunum vincere posset puer unus,
> Sitim et jejunium odi tanquam funus!
>
> Tales versus facio, quale vinum bibo,
> Neque possum scribere nisi sumto cibo;
> Nihil valet penitus, quod jejunus scribo,
> Nasonem post calices carmine præibo.
>
> Mihi nunquam spiritus prophetiæ datur,
> Nisi tum cum fuerit venter bene satur;
> Cum in arce cerebri Bacchus dominatur,
> In me Phœbus irruit, ac miranda fatur.

But, though this quiet satisfaction in sipping the blood of the grape, to the solitary toper is not without a certain lyrical value, yet so long as the drinking-song wants the element of sociality and conviviality, it falls short of its type; it is a bird without wings: "*Dulce cum sodalibus sapit vinum bonum*" gives the true key-note to the poetry of drinking-songs. Even in those verses of Mapes it is not the mere pleasure of the sipping that gives grace to the drinking, it is the emotional elevation that accompanies it and finds its utterance in verse :—

> "In my brain's high citadel, when Bacchus holds his sway, then
> Phœbus rushes into me, and pours a fervid lay then."

And in the same manner, Goethe in one of the versicles of the 'Saki-Nameh' expressly says, that unless the solitary cup is used to stimulate thinking, as the cigar is boasted to do by the devotees of the weed, it has no poetical value, and degenerates into mere calculated sottishness:—

> "Here sit I alone
>   With myself all my own;
>   And I sip my own wine,
>   And I thank God 'tis mine,
> And where no man can fret me with loud disputations,
> I sip and I spin here my own meditations."

Let these meditative drinkers enjoy their solitary potations exceptionally; but the rule holds, as we said, that drinking to be poetical must be social:—

> "Dulce cum sodalibus sapit vinum bonum,
>   Osculari virgines, dulcius est donum;
>   Donum est dulcissimum lyricen Maronum,
>   Si his tribus gaudeam sperno regis thronum."

Here the drink, even with the boon companions, is put in the lowest place, and, unless love and the lyre follow, it is not worthy of a man. This is the burden also of all the old drinking-songs in our song-books of the last century:—

> "To Anacreon in heaven, where he sat in full glee,
>   A few sons of harmony sent a petition
> That he their inspirer and patron would be;
>   When this answer arrived from the jolly old Grecian,
>   Voice, fiddle, and flute
>   No longer be mute,

I'll lend you my name, and inspire you to boot;
And besides, I'll instruct you like me to entwine
The myrtle of Venus with Bacchus's vine!"[1]

But this addition of the grace of Venus to the strength of Dionysus was not comprehensive enough to satisfy the sympathies of the triumphant drinking-song; for good liquor, whatever its sins and its dangers may be, has at least one good effect, of breaking down the conventional barriers that so often separate man from man, so that the trite proverb *in vino veritas* is scarcely more true than *in vino humanitas;* and among the grand human affections that find their expression in a social drinking-song, loyalty or devotion to the public weal, with faithful subjection to legitimate authority, seldom fails to take a prominent place. So in the popular old English song—

DOWN AMONG THE DEAD MEN.

Here's a health to the Queen, and a lasting peace,
  To faction an end, to wealth increase;
Come let us drink it while we have breath,
  For there's no drinking after death.
    And he that will this health deny,
      Down among the dead men,
      Down among the dead men,
        Down, down, down,
      Down among the dead men let him lie!

---

[1] The Edinburgh Musical Miscellany. Edinburgh, 1792.

Let charming beauty's health go round,
  In whom celestial joys are found,
And may confusion still pursue
  The senseless woman-hating crew.
    And they that woman's health deny, &c.

In smiling Bacchus' joys I'll roll,
  Deny no pleasure to my soul;
Let Bacchus' health round briskly move,
  For Bacchus is a friend to love.
    And he that will this health deny, &c.

May love and wine their rites maintain,
  And their united pleasure reign;
While Bacchus' treasures crown the board,
  We'll sing the joys that both afford.
    And they that won't with us comply, &c.[1]

But, with all these additions of loyalty and love, and whatever else of healthy sentiment may be thrown into the glass, it must be confessed that these drinking-songs stand low in lyrical value—are more apt to be abused than to be well used—and on the whole, quite worthy of the comparative neglect into which they have fallen. It is right to love gaiety and pleasure, and to sing gay songs; but the man who delights in them must, like Garrick, always know how to "temper his pleasures with refinement, and make them serve the business of life and pro-

---

[1] Old English Ditties. From W. Chappell's Popular Music of the Olden Time, 2 vols. London: Chappell, 50 New Bond Street.

moting friendship."[1] Sometimes these songs are redeemed from commonplace by a pretty conceit, as in that old song of "The brown Jug," where the singer boasts to have been made of the clay into which the body of Toby Filpot, a stout old toper, had been resolved after death; but generally speaking, there are only three ways in which a drinking-song can be elevated into the region of classical poetry, as distinguished from the mere rhythmical expression of nervous exhilaration. The first is by engrafting philosophy into it, of which the most notable example is Schiller's well-known

PUNCH SONG.

Mingle them kindly,
    Th' elements four,—
Mystical Nature
    Works by the four.

Press ye the citron
    Juicy and tart:
Life's inner kernel
    Harbours a smart.

Now with the sugar's
    Mild mellow power
Tame ye and temper
    Wisely the sour.

---

[1] Life of Garrick, by Fitzgerald (London, 1868), vol. i. ch. ii.

Pour then the water
　Flowing and clear,—
Water embraceth
　Calmly the sphere.

Now with the spirit
　Charm ye the bowl,—
Life of the living,
　Soul of the soul.

Ere it enhaleth,
　Swift be it quaffed :
Only when glowing
　Strengthens the draught—

a composition which not even the wise Greeks could have managed in better style. The second is by taking it on the humorous side, and amusing our fancy with an exhibition of frail humanity which, if seriously taken, would be purely painful. This humorous fashion of treating the drinker, who has lost the sober use of his senses in the titillation of his nerves, is admirably managed in the German song, "Gerad aus dem Wirthshaus," in which the toper is placed before us in the condition of the foolish juryman, who excused himself for always standing out against the verdict of his co-jurors, on the ground that he had the misfortune to be regularly the only wise man among fourteen fools. So in our German song, the devotee of Dionysus, coming out of the atmosphere of the tavern, big with beer and dim with tobacco, not recognising clearly his whereabout or his whatabout, forthwith concludes that the external world and all its accompaniments are in a state of intoxication. The streets, he says, are inverted, the right hand having become the left, and the left the right; the moon is making faces, with one eye open and the other shut; and the street-lamps—*Du lieber Gott!*—are all shaking and tumbling about, unable to stand on their legs, unquestionably drunk; everything in fact is become intoxicated, staggering and reeling into unreasonable chaos; a world in which no reasonable person can enjoy a tolerable existence: therefore he, the alone reasonable in a storm of unreason, as a wise man, will not venture farther, but go back into the tavern. Here it is:—

A Blessed Delusion.

Out from the tavern I come and stand here:
All things are looking so odd and so queer,
Right hand with left hand confounded, 'tis clear
The streets have been drinking too much of the beer.

And there's the moon, too, aloft in the sky,
Glinting and squinting, and shutting one eye:
Fie on you, fie! you old toper, 'tis clear,
Moon, you've been drinking too much of the beer.

And there's the lamps too, all flickering queer,
Some very far away, some very near,

Reeling and wheeling, now here and now there:
Lamps, you are drunk, this plain truth I declare!

Round about, round about, great things and small,
One only sober—myself—of them all;
With such a rout I'll not venture my skin,
Wisdom commands to go back to the inn.[1]

The third way in which a drinking-song can be redeemed from the cheapness of most of these old drinking-songs, is by scene, situation, and character; and here again we find that the Germans, our masters in music as well as in metaphysics, bear the bell. The character which in the drama of real life is most suited for a drinking-song, is that of a young man with an exuberant flow of unhampered spirits, plashing about like a young trout in a sunny pool, and in whom, as being, to use Aristotle's phrase, under the dominion of πάθος, or passion, the unbridled expression of the rapture of the moment, if not always reasonable, is natural and enjoyable; and the scene and situation which best suit this display of effervescent vitality is the student-life of the German universities. On the banks of the Rhine or the Neckar, amid grey old castles, ivy-grown monasteries, and vine-clad hills, the Academical Muse of Deutschland has found a stage where picturesque surround-

---

[1] Allgemeines Deutsches Commersbuch, 15te Auflage, Lahr, Moritz Schauenburg, p. 198. Englished by J. S. B.

ings, patriotic memories, intense vital enjoyment, and unconventional sociality unite to form a poetry of youthful life to which not even the merry Greeks, in the days of Socrates and Aristophanes, could boast anything superior. It is this atmosphere, this scenery, and this life which envelops and plays round us, as with a moral sunshine, when we peal forth from lusty lungs such *Burschen Lieder* as *Ça, ça, geschmauset!* and *Crambambuli!*—

> "Come, don't be mulish,
> March like men where you mean to go.
> *In loco* foolish,
> *Dulce* you know!
> *Edite, bibite, Collegiales,*
> *Post pauca sæcula*
> *Pocula nulla!*
>
> Pipes a-hand yarely,
> No Bursch is he who cries enough!
> Puff, puff away rarely,
> Drink while you puff!"

And so on. Then again—

> "Crambambuli, that is the liquor
> That fires the blood, makes tough the brains;
> My panacea is the beaker
> For every ill that earth contains.
> At morning bright, at noon, at night,
> Crambambuli is my delight;
> Crambimbambuli, Crambambuli!

Ye drink no wine, ye love no lasses,
  Teetotal men—heaven bless the fare!
Here being stamped and sealed for asses,
  How hope ye to be angels *there?*
    Drink water like the blessed swine,
    And dream it is the draught divine
    Of Crambimbambuli, Crambambuli!

Whoso at us Crambambulisten
  Proudly turns up his churlish nose,
He is a heathen, and no Christian,
  For God's best gift away he throws.
    The fool may bawl himself to death,
    I will not give to stop his breath
    One drop Crambambuli, Crambambuli!"[1]

So much for the general human prevalence and social significance of drinking-songs. Let us now see what crop

---

[1] Burschen Melodies, by J. S. B., in Tait's Edinburgh Magazine; Edinburgh, 1841. Of Scottish students' songs strictly so called, I know none; for the Academical songs that we have in College Songs (Edinburgh, 1886), and Musa Burchicosa, by J. S. B. (Edinburgh, 1869), are not by students, but by professors or physicians, notably in Edinburgh a very jovial fraternity. I believe that Professor Lindsay of the Free Church College, Glasgow, among other good deeds distinguished himself favourably by the encouragement which he gave to the practice of social song amongst the students. How far the students in the English universities may have succeeded in the production of a "Commersbuch" worthy to take rank with the German compends of convivial song, I do not know; but the musical indoctrination which they receive at Harrow and other great schools, certainly gives them an excellent start for brilliant advances in the same line at the University.—See Harrow School Songs, by John Farmer. London: Williams, 24 Berners Street.

of the same free revelry Scotland produces. And here, no doubt, one might be inclined to think, reasoning *a priori*, that a country of such severe religiosity and stern Sabbatic exercise would shrink from the exhibition of those purple blossoms of redundant vital enjoyment which drinking-songs contain. But it is not so. Rather the contrary. Nature is mighty, and will leap forth on the Monday with a more violent bound in proportion as the repressive force on the Sunday had been severe. Of this we have an admirable example in the song—

WILLIE WI' HIS WIG A-JEE.[1]

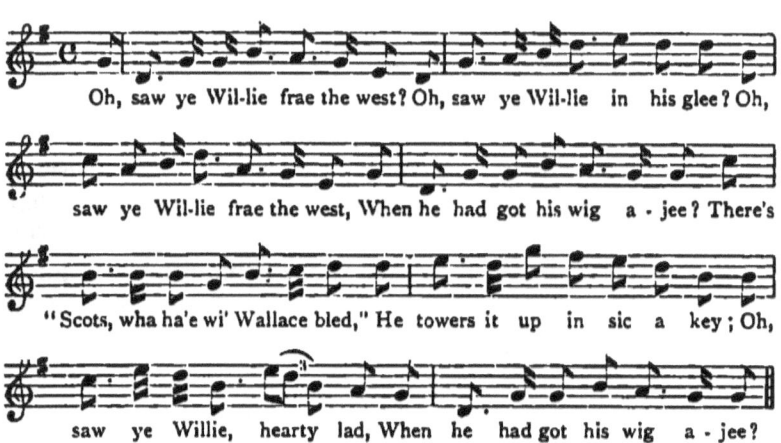

Oh, saw ye Willie frae the west? Oh, saw ye Willie in his glee? Oh, saw ye Willie frae the west, When he had got his wig a-jee? There's "Scots, wha ha'e wi' Wallace bled," He towers it up in sic a key; Oh, saw ye Willie, hearty lad, When he had got his wig a-jee?

    To hear him sing a canty air,
      He lilts it o'er sae charmingly,
    That in a moment aff flies care,
      When Willie gets his wig a-jee.

---

[1] Air by kind permission from J. Ferrie, Glasgow.

> Let drones croon o'er a winter night,
>   A fig for them, whate'er they be,
> For I could sit till morning light,
>   Wi' Willie and his wig a-jee.
>
> At kirk on Sundays, sic a change
>   Comes o'er his wig, and mou', and e'e,
> Sae douce—you'd think a cannon-ba'
>   Wad scarce ca' Willie's wig a-jee.
> But when on Mondays he begins,
>   And rants and roars continually,
> Till ilk owk's end, the very weans
>   Gang daft—when Willie's wig's a-jee.

In this song it is notable that there is no mention of drink; but in harmony with the general tone of such exhibitions of lyrical revel in Scotland, it is difficult to conceive how, after a long travel from the west, any Scotch Willie, Jamie, or Sandy could recreate himself and his entertainers with a dry throat, or a throat moistened only with water from the well. We venture to suggest, therefore, that the author, William Chalmers, a Paisley man, like so many of our best song-writers, would have done better had he shaped his last four lines somewhat thus:—

> But when on Monday he begins,
>   And laughs and quaffs wi' bickering glee,
> And sips and sings, the very weans
>   Gang daft, when Willie's wig's a-jee.

Of regular drinking-songs, one of the best known is "There's cauld Kail in Aberdeen," sometimes, but erroneously, attributed to Alexander, Duke of Gordon, the same who was husband to the genial social Duchess who lionised Burns so grandly in his year of Edinburgh sojourn.[1] This song, though not expanding beyond the pure social enjoyment of "the cogie" (Gaelic, *cuach*), æsthetically, if not morally, has a charm to the song-lover, not only from the completeness of the enjoyment expressed by the toper, but from the dramatic contrast so vividly presented between the drinker with his cogie and boon companions in the ale-house, and the jealous niggardliness of a certain class of wives who would restrict their devoted lords to the sober monotony of the wife, the fireside, and the bairns :—

THERE'S CAULD KAIL IN ABERDEEN.

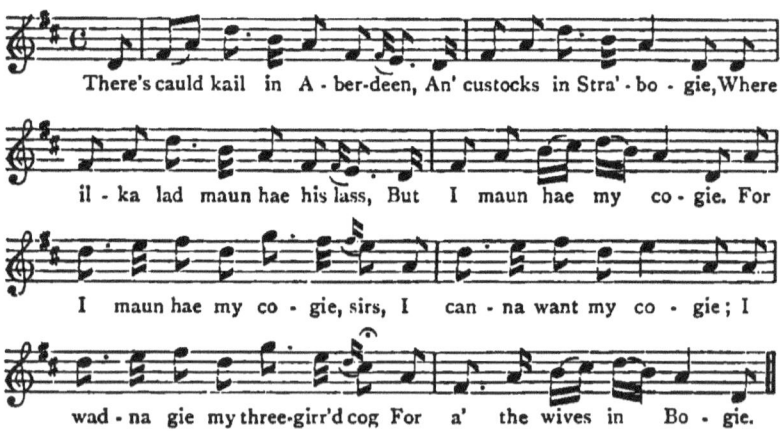

There's cauld kail in A-ber-deen, An' custocks in Stra'-bo-gie, Where il-ka lad maun hae his lass, But I maun hae my co-gie. For I maun hae my co-gie, sirs, I can-na want my co-gie; I wad-na gie my three-girr'd cog For a' the wives in Bo-gie.

---

[1] The words of this song in Johnson's Musical Museum, vol. ii., 1788, and marked in the index as by the D—— of G——, are quite different.

There's Johnnie Smith has got a wife
   Wha scrimps him o' his cogie;
But were she mine, upon my life,
   I'd dook her in a bogie.
For I maun hae my cogie, sirs,
   I canna want my cogie;
I wadna gie my three-girr'd cog
   For a' the wives in Bogie.

An' twa three todlin' weans they hae,
   The pride o' a' Stra'bogie;
Whene'er the totums cry for meat,
   She curses aye his cogie;
Crying, "Wae betide the three-girr'd cog!
   O wae betide the cogie!
It does mair skaith than a' the ills
   That happen in Stra'bogie."

She fand him ance at Willie Sharp's,
   An' what they maist did laugh at,
She brak' the bicker, spilt the drink,
   An' tightly cuff'd his haffet;
Crying, "Wae betide the three-girr'd cog!
   O wae betide the cogie!
It does mair skaith than a' the ills
   That happen in Stra'bogie."

Yet here's to ilka honest soul
   Wha'll drink wi' me a cogie;
An' for ilk silly, whinging fool,
   We'll dook him in a bogie.
For I maun hae my cogie, sirs,
   I canna want my cogie;
I wadna gie my three-girr'd cog
   For a' the wives in Bogie.

As a contrast to this song, and remarkable for the subordination of the mere element of stimulating liquor, to the large catholic humanities and kindly social feelings of which it is the bearer, we fitly place here—

SAE WILL WE YET.

Sit ye down here, my cronies, and gie us your crack, Let the win' tak' the cares o' this life on its back; Our hearts to despondency we never will submit, For we've aye been provided for, and sae will we yet.

Chorus.
And sae will we yet, and sae will we yet, For we've aye been provided for, and sae will we yet.

Success to the farmer, and prosper his plough,
Rewarding his eident toils a' the year through;
Our seed-time and harvest we ever will get,
For we've lippened aye to Providence, and sae will we yet.
        And sae will we yet, &c.

Lang live the king, and happy may he be,
And success to his forces by land and by sea!

His enemies to triumph we never will permit,
Britons aye hae been victorious, and sae will they yet.
   And sae will they yet, &c.

Let the glass keep its course and go merrily roun',
For the sun it will rise tho' the moon has gane down;
When the house is rinnin' round about it's time enough to flit,
When we fell we aye got up again, and sae will we yet.
   And sae will we yet, &c.

This is one of those songs with which the late lamented Scottish vocalist, Mr Kennedy, for so many years recreated the souls of the Scot at home, and refreshed the memories of the Scot abroad, in a fashion not likely soon to be met with again. In Kennedy's musical evenings, given frequently in the Music Hall, Edinburgh, the hearty humour of the father and the graceful sweetness of the daughters united to produce an æsthetical and a moral effect of the rarest kind, which all the artillery of the most highly paid virtuosos in an orchestral entertainment might in point of volume have overwhelmed, but in point of purity and depth of emotion could not have approached. In this admirable drinking-song it will be observed that not only the king on the throne, the army, the navy, and the producers of the staff of life, receive the loyal and grateful recognition that they deserve, but there is a vein of contentment and cheerful resignation running through it, which elevates the drinking-song into a sermon; and a sermon, too, preached on a text not the least prominent in a discourse (Matthew vi. 25-34) full of that mellow wisdom which all Christians profess to admire, but only a few attempt to realise. Another drinking-song not less redolent of a cheerful human piety is—

A WEE DRAPPIE O'T.[1]

The trees are a' stript o' their mantle sae green,
The leaves o' the forest nae langer are seen,
Winter draws near wi' its cauld icy coat,
And we're a' met thegither owre a wee drappie o't.
    A wee drappie o't, a wee drappie o't,
    And we're a' met thegither owre a wee drappie o't.

We're a' met thegither owre a glass and a sang,
We're a' met thegither by special command,
Free frae all ambition and frae every evil thocht,
We're a' met thegither owre a wee drappie o't.
    A wee drappie o't, &c.

When freendship and truth and gude-fellowship reign,
And folk, growin' auld, are made youthfu' again,
When ilka heart is happy and a' warldly cares forgot,
Is just when we're met thegither owre a wee drappie o't,
    A wee drappie o't, &c.

Job, in his lamentation, says that man was made to mourn,
That there's nae sic thing as pleesure frae the cradle to the urn;
But in his lamentation, oh, he surely has forgot
The warmth that spreads so sweetly in a wee drappie o't.
    A wee drappie o't, &c.

---

[1] Air same as "Sae will we yet," p. 320.

The version here given is as I have heard it sung by the late Mr Tod of St Mary's Mount, Peebles, a gentleman well known on the banks of the Tweed not less for his catholic generosity than for his genial hospitalities and graceful surroundings. The air, with other words, will be found in the song as arranged by Gleadhill, and published by Ferrie, Bath Street, Glasgow.

Our great national song-writer, Robert Burns, as an intensely social man, and living in an extensively drinking age, though he indulged largely in the social glass, and paid dearly for his indulgence, did not write many drinking-songs, certainly none that equal in popularity or approach in excellence the classical perfection of his love-songs. I have no doubt he felt that, though the society of jovial topers in the Freemasons' Hall at Tarbolton, or of jolly beggars in Poosey Nancy's ale-house, was highly enjoyable for the moment, yet that songs of the type of "Andrew with his cutty gun and sappy kisses" were not of the class to satisfy the ambition of a man who had tuned his lyre to the key-note supplied by such models of female beauty and chasteness as Miss Burnett of Monboddo, Mrs M'Lehose, Miss Peggy Chalmers, and Mrs Riddell of Woodley Park. Nevertheless he did write drinking-songs, and drinking epistles too; his works, indeed, would have given the lie to his life had no such compositions been in the record; and two of these, one in the humorous vein, and the other consecrated by general acceptance as the symbol of Scottish brotherhood and Scottish patriotism all over the globe, are sure to survive with the best love-songs of the poet wherever Scotsmen do congregate :—

WILLIE BREWED A PECK O' MAUT.

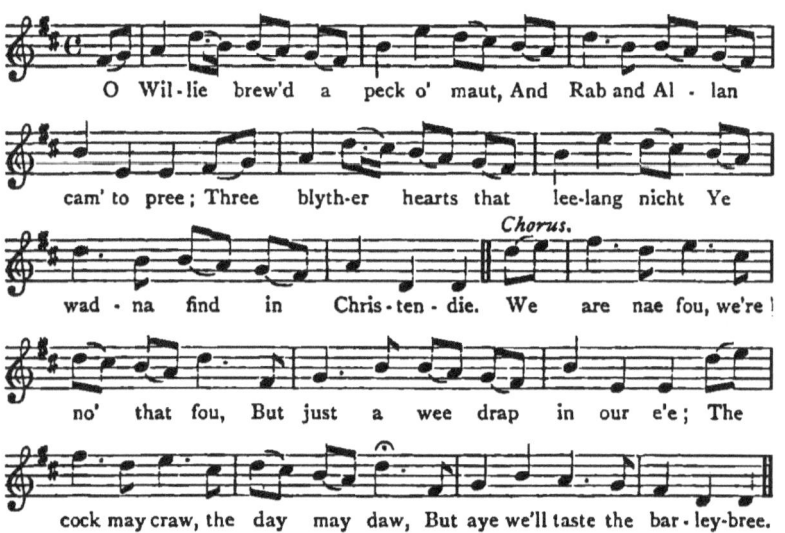

O Willie brew'd a peck o' maut, And Rab and Allan cam' to pree; Three blyther hearts that lee-lang nicht Ye wadna find in Christendie. We are nae fou, we're no' that fou, But just a wee drap in our e'e; The cock may craw, the day may daw, But aye we'll taste the barley-bree.

> Here are we met three merry boys,
>   Three merry boys I trow are we;
> And mony a nicht we've merry been,
>   And mony mae we hope to be.
>   We are nae fou, &c.
>
> It is the moon—I ken her horn,
>   That's blinkin' in the lift sae hie:
> She shines sae bricht to wile us hame,
>   But by my sooth she'll wait a wee.
>   We are nae fou, &c.

"Auld Langsyne."

> Wha first shall rise to gang awa',
> A cuckold, coward loon is he;
> Wha last beside his chair shall fa',
> He is the king amang us three.
> We are nae fou, &c.

This admirable skit of Bacchanalian humour, which forms a worthy pendant to the German "Gerad aus dem Wirthshaus" above mentioned (p. 311), first appeared in Johnson's Museum, 1790, vol. iii. p. 301, and was written in commemoration of a jovial meeting which the poet had at Moffat with his old travelling companion in his Highland tour, William Nicol, one of the masters of the High School, Edinburgh. The next song, "FOR AULD LANGSYNE," requires no comment. It is as characteristically Scottish as the heather on the brae, or the pine-tree in the glen; and the Scot who does not sing it heartily whenever he has a fine social opportunity, is a poor creature, though he had all the symphonies of Beethoven and all the Greek of the Athenian dramatists reeling through his brain.

AULD LANGSYNE.

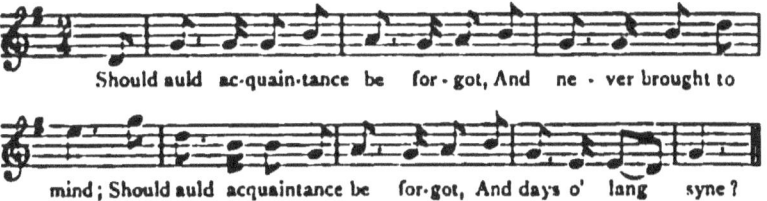

We twa hae ran about the braes,
    And pu'd the gowans fine ;
But we've wander'd mony a weary foot
    Sin' auld langsyne.
        For auld, &c.

We twa hae paidl'd in the burn
    Frae morning sun till dine ;
But seas between us broad hae roar'd
    Sin' auld langsyne.
        For auld, &c.

And there's a hand, my trusty friend,
    And gie's a hand o' thine ;
And we'll tak' a richt guid-willie waught
    For auld langsyne.
        For auld, &c.

And surely ye'll be your pint stoup,
    And surely I'll be mine ;
And we'll tak' a cup o' kindness yet
    For auld langsyne.
        For auld, &c.

We have now to append a humorous old drinking-song of the time before Burns, which leads to reflections of a very different description, and brings before us a most striking illustration of the adage, *corruptio optimi pessima*.

If a glass of wine is a good thing, and tends to recreate the weak and to enliven the dull, it does not in any wise follow that a bottle is a better thing. Here, as in every other province of vital action, Aristotle's famous ethical principle approves itself an absolute law — all right conduct, and, indeed, all excellence of every kind, is a mean between too much and too little, or, in other words, all extremes are wrong :—

MY WIFE HAS TA'EN THE GEE.

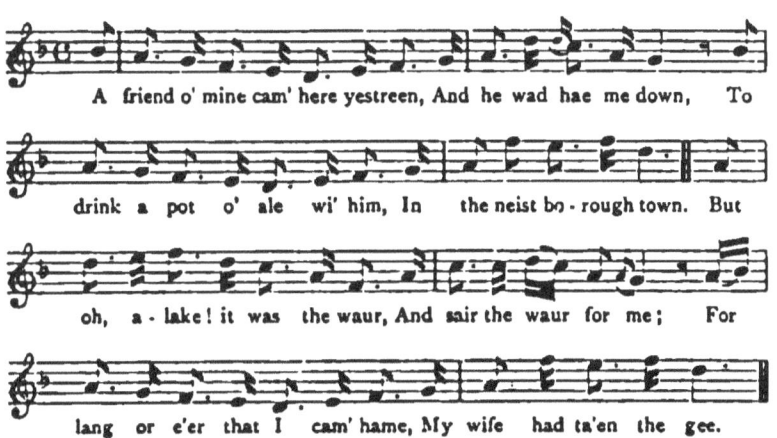

A friend o' mine cam' here yestreen, And he wad hae me down, To drink a pot o' ale wi' him, In the neist bo-rough town. But oh, a-lake! it was the waur, And sair the waur for me; For lang or e'er that I cam' hame, My wife had ta'en the gee.

> We sat sae late, and drank sae stout,
>   The truth I'll tell to you,
> That lang or ever midnight cam'
>   We baith were roarin' fou.
> My wife sits by the fireside,
>   And the tear blinds aye her e'e;
> The ne'er a bed will she gae to,
>   But sit and tak' the gee.

In the morning soon, when I come down,
    The ne'er a word she spak';
But mony a sad and sour look,
    And aye her head she'd shake.
"My dear," quo' I, "what aileth thee,
    To look sae sour at me?
I'll never do the like again,
    If ye'll ne'er tak' the gee."

When that she heard, she ran, she flang
    Her arms about my neck,
And twenty kisses in a crack,
    And, poor wee thing, she grat.
"If ye'll ne'er do the like again,
    But stay at hame wi' me,
I'll lay my life, I'se be the wife
    That never tak's the gee."

Here we have in the form of a song the identical story so often brought home to respectable firesides by benevolent ladies, or home missionaries, from the haunts of the slums and dark places of our great cities. The husband spends his day's wages at night in some tippling-shop, while his wife sits in misery and rags, and his bairns, instead of going to school, infest the streets with the "evening paper"! or any catalogue of the devil's doings that may be the talk of the hour. Now, no doubt this is a very serious business, and ought to be seriously weighed by all singers of drinking-songs. They are not to be sung on all occasions or in all companies; never, where they might add a spur when a rein is more necessary, or where they might be construed to fling a pseudo-halo of glorification over the beastly vice of drunkenness. But the fact is, I believe that as drinking-songs are never made by drunkards—who indeed are not capable of writing anything—so they very seldom have been the occasion to any man of sinking to the low level of bibulous degradation or Bacchanalian riot. It is weakness of the spiritual principle—the τὸ ἡγεμονικόν as the Stoics called it —the feeling of a void that cries out for being filled, or a lassitude craving a stimulus, that leads people to drown their reason in the sensualities of the gin-palace or the wine-vault. The worst that can be said of them in the way of being an incentive to drunkenness, is that the drinking-song of the lowest style, containing nothing but the element of drink, though intended humorously, may, when taken seriously by a low class of topers, add a certain poetical charm to the prose of drinking, which makes the carnal indulgence look a little more respectable for the nonce. On the other hand, the best drinking-songs, where the social element, as in "Auld Langsyne," prevails, are never sung by drunkards; and "A wee Drappie o't" will sound rather as a reproach in the ear of those swashbucklers of drink who are never content till they drown their reason in the element which was meant only to enliven their fancy. Certainly the above ditty, describing so vividly the situation of the drinking husband whose wife had "ta'en the gee," could never be sung by a regular drunkard at any ale-house: it is rather like so many of the best Scotch popular ditties, a sermon in the guise of a song; and might be used with the best effect by any society of total abstainers ambitious to enlist a witness from the classic age of Scottish song in favour of their ascetic evangel. And with regard to abstinence generally, though it is not so great a virtue as temperance, is rather, strictly judged, a refuge of despair for those who are not strong enough to practise moderation, yet we have the highest authority for saying that in certain cases, and for certain persons, it is not only a wise precaution, but an imperative duty to abstain from the enjoyment of that which cannot be used without the certainty or the near probability of its abuse. For "if thy right eye offend thee," said He who spake as never man spake, "pluck it out, and cast it from thee: it is profitable for thee that one of thy members should perish, and not that thy whole body should be cast into hell." And this law holds good, not only for the sake of the individual himself, but in certain special cases where a man may wisely curtail himself of his natural liberties for the sake of others, or a good landlord will often stint himself of his just rent for the respect which he loves to show to a good tenant. "For it is good," says the great apostle of the Gentiles, "neither to eat flesh, nor to drink wine, nor do anything whereby thy brother stumbleth, or is offended, or is made weak." But on this side of the question also, of course, moderation must be used in a reasonable discrimination of cases; for the difficulty here, as in all moral questions, lies not so much in the rule as in the application of the rule: *when*, *where*, *how*, and *how much*,—these are the words that give the wise doer pause. The ancient Romans, who, before they became infected with those Oriental and Hellenic sensualities which St Paul in the introduction to Romans lashes with such effective indignation, were no doubt, like the Scotch, a very stout, sturdy, serious, and sober people; but, when at the middle of the second century B.C. they had humbled their great commercial adversary in the command of the Mediterranean seas, a wide door was opened to foreign influences, which speedily rushed in like a restrained flood from the removal of a dam. Accordingly we find in the year 188 B.C. a remarkable notice in Livy to the effect that among other foreign importations the peace and purity of old Rome had been invaded by a band of ignoble Greeklings, who, passing through Tuscany, brought with them to the capital of the empire certain Bacchanalian rites, characterised not only by riotous drinking and sensual excess, but by the practice of such gross impurities and lustful licence as went directly to poison the blood of the people, and to pull up by the root the sound-hearted growth of the family, which the Romans justly cherished with a holy jealousy as the seminary of the commonwealth. Against this monstrous apparition of a worship destitute of every spiritual element, the Roman Senate passed a celebrated decree;[1] an act of wise interference with what the devotees of Dionysus might, in modern language, have styled their liberty of conscience, but which as necessarily called for repression by a wise government, as the city police is entitled to treat as criminals those persons who block the streets with filth, or taint the atmosphere with poisonous fumes. But the same Romans who acted thus wisely in stamping out the grossness of sensualism in the worship of the foreign Dionysus, did not interfere with the kindly festivities of the old Latin LIBER, or wine-god, in whose honour annual processions were made, with priests and priestesses adorned with ivy, and carrying wine, and honey, and cakes, and sweetmeats, in grateful acknowledgment of the gods, whom the Greeks loved to name δωτῆρες ἐάων,

---

[1] Livy, xxxix. 8 and 18.

givers of good things. Let this moderation be our rule; and, while we give all liberty to those who, from whatever motives, prefer water-drinking to wine, let us beware of raising the exceptional restraint in favour of a few into the dignity of a law to tyrannise over the many. The charity which condescends to prop up the weakness of the weak loses half its virtue when it conspires to paralyse the strength of the strong.[1]

[1] There cannot be any doubt that in a country like Scotland, where the drinking of strong intoxicating liquors, without any redeeming element, has long exercised a debasing influence on large classes of the people, Total Abstinence Societies have acted and continue to act with the most excellent social results; and in discarding strong drinks, let it be mentioned with praise that the teetotallers have not discarded popular song, but taken care to supply that musical relish to the drinkers of water which the mass of embruted tipplers of strong drink are not in a condition to enjoy. Of this excellent wisdom, 'The Scottish Temperance Songs, to Scottish Airs,' by the late Thomas Knox, a man whose memory is fragrant in Edinburgh, and 'Songs and Hymns for the Band of Hope,' both published by Parlane in Paisley, give the most pleasing evidence.

CHAPTER VI.

SEA-SONGS, NAVAL SONGS, AND BOAT-SONGS.

> Ho, my bonnie boatie !
> Thou bonnie boatie mine !
> So trim and tight a boatie
> Was never launched on brine !
> Ho, my bonnie boatie !
> My praise is justly thine,
> Above all bonnie boaties
> Were builded on Loch Fyne.
> —JOHN MACLEOD of Morvern.

IN this chapter, for the first time, we find our rich and various Scottish Muse at a discount. Except in the domain of the formal lament, coronach, wail, or *Marbrann* as the Highlanders call it, which is a purely Gaelic phenomenon, there is no department of popular song in Scotland so meagrely furnished as the sea-song, boat-song, or nautical song. All the most popular compositions that smell of the sea, from "Ye Gentlemen of England that live at home at ease," which dates from the early period of the seventeenth century, and "Hearts of Oak are our Men," of which the words came from Garrick and the music from Boyce, down to "Tom Bowling" and whatsoever of good nautical stuff has taken possession of the popular ear since the death of Charles Dibdin, have an English ring about them with which a Scotsman may be proud to sympathise, though he must be conscious that he had no share in their production. Even those Dioscuri of nautical poetry, "The Battle of the Baltic" and "Ye Mariners of England," though written by a Scotsman with one of the most widely spread of Scottish names, are altogether English, as the very first line declares, "Ye Mariners of England"; and it is well that it should be so. If England is upon the whole not such a songful country in the popular heritage as Scotland, it is good that it should be able to claim, in one highest department of national song, an undisputed pre-eminence; and every large-hearted Scot will feel his pulse beat as warmly to the praises of Nelson and the Nile, as the generous Englishman is proud to acknowledge the heroism of the Scot in the glories of the blue bonnet at Waterloo and the Crimea. How it came about that the poetical side of the life of the sailor should have been so left in the shade by the Muse of Coila, may be difficult to explain: in this, as in every other region of human sentiment, contagion is strong, and example imperious; and, if a great singer of the people gains the lordship of the popular ear, with a constant reference to the plough and the threshing-floor, and not a word in favour of the oar and the helm, there are sure to be hundreds following in his track for one that is stirred by a counter-inspiration.[1] Long before Burns, however, the destiny of Scottish song in the rural, rather than in the nautical direction, was fixed. The typical seamen of the middle ages, before the battle of Largs in 1263, were strangers and rovers, and besides, for four hundred years, held their own so stoutly in the Western seas that the Saxon of the Lowlands was content to be dumb in a region where he had no glories to celebrate. The field which Fortune kept open for him was in the debatable land of the Border, where the Scotts, the Douglases, the Pringles, the Riddells, and the Rutherfords furnished materials enough for those ballads of daring adventure and pathetic incident which fed the early genius of Sir Walter Scott. As little do the Celts of the northern half of the island ever seem to have maintained their position on the watery element against those

[1] How entirely the sea and sailor life is ignored by Burns has been set forth in detail, along with other interesting local features of his poetry, in a valuable pamphlet, 'Burns and his Times,' by J. O. Mitchell, originally published in the 'Glasgow Herald,' 25th January 1888.

potent sea-rovers who possessed the coasts and the islands of the North and West, and baptised the fringe of the land all round with Scandinavian names, patently legible in the topographical nomenclature of the present day. The Highlander was a soldier, not a sailor, and as such, has approved himself, from Fontenoy and Waterloo to the Indies and the Soudan, as the right arm of British soldiership; but in the sea service he is an altogether secondary figure, represented by an occasional marked personality, as a M'Clintock or a Maclure, but not typically dominant in the waters of the deep.

By Scottish song, I mean generally in this book Lowland song—song composed originally in the language of the Saxon of the Lowlands, familiarly known as such, in distinction from the Celt of the Highlands. But the distinction, as the reader will have noted, and specially in the case of the Jacobite ballads, is not always strictly to be observed. Not a few Highland airs have been adopted by Scottish song-writers; and the genuine popular songs of the Highlands, too long neglected by foolish fashion and ignorant prejudice, are coming yearly more and more into the great stream of national Scottish poetry. We find in them not a little that has a distinct kinship with our native songs—a marked originality both in the music, in the scenery, and in the subjects, with which we should be fools not to enrich ourselves.[1] Let us take, therefore, one of their boat-songs—*iorram*, as they call them: for boat-songs, they must have plashing about habitually like ducks in those West waters, though the majesty of the nautical ode and the glory of the naval victory have been denied. Here is one in the true Gaelic style, not even rhymed, but delighting in loose assonance, after the fashion of the Spaniards, not always lightly caught by the English ear; but this does not affect the rhythmical flow, which is pleasant enough :—

Ho ro, Clansmen!

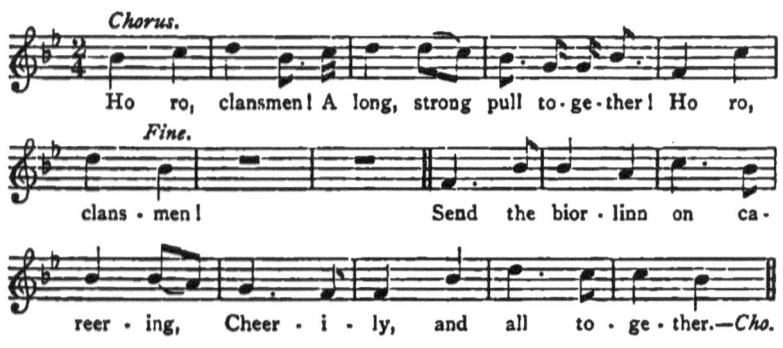

Ho ro, clansmen! A long, strong pull to-ge-ther! Ho ro, clans-men! Send the bior-linn on ca-reer-ing, Cheer-i-ly, and all to-ge-ther.—*Cho.*

Bend your oars and send her foaming
O'er the dashing, swelling billows.
   Ho ro, &c.

---

[1] On the poetry and songs of the Highlands generally, see The Language and Literature of the Scottish Highlands, by J. S. B. Edinburgh: Douglas, 1876.

Give her way and show her wake,
'Mid showering spray and curling eddies.
   Ho ro, &c.

Through the eddying tide we'll guide her,
Round each isle and breezy headland.
   Ho ro, &c.

O'er the wave we'll send her bounding,
As the staghound bounds o'er the heather.
   Ho ro, &c.

See the diver as he eyes her
Dips with wonder under water.
   Ho ro, &c.

The gannet high in midway sky
Triumphs wildly as we're passing.
   Ho ro, &c.

The sportive sunbeams gleam around her
As she bounds through shining waters.
   Ho ro, &c.

Clansmen, cheer! the wind is veering,
Soon she'll tear and clear the billows.
   Ho ro, &c.

Soon the flowing breeze will blow,
We'll show the snowy canvas on her.
   Ho ro, &c.

Wafted by the breeze of morn
We'll quaff the joyous horn together.
   Ho ro, &c.

>   Another cheer ! our isle appears—
>   Our biorlinn bears her on the faster.
>   Ho ro, &c.
>
>   Ahead she goes ! our biorlinn knows
>   What eyes on shore are gazing on her.
>   Ho ro, &c.
>
>   Ahead she goes ! the land she knows—
>   She holds the shore, she holds it bravely.
>   Ho ro, clansmen !
>   Stoutly did we pull together,
>   My brave clansmen ! [1]

The author of this spirited song was the late Dr John Macleod of Morvern, in the Sound of Mull, not far from Tobermory. This reverend gentleman, commonly known in the district, from his majestic personal presentment,[2] as the high priest of Morvern, was brother to the celebrated Dr Macleod of St Columba, Glasgow, author of the classical Gaelic work 'Caraid nan Gaidheal,' father of the celebrated Dr Norman Macleod, the Queen's friend, and uncle of the present talented editor of 'Good Words.' Like every active servant of God in those parts, he had to

---

[1] From the Killin Collection of Gaelic Songs. By Charles Stewart, Killin. Music here by kind permission of Messrs Maclachlan & Stewart, Edinburgh.

[2] I am informed on the best authority that the stature of this bishop of the Isles was six feet eight inches ; but he was so well proportioned that the majesty of his appearance did not suffer, as with tall men it so often does, by the intrusive analogy of a May-pole.

perform his round of parochial visitations as much by sea as by land; and in performing these rounds, the sympathy which he showed with sea life and sea danger served to endear him so much the more to the stout fellows under his pastoral care; for the pious people in those far regions, though they object to fiddling and dancing in a preacher of the Gospel generally, would not object to boating—though they might perhaps find a scruple about boat-songs on Sunday. As an illustration of the lusty nautical spirit which fired the bosom, not only of this Dr John, but of the minister of St Columba, we may give here the following lines by him addressed to his favourite boatman, Roderick or Rory:—

RORY BEAG SABHAIRI.

Hail to the boy
With the sharp twinkling eye,
In coat and in breeches
So gallantly dressed!
You may read in his face
His descent from the race
That rules o'er the mist-mantled
Isle of the West.

O Angus MacRory,
How proud wouldst thou be
If thou wert alive
Such a brave boy to see!

There's none in the parish
  With him may compare;
A gentleman quite,
  With a style and an air—
Our brave little Rory,
Our brave little Rory—ho-i-ho-ro!

No clerk in the land
  Hath a sturdier pace;
Without panting or puffing,
  He's first in the race.
No clerk in the Synod
  More proudly will ride
O'er the hissing white crests
  Of the billowy tide.
When the mast and the sail
  Are pressed by the sway
Of the strong-wingèd blasts
  As they bluster and bray,
Then each sailor cries,
  Yarely, boys, yarely!
O'er mountains of billows
  We'll bowl along rarely,
With brave little Rory—ho-i-ho-ro!

When he raises the *iorram*,
  Whose soul-stirring note
Gives strength to the arms
  And gives wings to the boat,
'Tis then I'd be sitting
  Beneath his command,
With a song in my breast
  And a flask in my hand!

There's no man in Suinart,
  Or in Tobermory,
Who can handle an oar
  With a swing like our Rory;
And all the lads cry,
  Be guerdon and glory
To the blood of Macleod,
    In the stout heart of Rory!
Our brave little Rory—ho-i-ho-ro![1]

Another beautiful boat-song, from the author of "Ho ro, Clansmen!" to the tune of a popular love-song, "Mairi Laghach," we shall give here; and with a reference back to the Skye boat-song given in our third chapter (p. 239), feel that we have done enough to induce the song-lover in the Lowlands to drink more largely than he has hitherto done from the refreshing wells of such manly music:—

HO, MY BONNIE BOATIE!

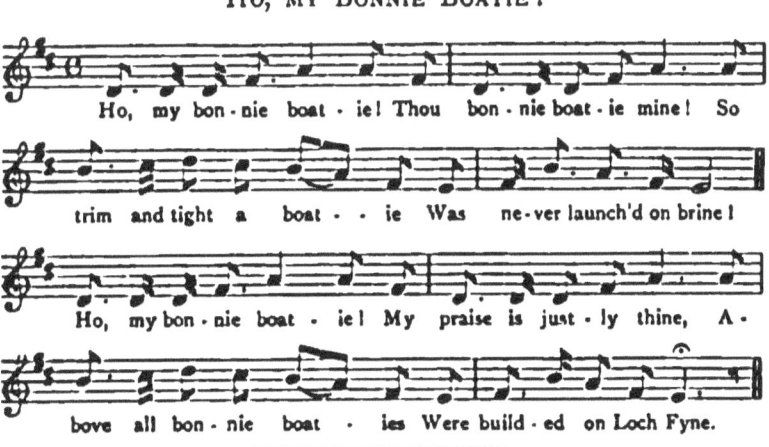

Ho, my bon-nie boat-ie! Thou bon-nie boat-ie mine! So trim and tight a boat-ie Was ne-ver launch'd on brine! Ho, my bon-nie boat-ie! My praise is just-ly thine, A-bove all bon-nie boat-ies Were build-ed on Loch Fyne.

---

[1] From Altavona, by J. S. B., p. 416.

To build thee up so firmly,
    I knew the stuff was good;
Thy keel of stoutest elm-tree,
    Well fixed in oaken wood;
And timbers ripely seasoned
    Of cleanest Norway pine,
Well cased in ruddy copper,
    To plough the deep were thine!

How lovely was my boatie
    At rest upon the shore,
Before my bonnie boatie
    Had known wild ocean's roar!
Thy deck so smooth and stainless,
    With such fine bend thy rim,
Thy seams that know no gaping,
    Thy masts so tall and trim!

And bonnie was my boatie,
    Afloat upon the bay,
When smooth as mirror round her
    The heaving ocean lay;
While round the cradled boatie
    Light troops of plumy things,
To praise the bonnie boatie
    Made music with their wings.

How eager was my boatie
    To plough the swelling seas,
When o'er the curling waters
    Full sharply blew the breeze!
O, 'twas she that stood to windward,
    The first among her peers,

When shrill the blasty music
  Came piping round her ears!

And when the sea came surging
  In mountains from the west,
And reared the racing billow
  Its high and hissing crest,
She turned her head so deftly,
  With skill so firmly shown,
The billows they went their way,
  The boatie went her own.

And when the sudden squall came
  Black swooping from the Ben,
And white the foam was spinning
  Around thy top-mast then,
O never knew my boatie
  A thought of ugly dread,
But dashed right through the billow,
  With the hot spray round her head!

Yet wert thou never headstrong
  To stand with forward will,
When yielding was thy wisdom
  And caution was my skill.
How neatly and how nimbly
  Thou turned thee to the wind,
With thy lee-side in the water,
  And a swirling trail behind!

What though a lowly dwelling
  On barren shore I own,
My kingdom is the blue wave,
  My boatie is my throne!

> I'll never want a dainty dish
> To breakfast or to dine,
> While men may man my boatie,
> And fish swim in Loch Fyne![1]

In one other direction we are entitled to look for good specimens of the Scottish boat-song, though even more remote from the classical fellowship of Burns, and the bards of Ayrshire and Renfrew, than the sea-songs of the Macleods,—in Orkney and in Shetland and in Caithness, where the Norsemen made permanent settlements, and either supplanted or obliterated the original Celtic population—if indeed a firmly rooted Celtic population ever was there. How rich the repertory of native Norse song in those parts may be, I do not personally know; but here follows one recommended to me by a gentleman well versed in the life and converse of "Ultima Thule," and which certainly, both in conception and in tone, is worthy to take its place with the most popular productions of Burns or Tannahill. "The Tooin' o' wir Boat" is no doubt, in its inspiration, like the well-known Gaelic song "Fearabhata"—the Boatman—a love-song; but whereas in the Gaelic song the boat is altogether lost in the love, in this Shetland ditty the boat dominates throughout, and the "too, too, too!" of the refrain keeps the ear possessed with the music of the sea and the shore from beginning to end of the chant:—

---

[1] From the Gaelic, by J. S. B. *Language and Literature of the Highlands*, p. 279.

THE TOOIN' O' WIR BOAT.[1]

My faither aye weel steers the boat,
    Wi' him are brithers three,
An' Sandy cam' at Beltane time,
    An' just gangs for a fee.
        The tooin', &c.

O Sandy is a bonnie lad,
    An' saft blue is his e'e,
An' though oor folk kens naething o't,
    He's unco fond o' me.
        The tooin', &c.

Sometimes when we gang in the ebb,
    An' when there's nane to see,
He puts his airm aroond my waist,
    An' aft he kisses me.
        The tooin', &c.

---

[1] By kind permission of Roy Paterson & Sons, Edinburgh.

Whene'er our men are lang lang oot,
   Sic fears come to my heart,
I canna rest within the hoose,
   But glower in every airt.
      The tooin', &c.

But when I see her weel-kent sail—
   Her sail is barkit broon—
My heart is so o'ercome wi' joy,
   The tears come rinnin' doon.
      The tooin', &c.

My faither says that summer neist
   My Sandy 'ill hae a share,
For weel he can baith set an' hale,
   An' row upon an aire.
      The tooin', &c.

An' then when Hallowmas comes roond,
   An' Sandy marries me,
I'll no' think ony shame to greet
   When he's owre lang at sea.
      The tooin', &c.

As a contrast to the *allegretto* tone of this beautiful song, we may take "The Tempest is Raging," by David Vedder, where, however, Eros, the most insinuating of all the gods, is not altogether wanting, as in not a few other songs of storm and tempest:—

"Lashed to the helm,
   Should seas o'erwhelm,
     I'd think of thee, my love!"

David Vedder, the author of the song which we now insert, was an Orkney man, born in the parish of Burness. Having had the misfortune to lose both his parents at an early age, he earned his livelihood as a seaman, and with the rank of captain performed several voyages to Greenland. He afterwards entered the Revenue service, and was raised to the post of tide-surveyor, the duties of which office he continued to discharge at Montrose, Kirkcaldy, Dundee, and Leith, till his death at Edinburgh in 1854. He united the faithful performance of his tidal duties with the assiduous cultivation of the Muse, and secured for himself a place in the lyrical literature of the day, of which Orkney is justly proud, and Scotland will not be wise to forget :—

THE TEMPEST IS RAGING.

The tempest is raging,
   And rending the shrouds;
The ocean is waging
   A war with the clouds;
The cordage is breaking,
   The canvas is torn,
The timbers are creaking,
   The seamen forlorn.

The water is gushing
   Through hatches and seams,
'Tis roaring and rushing
   O'er keelson and beams;

And nought save the lightning
  On mainmast or boom,
At intervals brightening
  The depth of the gloom.

Though horrors beset me,
  And hurricanes howl,
I may not forget thee,
  Beloved of my soul!
Though soon I must perish
  In ocean beneath,
Thine image I'll cherish,
  Adored one, in Death.[1]

When we turn from these echoes of the old Scandinavian scalds, to the boat-song of genuine Saxon growth, we seek for them, as the botanist does for rare herbs in the crevices of the rock, or as the Muse of Virgil did for a few heads keeping themselves up buoyantly above the multitudinous roll of waters that overwhelmed the sinking ship:—

"Apparent rari nantes in gurgite vasto;"

and the one, generally the only one, that peeps forth from the musical memory of a Scot, when you ask him for a boat-song, though it smells distinctly of the salt water, transports the singer more into the region of domestic joys and connubial loves than into the stormy element of the sea:—

[1] Dr Rogers's Scottish Minstrel, p. 233.

THE BOATIE ROWS.

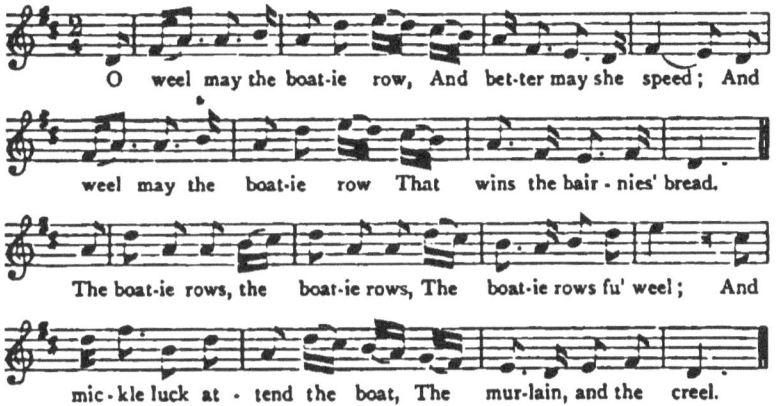

O weel may the boat-ie row, And bet-ter may she speed; And weel may the boat-ie row That wins the bair-nies' bread. The boat-ie rows, the boat-ie rows, The boat-ie rows fu' weel; And mic-kle luck at-tend the boat, The mur-lain, and the creel.

    I cuist my line in Largo bay,
      And fishes I caught nine;
    There's three to boil, and three to fry,
      And three to bait the line.
        The boatie rows, the boatie rows,
          The boatie rows indeed;
        And happy be the lot o' a'
          That wish the boatie speed.

    O weel may the boatie row
      That fills a heavy creel,
    And cleeds us a' frae head to foot,
      And buys our parritch meal.
        The boatie rows, the boatie rows,
          The boatie rows indeed;
        And happy be the lot o' a'
          That wish the boatie speed.

    When Jamie vow'd he wad be mine,
      And won frae me my heart,
    O mickle lighter grew my creel;
      He swore we'd never part.

The boatie rows, the boatie rows,
  The boatie rows fu' weel;
And mickle lighter is the boat,
  When love bears up the creel.

My kertch I put upon my head,
  And dress'd mysel' fu' braw;
But dowie, dowie was my heart,
  When Jamie gaed awa'.
    But weel may the boatie row,
      And lucky be her part;
    And lightsome be the lassie's care,
      That yields an honest heart.

When Sandy, Jock, and Janetie,
  Are up an' gotten lear,
They'll help to gar the boatie row,
  And lighten a' our care.
    The boatie rows, the boatie rows,
      The boatie rows fu' weel;
    And lightsome be her heart that bears
      The murlain and the creel.

And when we're auld and sair bow'd down,
  And hirplin' round the door,
They'll row to keep us hale and warm,
  As we did them before.'
    Then weel may the boatie row,
      And better may she speed;
    And happy be the lot of a'
      That wish the boatie speed.

The author of this song was a Montrose man, John Ewen by name, born in 1741, and who afterwards transferred his services as a merchant and a philanthropist to the granite metropolis of the North. The song, deservedly placed by Burns in the very first rank of our rich songful array, stands as a solitary instance of the author's lyrical genius.[1]

But the real glory and crown of the Scottish sea-song of Lowland origin is "The Rover of Lochryan," a song which, notwithstanding the classical excellence both of its music and its words, rarely appears in the programme of our musical entertainments—a fact which I mention as a striking proof of the degree in which the pastoral tone of Burns's poetry has overmastered the popular ear, so as to throw into comparative obscurity any ballad, however excellent, of which the sea-rover, not the plough-follower, is the hero. It is worthy of note in this case that the author, Hew Ainslie, was born and schooled as a boy in Ballantrae in Ayrshire, a village on the shore of those very seas where the predominance of the Vikings of the ninth century is distinctly traced in the names of Wigton, the Fleet, and other philological witnesses of Scandinavian settlements, in a country originally peopled by Celts. Ainslie, like the father of Burns when he came to the South, commenced life as a gardener: thence moving upwards in the social scale, he became first a clerk to a legal gentleman, and by

[1] See Songs of Scotland. By J. D. Ross. New York, 1887.

this training in the dexterities of the pen, fitted himself for an appointment in the General Register House, Edinburgh; but having entered into the married state, and finding the salary of subordinate officials in that establishment insufficient for the comfortable maintenance of his family, he transported himself, in the year 1822, to America, where he engaged in various farming and manufacturing schemes. Like Ballantine, he knew to combine the effective performance of the duties of a business life with the devout worship of the Muse. At Redfield, New York, in the year 1855, he published two volumes of Scottish songs and ballads, which will secure him a high place among the lyric poets of his country; and he died at Louisville in the year 1878, in the eighty-sixth year of his age, adding another proof to the many already brought forward in these pages, of the falsity of the vulgar notion that poets die young. If they die young sometimes, as they will do, like other people, it will not be because they have more vitality to expend, but because they do not spend it wisely. In the song as we now give it, and with which we conclude this short chapter, let the reader note the vivid dramatic picturesqueness of the descriptive lines—lines worthy of Homer, and which were not surpassed by Burns in his most favoured hour:—

THE ROVER OF LOCHRYAN HE'S GANE.

The rover of..... Lochryan he's gane, Wi' his merry men sae brave: Their hearts are o' the steel, an' a better keel Ne'er bowl'd on the back o' a wave. It's no' when the loch lies dead in its trough, When naething disturbs it ava; But the rack an' the ride o' the restless tide, Or the splash o' the gray sea-maw.

It's no' when the yawl an' the light skiffs crawl
    Owre the breast o' the siller sea,
That I look to the west for the bark I lo'e best,
    An' the rover that's dear to me.
But when that the clud lays its cheeks to the flood,
    An' the sea lays its shouther to the shore;
When the win' sings high, an' the sea-whaups cry
    As they rise frae the whitening roar.

It's then that I look to the thickening rook,
    An' watch by the midnight tide;
I ken the wind brings my rover hame,
    An' the sea that he glories to ride.

O merry he sits 'mang his jovial crew
  Wi' the helm-heft in his hand;
An' he sings aloud to his boys in blue,
  As his ee's upon Galloway's land.

Unstent an' slack each reef an' tack,
  Gie her sail, boys, while it may sit;
She has roar'd through a heavier sea afore,
  An' she'll roar through a heavier yet.
When landsmen sleep, or wake an' creep,
  In the tempest's angry moan,
We dash through the drift, an' sing to the lift
  O' the wave that heaves us on.

CHAPTER VII.

SONGS OF THOUGHT AND SENTIMENT.

"Imprimis hominis est propria veri inquisitio atque indagatio; ex quod intelligitur, quod verum, simplex sincerumque sit, id esse naturæ hominis aptissimum: Huic veri videndi cupiditati adjuncta est appetitio quædam principatus, ex quo animi magnitudo, humanarumque verum contemptio."—CICERO.

BY songs of thought and sentiment, I mean songs of which the object and the purpose, not merely the atmosphere, the situation, and the incidents, are a thought, sentiment, idea, or principle, what in the formal language of the schools might be called a proposition. Of course, there is no reason why any great moral truth, or elevating human idea, should not take the form of a song: in the oldest Greek times all wisdom was clothed in verse; and didactic poetry was as legitimate as any other form of rhythmical expression.[1] But in the course of time, when the minstrel

[1] "Quis ignorat musicen tantum antiquis temporibus non studii modo, verum etiam venerationis habuisse, ut iidem musici, et vates, et sapientes judicarentur."—Quinctilian, i. 10.

had ceased to be the only popular instructor, and a distinctly marked prose literature, from Pherecydes of Syros downwards, had asserted its separate position, philosophical ideas or great pervading principles of the universe, and forces of society, were formally set forth in prose; while the impassioned and dramatic expression of the principle in the actual encounters and conflicts of life was left in the hands of the singer. So little, however, did the modern idea of drawing a broad line of demarcation betwixt instruction and song receive acknowledgment from the Greek mind, that even in the most flourishing period of Attic prose, the choral ode, which was the most effective element in the Greek drama, had, both as respects substance and attitude, more in it of what we should call a sermon than a song. The formal intention to teach as in a modern lecture or sermon, is indeed wanting in all song properly so called; nevertheless the solemn chorus in the 'Eumenides' of Æschylus, beginning with—

"Mother Night, that bore me,
A scourge to go before thee,"

is as much a sermon on conscience as any ever preached by the most serious gospeller in a Christian pulpit. And in the same way, the choral ode in the 'Antigone' of Sophocles, starting from the sentence—

"Πολλὰ τὰ δεινὰ καὶ οὐδὲν
ἀνθρώπου δεινότερον πέλει,"

might be adopted word for word by any Christian preacher, enlarging on the familiar text of Ecclesiastes, "God hath made man upright; but he hath sought out many inventions." And in consideration of his function as a great popular teacher, the poet was always spoken of by the Greeks as a σοφός or wise man, no less than the philosopher. And amongst the Hebrews, though in the Book of Proverbs and that singular work just quoted a separate school of strictly didactic prose literature had taken shape, it is plain that in the time of David, or of the sacred songsters, of whom he was the most prominent type, the psalm required to make no apology for presenting itself as the exponent of moral truth rather than as the expression of lyrical passion. Thus the 1st Psalm is simply a pious meditation on the favourite Hebrew text, that even in this world the way to lasting prosperity is the way of righteousness, while the apparent strength of the wicked is only for a season, to be blown away as chaff before the wind in the day of the Lord's judgment. In the same way, the 8th Psalm is a discourse on the grand order of the universe, and the significant place of man as the crown and master of the animated creation. Not less admirable in the same view is the familiar 19th Psalm, in whose well-balanced roundness the wisdom of the great author of the universe is recognised with equal fairness in what the Greeks called the ἀνάγκαι, or necessary laws of the physical world, and the liberty or responsible individualism of the moral world; two spheres of divine energy which, with the narrowness of view so notable in scientific specialists, not a few modern thinkers have been foolishly studious to confound, while with the great Hebrew poet-king they stood wisely apart, like the right hand and the left of the human body in the service of the common brain. In modern times the existence of a separate popular school of ethics in the Christian Church has caused the serious wisdom of the Greek dramatic ode to confine itself in the main, under the name of hymns, to the service of the Church; and this has been especially the case in Scotland, where the severity of a sternly Calvinistic creed stiffly refused to have any communion with the lightness and brightness of human joy, which characterised the popular song. The consequence was, of course, that the popular song became more and more secular; and the Monday, as we had occasion in a previous chapter to remark, with its riotous and sometimes not over-dainty mirth, strove to compensate itself for the enforced awfulness of the Sunday. But the Church was not to be out-manœuvred in this way; so it borrowed the love-songs of the peasantry, and with a few verbal changes, and a direct spiritual application, made the inspiration of the devil in the popular song serve the cause of God, as Balaam was made to pour forth a prophetic blessing on the Israelites, whom he had been sent to curse. So in the "gude and godly ballad" that was published in Edinburgh some three hundred years ago and more, we find the young lady who had been besieged by amorous addresses from an old Highland gentleman, by the single change of *Donald* into *Deil*, turn a secular love-song into a ballad of stout spiritual denunciation :—

> "Haud awa', bide awa',
> Haud awa' frae me, Deilie!"

And to the lover who appealed eagerly to be admitted by the window to his fair one, translated by the craft of the godly Muse into the character of the great spiritual bridegroom, not the window only is opened furtively, but the door is freely thrown on its hinges :—

> "Quho's at the window? quho?
> Go from my window, go!
> Cry no more like a stranger,
> But in at my door thee go."[1]

All this was very natural and very fair, and might serve

---

[1] Dauney's Ancient Scottish Melodies, Edinburgh, 1838, p. 37. Gude and Godly Ballads, Edinburgh, 1578; republished by David Laing, Edinburgh, 1868.

a good purpose here and there in its day; but it is evident that, however good the intentions were of those spiritualisers of the secular songs, they had too much the aspect of travesty and caricature to become popular with the great mass of the people, who in matters of moral instinct and æsthetic propriety have not seldom more good taste than the persons who put themselves forward as their guides. Anyhow, it seems certain that after all these attempts of enforced assimilation, the divorce between sacred and secular song remained as it was, and has remained down to the present day in Scotland in a very notable degree. To such an extreme, indeed, did the Bibliolatry of the Scottish Covenanters go, as the natural rebound from the enforced Laudian ritualism, that it was looked upon as a sin to sing any song in church but the Psalms of David, and every utterance of free evangelical spontaneity in the domain of song was systematically smothered; and it was not till the year 1751[1] that a successful attempt was made to enlarge the domain of Presbyterian hymnology in Scotland by introducing into the Church service those metrical versions of certain passages of Scripture commonly called Paraphrases. These lyrical adaptations of the sacred text have now been received into full brotherhood with the Book of Psalms; but, though recently even hymns by vari-

[1] Acts of Assembly, May 20, 1751.

ous modern poets have been received into the singing service both of the Free and the Established Churches, there remained a strong feeling against any extension of the Davidic hymnology among the more strict adherents of the religious traditions of the country; and I remember having read in the life of one of those travelling pedlars who, before the day of steam-engines and steam printing-presses, used to perambulate the country as dispensers of knowledge, that when, after a day's weary travel through vale and village, he sat down in the evening before a comfortable fire in a hospitable farmhouse, so soon as he felt himself refreshed by a stout glass of "the nappy," he forthwith waxed eloquent against the dominant evils of the time, and specially against the two deadly P's — Popery and the Paraphrases. And even to the present hour, in the region north of Inverness, the Psalms of David maintain so firmly their exclusive hold of the devout ear, that, though the worshippers have no objections to listen to uninspired sermons and uninspired prayers of any length or of any solemnity, they look upon the proposed introduction of uninspired songs under the name of hymns into the Church service as a profanation and a horror. These facts sufficiently indicate the reasons why songs of religious thought and sentiment are so rare in the rich repertory of the Scottish lyre. They are not sung on Sunday because they are secular; and they are not sung on Monday because they are in a serious key, with which the associations of a Monday audience are not in tune. But there is another reason why really pious and devout Scottish songs cannot be sung in the church; they are in the Scottish dialect, and the Scottish dialect is not the language of the pulpit. This reason is good. Not every language is cultivated on every side; and to use a language in a sphere foreign to the range of its historical growth, is to call up a whole army of hostile associations to disturb the effect of your address. It is different with Gaelic. Gaelic is the language not only of the fireside, and the familiar colloquy of friend with friend, but of the pulpit; and so, if it had been the will of the Gaelic Christians to have adopted the sacred songs of Dugald Buchanan or other Gaelic bards into their Church service, no ludicrous or undignified associations could have interfered with the devout sentiments which they are calculated to inspire. But in the Lowlands a sermon in the Scottish dialect, even from the mouth of the most uneducated street preacher, would be looked upon as irreverent and profane; as any one may prove to himself by casting a glance over the Scottish version of the Psalms put forth by that eloquent expounder of Burns, the Rev. Hately Waddell, Glasgow. Associations are spoiled children, whom neither the gravity of the Bench nor the sanctity of the pulpit will prevent from having their sport in the presence-chamber of the brain.

These remarks seemed necessary in order to account for the very small amount of purely gnomic, reflective, or meditative poetry to be found in the popular currency of Scottish song. The Psalms of David had preoccupied the ground; and, were it not for the prevalent notion that the popular song was meant mainly for recreation, while the sacred song was meant for edification, there was nothing but the associations connected with the Scottish language to prevent the following beautiful song on trust in Providence from being sung in all the churches alongside of the most devout utterances to the same effect in the Psalms and other familiar passages of Scripture:—

ILKA BLADE O' GRASS KEPS ITS AIN DRAP O' DEW.[1]

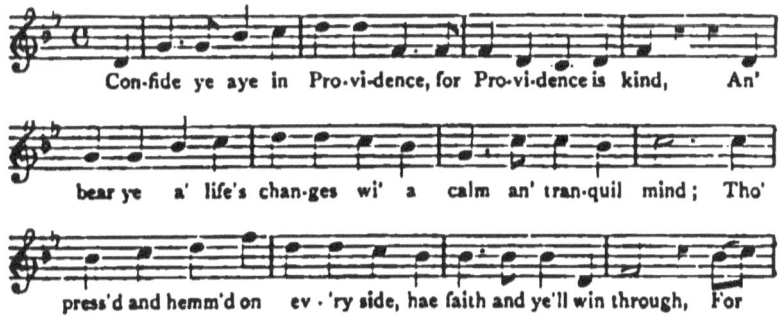

---

[1] Melody by kind permission of Blockley, London.

Gin reft frae friends, or cross'd in love, as whiles nae doubt
  ye've been,
Grief lies deep hidden in your heart, or tears flow frae your
  e'en;
Believe it for the best, an' trow there's gude in store for you,
For ilka blade o' grass keps its ain drap o' dew.

In lang lang days o' simmer, when the clear an' cludless sky
Refuses ae wee drap o' rain to Nature parch'd an' dry,
The genial night, wi' balmy breath, gars verdure spring anew,
An' ilka blade o' grass keps its ain drap o' dew.

So lest 'mid Fortune's sunshine we should feel owre proud an'
  hie,
An' in our pride forget to wipe the tear frae poortith's e'e;
Some wee dark cluds o' sorrow come, we ken nae whence or
  how,
But ilka blade o' grass keps its ain drap o' dew.

The author of this pious effusion, James Ballantine, or "Jamie Ballantine," as he was familiarly called by those who had the pleasure to know and to love him, is in many views, next to Robert Burns, perhaps the most notable of Scottish song-writers. An exception to what appears to me the general rule, that the fervid force of Scottish song comes from the West, and not from "cold and stately Edinburgh," Ballantine was born in the very historic gateway to the capital of his native country, the notable West Port. Like Burns, he was of humble parentage, and, like him, destined in vivid portraiture to prove how little Latin and Greek, and other academical appliances, have to do with the formation of a manly character and the inspiration of an elevating Muse. His father, who was a brewer, died young; and the boy, thus left with a mother and three sisters, had to fight his way through the world in the noble style which has so long been the boast of our Scottish youth. He was bound apprentice to a house-painter, and the passion for the beautiful which made him so distinguished as a lyrical poet, led him to transfer his imaginative colouring to glass, and so he became an artist in the elegant craft of decorating window-lights. In this capacity he attained such eminence that the designs made by him were selected by the Royal Commissioners of the Fine Arts for the decoration of the windows of the House of Lords, executed under his superintendence. In this way he stands before us like Goethe and other poets of well-balanced character; his imagination did not become wild by being divorced from practical good sense, nor his sense debased by being divorced from imagination. He was thus, if not as a poet, certainly in character, superior to the great Coryphæus of our national quire; for, while Burns failed as a farmer, Ballantine prospered as a glass-painter; and thus, to use Lord Cockburn's happy phrase, he succeeded in solving the rare practical problem of making his business feed the Muses, while the Muses graced his business.

Hardly less wise, if not quite so evangelical, is another familiar ditty of our wise-thoughted and kindly-hearted glass-artist. How many pilers of hydropathic palaces, and other investors in schemes which had only daring and distance and novelty to recommend them, might have saved themselves and hundreds of innocent people from ruin, had they been alive to the wisdom which lies in the song of—

CASTLES IN THE AIR.[1]

The bon-nie, bon-nie bairn, wha sits po-kin' in the ase,
Glow'r-in' in the fire wi' his wee round face;
Laugh-in' at the fuf-fin' lowe, what sees he there?
Ha! the young dreamer's big-gin' cas-tles in the air.

[1] Air inserted here by kind permission of Swan & Co., Berners Street, Oxford Street, London.

"Castles in the Air."

His wee chubby face, and his touzie curly pow, Are laughin' and noddin' to the dancin' lowe; He'll brown his rosy cheeks, and singe his sunny hair, Glow'rin' at the imps wi' their castles in the air.

He sees muckle castles tow'rin' to the moon:
He sees little sodgers pu'in' them a' doun!
Worlds whomblin' up and doun, bleezin' wi' a flare,—
See how he loups! as they glimmer in the air.
For a' sae sage he looks, what can the laddie ken?
He's thinkin' upon naething, like mony mighty men;
A wee thing mak's us think, a sma' thing mak's us stare,—
There are mair folk than him biggin' castles in the air.

Sic a night in winter may weel mak' him cauld:
His chin upon his buffy hand will soon mak' him auld;
His brow is brent sae braid, O, pray that daddy Care,
Would let the wean alane wi' his castles in the air!
He'll glower at the fire! and he'll keek at the light!
But mony sparklin' stars are swallow'd up by night;
Aulder een than his are glamour'd by a glare,
Hearts are broken, heads are turn'd wi' castles in the air.

One more ditty from our brave glass-stainer to show how wisely a song-singer can philosophise on our great national virtue, the power of work:—

The mair that ye Wark, aye the mair will ye Win.[1]

Be eident, be eident, fleet time rushes on;
Be eident, be eident, bricht day will be gone;
To stand idle by is a profitless sin,
The mair that ye wark, aye the mair ye will win.

The earth gathers fragrance while nursing the flower,
The wave waxes stronger while feeding the shower,
The stream gains in speed as it sweeps o'er the linn,
The mair that ye wark, aye the mair will ye win.

There's nought got by idling, there's nought got for nought,
Health, wealth, and contentment by labour are bought;
In raising yoursel' ye may raise up your kin,
The mair that ye wark, aye the mair will ye win.

Let every man aim in his heart to excel,
Let every man ettle to fend for himsel';
Aye nourish ye stern independence within,
The mair that ye wark, aye the mair will ye win.[2]

Of pious songs bearing on their face the distinct stamp of Scottish religious tradition, though there are not a few in the published poetry of the country worthy to maintain their ground against the Cavalier Lays of Professor Aytoun,[3]

---

[1] From Rogers's Scottish Minstrel, p. 413.

[2] The same gospel is preached in an excellent song, "Aye work awa'," composed by Joseph Wright, the great Glasgow umbrella-maker, 48 Argyle Arcade, Glasgow.

[3] See Songs of the Kirk and Covenant, by Mrs Menteith; Edinburgh, 1850. Songs of the Covenanters, by James Dodds; Edinburgh, 1880. Songs of the Scottish Worthies, by T. Wellwood; Paisley, 1881.

there is only one that I ever heard sung in a public concert of popular Scottish music, and the singer was that same David Kennedy who has done so much to give a world-wide reputation to that rich treasure of native song which not a few persons at home, trained in the school of fashionable false culture, are ignorant or shallow enough to ignore. The Covenanters, to whom with all their faults we owe the manliness and the moral seriousness of our national character, received from Robert Burns in a passing stanza that recognition which a man of his healthy moral and religious up-bringing could not fail to bestow :—

> "The Solemn League and Covenant
> Cost Scotland blood, cost Scotland tears,
> But faith sealed freedom's sacred cause ;
> If thou'rt a slave, indulge thy sneers."

But he was too deeply involved in the theological controversies of the day, and had too little of distinctively Presbyterian piety in his tone, to induce him to come forward as a minstrel of the noble army of martyrs in "the killing times." The Covenanting song to which I allude, called "The Covenanter's Lament," was the composition of a man whose name brings us back to Tannahill, R. A. Smith, and the other notable company of native singers in the Celtic West. Robert Allan was born in Kilbarchan, Renfrewshire, the son of a flax-dresser, in the year 1774, and so contemporary with Scott, Coleridge, and other distinguished men, whose youth fell into the stirring period of the French Revolution. As a muslin-weaver in his native town, he knew, like Ballantine, to unite a laborious trade with the worship of the Muse; but, not so happy as Ballantine in a career either of worldly prosperity or literary recognition, he conceived that he could breathe more freely, and work more effectively, and sing more cheerily, in the far free land beyond the Atlantic; and so, though advanced in years, he set sail for New York, but alas! destined to find there, not a new start to a new career, but a sad end to an old one. He died at New York on 1st June 1841, only six days after his arrival:—

THERE'S NAE COV'NANT NOW, LASSIE.

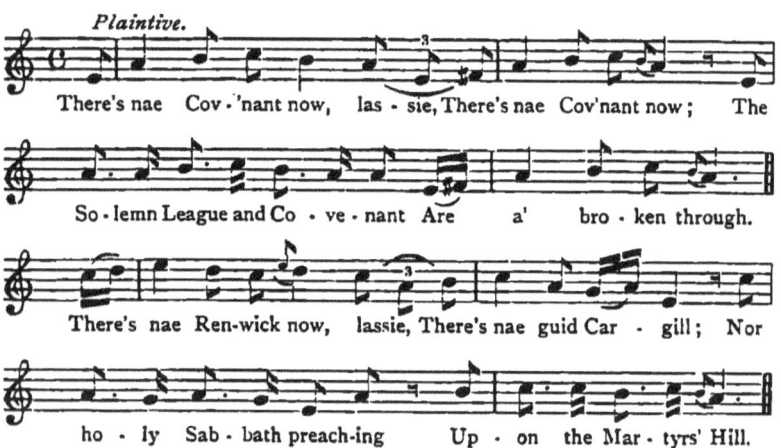

> It's naething but a sword, lassie—
>   A bluidy, bluidy ane—
> Waving owre puir Scotland
>   For her rebellious sin.
> Scotland's a' wrang, lassie,
>   Scotland's a' wrang ;
> It's neither to the hill nor glen,
>   Lassie, we daur gang.
>
> The Martyrs' Hill's forsaken,
>   In simmer's dusk sae calm ;
> There's nae gathering now, lassie,
>   To sing the e'enin' psalm.
> But the martyrs' grave will rise, lassie,
>   Aboon the warrior's cairn ;
> An' the martyr soun' will sleep, lassie,
>   Aneath the wavin' fern.

Pleasantly chiming with this grateful recognition of what our brave Covenanting forefathers did for Scottish independence, Scottish character, and Scottish piety, is the following song by George Paulin, a Berwickshire bard, and distinguished member of the scholastic profession, whose name, along with that of Ballantine, contributes not insignificantly to swell the meagre records of the Lyrical Muse of Scotland in the East, which we have more than once had occasion to mention, as contrasted with the luxuriance and fertility of her achievements in the West.[1] The

---

[1] See a sketch of his life and work in Murdoch's Scottish Poets (Glasgow : Morison, 1883), p. 38.

music is by Alan Reid, a rising young composer in "our own romantic town," and distinguished for his zeal in the musical indoctrination of our schools and the popularisation of national music, by cheap publications throughout the land :—

AUNTIE'S SANGS.[1]

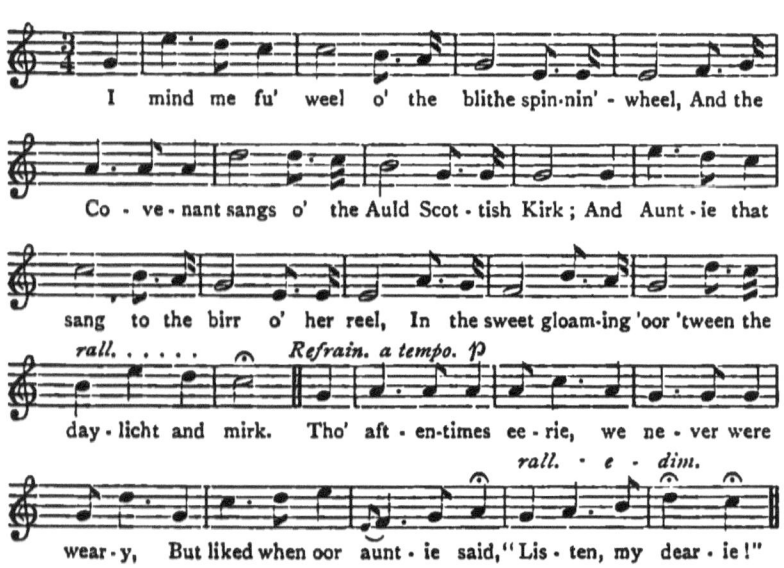

I mind me fu' weel o' the blithe spin-nin'-wheel, And the Co-ve-nant sangs o' the Auld Scot-tish Kirk; And Aunt-ie that sang to the birr o' her reel, In the sweet gloam-ing 'oor 'tween the day-licht and mirk. Tho' aft-en-times ee-rie, we ne-ver were wear-y, But liked when oor aunt-ie said, "Lis-ten, my dear-ie!"

She'd mony a rhyme o' the Covenant time,
O' the mosses and muirs where the brave martyrs fell,
In dark days o' yore when to pray was a crime,
And the red blude o' saints was the dew o' the dell.
    Tho' oftentimes eerie, &c.

And sometimes she'd greet—for the mem'ry was sweet
O' the psalm o' the glen, and the voice o' the heart—

---

[1] By permission from the National Choir (Parlane, Paisley, 1888), vol. i. p. 48.

That the banner should lie in the dust o' the street,
And the Covenant life frae the land should depart.
    Tho' oftentimes eerie, &c.

But Auntie is gane and I croon a' alane
O'er the lilt that was wed to the birr o' the reel;
The bonnie birk waves o'er the cauld grave-stane,
But her spirit's awa' to the land o' the leal;
    And noo I am eerie, and dowie, and weary,
    I'll ne'er again hear her say, "Listen, my dearie!"

But perhaps the very top and crown of all Scottish devout songs, and one which, no doubt partly from the celebrity of the authoress, has earned for itself a fair currency, even in fashionable drawing-rooms and saloons, is "The Land o' the Leal," by the Baroness Nairne, with whom we have already made, on more occasions than one, such inspiring acquaintance. Here it is:—

THE LAND O' THE LEAL.[1]

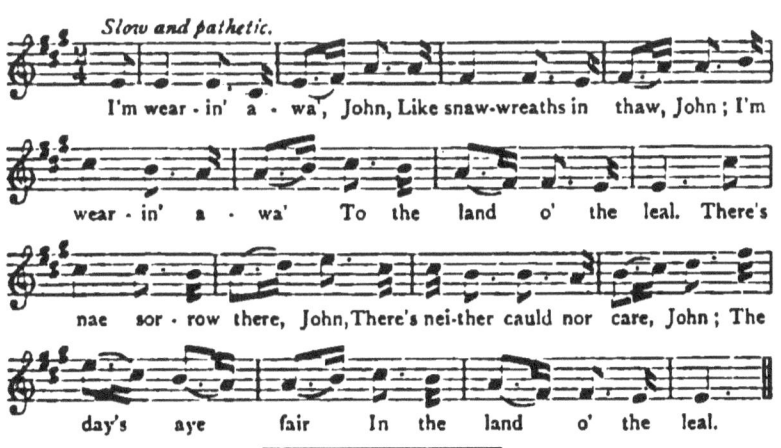

[1] By permission from Paterson & Sons.

Our bonnie bairn's there, John,
She was baith guid and fair, John;
And oh! we grudged her sair
   To the land o' the leal.

But sorrow's sel' wears past, John,
And joy's a-comin' fast, John;
The joy that's aye to last
   In the land o' the leal.

Sae dear's that joy was bought, John,
Sae free the battle fought, John,
That sinfu' man e'er brought
   To the land o' the leal.

Oh! dry your glist'nin' e'e, John,
My saul langs to be free, John,
And angels beckon me
   To the land o' the leal.

Oh! haud ye leal and true, John,
Your day it's wearin' through, John,
And I'll welcome you
   To the land o' the leal.

Now fare-ye-weel, my ain John,
This warld's cares are vain, John;
We'll meet, and we'll be fain
   In the land o' the leal.

So much for the more strictly, or at least approximately, religious section of the Scottish contemplative songs. But all contemplation, though reverential, is not necessarily religious; a Pythagoras and an Empedocles may dress their wisdom in verse as fitly as an Orpheus and an Olen. Nay, even science—modern physical science—so sharp, so severe, and so exact, may, in the hands of a great master, know to present itself in the dress of the Muses, with all the grace and sweetness that belongs to the spontaneous outflowing of natural song : of this, Goethe's well-known poem, "The Metamorphosis of Plants," is a capital example. In this poem all that is true in the Darwinian doctrine of development is set forth lucidly, free from all the narrowness of view and one-sided dogmatism which is the besetting sin of the purely scientific mind. Against this tendency of the scientist, Scottish poetry has a weapon called humour, as potent to expose the falsehood as the constructive Muse of the great German is to commend the truth that may lie in the stimulant novelty of the hour. Of the application of this weapon to prune the rampancy of an ingenious physical speculation, passing itself off for a philosophy, we could imagine no more classic specimen than the following song, familiar to not a few of the most cultivated Edinburgh ears, and well deserving of a world-wide circulation :—

THE ORIGIN OF SPECIES.

A New Song.

Have you heard of this question the Doctors among,
Whether all living things from a Monad have sprung?
This has lately been said, and it now shall be sung,
        Which nobody can deny.

Not one or two ages sufficed for the feat,
It required a few millions the change to complete;
But now the thing's done, and it looks rather neat,
        Which nobody can deny.

The original Monad, our great-great-grandsire,
To little or nothing at first did aspire;
But at last to have offspring it took a desire,
        Which nobody can deny.

This Monad becoming a father or mother,
By budding or bursting, produced such another;
And shortly there followed a sister or brother,
        Which nobody can deny.

But Monad no longer designates them well—
They're a cluster of molecules now, or a cell;
But which of the two, Doctors only can tell,
        Which nobody can deny.

These beings, increasing, grew buoyant with life,
And each to itself was both husband and wife;
And at first, strange to say, the two lived without strife,
        Which nobody can deny.

But such crowding together soon troublesome grew,
And they thought a division of labour would do;

So their sexual system was parted in two,
           Which nobody can deny.

Thus Plato supposes that, severed by fate,
Human halves run about, each in search of its mate,
Never pleased till they gain their original state,
           Which nobody can deny.

Excrescences fast were now trying to shoot;
Some put out a finger, some put out a foot;
Some set up a mouth, and some sent down a root,
           Which nobody can deny.

Some, wishing to walk, manufactured a limb;
Some rigged out a fin, with a purpose to swim;
Some opened an eye, some remained dark and dim,
           Which nobody can deny.

Some creatures grew bulky, while others were small,
As nature sent food for the few or for all;
And the weakest, we know, ever go to the wall,
           Which nobody can deny.

A deer with a neck that was longer by half
Than the rest of its family's (try not to laugh),
By stretching and stretching, became a Giraffe,
           Which nobody can deny.

A very tall pig, with a very long nose,
Sends forth a proboscis quite down to his toes;
And he then by the name of an Elephant goes,
           Which nobody can deny.

The four-footed beast that we now call a Whale,
Held its hind-legs so close that they grew to a tail,
Which it uses for threshing the sea like a flail,
           Which nobody can deny.

Pouters, tumblers, and fantails are from the same source;
The racer and hack may be traced to one Horse:
So Men were developed from monkeys, of course,
        Which nobody can deny.

An Ape with a pliable thumb and big brain,
When the gift of the gab he had managed to gain,
As a Lord of Creation established his reign,
        Which nobody can deny.

But I'm sadly afraid, if we do not take care,
A relapse to low life may our prospects impair;
So of beastly propensities let us beware,
        Which nobody can deny.

Their lofty position our children may lose,
And reduced to all-fours, must then narrow their views,
Which would wholly unfit them for filling our shoes,
        Which nobody can deny.

Their vertebræ next might be taken away,
When they'd sink to an oyster, or insect, some day,
Or the pitiful part of a polypus play,
        Which nobody can deny.

Thus losing Humanity's nature and name,
And descending through varying stages of shame,
They'd return to the Monad, from which we all came,
        Which nobody can deny.[1]

The author of this admirable exposition of the vagaries of a godless science was Charles Neaves, well known as a contributor to 'Blackwood's Magazine,' and as a man

---

[1] Songs and Verses. By an Old Contributor to Maga. Edinburgh: Blackwood, 1869.

who, like Lord Jeffrey, and other distinguished Scottish judges, knew to temper the severity of the Law with the grace of poetry and the warmth of song. But Neaves did more in this respect than Outram, or any other of the contributors to the Parliament House Garland. He made severe scientific studies the seed out of which his song grew; and whether it were a metaphysical whim of Lord Monboddo, or a grand linguistic law of Jacob Grimm, or the Darwinian rage of drawing one thing out of another thing in a straight line, and all things out of one thing by a blind force or blind dance of forces, you saw that he was not merely blowing soap-bubbles, or flinging about squibs and crackers, with which inferior wits content themselves, but he built up his growth of song from a living root, and showed, even in his most humorous vein, that he was well aware of the germs of truth that lay beneath the exuberance of pampered speculation which he so gracefully pruned. He had not only, as this song shows, made a careful study of the facts of the Darwinian theory, but he was an excellent philologer, read Greek with pleasurable ease, which very few Scotsmen can do, and was one of the first who, in the pages of 'Blackwood's Magazine,' introduced to Scottish readers the far-reaching conclusions of Bopp and other German scholars, on the attractive new science of comparative philology.

We cannot do better than conclude this chapter and this little book with that song of Burns which, along with the patriotic strain of "Scots wha hae" and the genial conviviality of "Auld Langsyne," forms what, to borrow a phrase from the musicians, we may call the major third of melody, to stir the blood of all true Scotsmen, from the extreme West to the extreme East of their multifarious wanderings. In "A Man's a Man for a' that," we have the finest combination of practical philosophy, evangelical piety, and political wisdom that ever was put into a popular song. It is grandly human, and therefore philosophical; its key-note of moral brotherhood makes it evangelical; its assertion of the worth of individual character, as opposed to conventional distinctions, makes it politically wise. It is, moreover, eminently Scotch in the prominence which it gives to that estate of honest, and laborious, and self-sustaining poverty, the stout root out of which so many Scottish virtues have grown and so much social eminence has been achieved. I have known persons who in the words—

> "A king can mak' a belted knight,
> A marquis, duke, and a' that,"—

saw that narrow jealousy of superior rank and social position which shows itself so lovelessly in some specimens of the Radical politician. But it is not so. Burns was a

Liberal; but there was no touch of envy, or jealousy, or social bitterness in his composition. Certainly in this song he soars far above all party feelings, and merely announces plainly what is the poet's mission no less than the prophet's, to preach from the house-top that there is no respect of persons with God, and that whosoever pays worship to anything in any human being independent of personal worth and character, is an idolater and a heretic, with whom no professor of a moral and catholic Christianity can hold any fellowship. "How can ye believe, who receive honour one from another, and seek not the honour which cometh from God only?" is the weighty text that stamps with a truly evangelical significance this wise song of our national bard :—

A MAN'S A MAN FOR A' THAT.

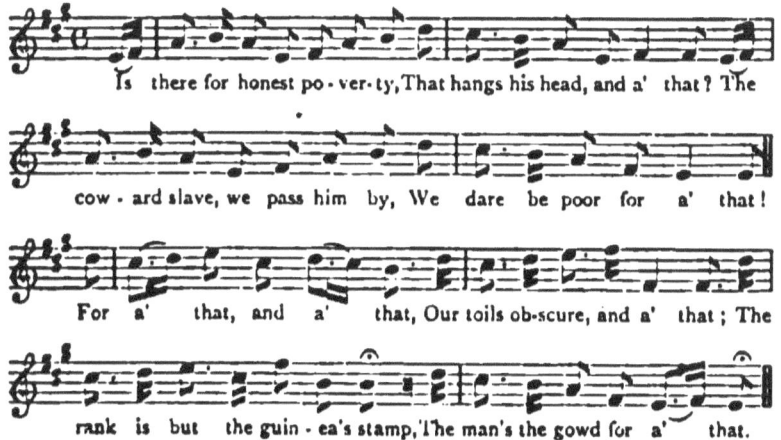

What though on hamely fare we dine,
    Wear hoddin grey, and a' that;
Gie fools their silks, and knaves their wine
    A man's a man for a' that.
For a' that, and a' that,
    Their tinsel show, and a' that;
The honest man, though e'er sae poor,
    Is king o' men for a' that.

Ye see yon birkie, ca'd a lord,
    Wha struts, and stares, and a' that;
Though hundreds worship at his word,
    He's but a coof for a' that.
For a' that, and a' that,
    His riband, star, and a' that;
The man of independent mind
    He looks and laughs at a' that.

A king can mak' a belted knight,
    A marquis, duke, and a' that;
But an honest man's aboon his might,
    Guid faith! he maunna fa that.
For a' that, and a' that,
    Their dignities, and a' that;
The pith o' sense, and pride o' worth,
    Are higher ranks than a' that,

Then let us pray that come it may,
    As come it will, for a' that,
That sense and worth, o'er a' the earth,
    May bear the gree, and a' that.
For a' that, and a' that,
    It's coming yet, for a' that,
That man to man, the warl' o'er,
    Shall brithers be for a' that.

GLOSSARY.

THE Scotch, as the Doric or musical dialect of our common English tongue, is characterised (1) by the prominence of the broad open *a*, as in *daur* for *dare;* (2) by the smooth and softly sounded *oo*, for the canine sound of *ou*, as in *hoose* for *house*, *doon* for *down;* (3) by the dropping of the final consonant to procure a soft vocalic ending, as *ha'* for *hall*, *loe* for *love*, *doo* for *dove*, and suchlike; (4) by the dainty and delicate labial sound of the Greek ὐψιλόν, identical with the *ue* of the Germans, for the English *oo*, or *ew* in *yew*, as in *guid* for *good*, *puir* for *poor;* (5) by the slurring of two consonants into one long vowel or diphthong with a single consonant, as *gowd* for *gold*, *stown* for *stolen;* and (6) by the soft aspirate χ in Greek and *ch* in German, for the sharp English *k*, as in *loch* for *lake*—and in general, preserving that Hellenico-Teutonic aspirate where the English have systematically swamped it, as in *richt* for *right*, *fecht* for *fight*. Attention to these well-pronounced features will in the general case enable the Englishman to understand Scotch without any help from a glossary; but there are some changes, and some radically different words, which cannot be subsumed under any orthoepic category, and for these I have endeavoured to provide in the following list:—

Glossary.

Aboon—above.
Ahint—behind.
Ail—vex, annoy.
Airt—direction, quarter.
Aise—ashes, hearth.
A-jee. See Jee.
Ava—at all.

Bairns—children.
Bauk—a cross-beam.
Bawbee—halfpenny.
Bawsand—having a white spot on the forehead or face.
Befyle—to soil, dirty.
Ben—the inner apartment of the house.
Bien—good, comfortable.
Big—to build.
Bigonet—coif, head-dress.
Bing—bend, duck, bow.
Bink—a bench or seat beside the fire.
Birk—birch.
Birkie—a smart young fellow, a puppy.
Birl—to toss down.
Birr—to make a whirring noise.
Birse—bristles.
Blaeberry—bilberry.
Blaw—to boast.
Bogle—a play of young people, in which one hunts the other round the stacks of corn in a barn-yard.
Bothie—a small wooden hut for labourers.
Bouk—bulk, body, carcass.
Brae—hill, slope.
Braw—well dressed, trim, handsome.
Brawly—well, very well.
Braws—fine dress.
Breckan—ferns.
Brent—smooth.
Brose—a kind of pottage made by pouring water or broth on meal, which is stirred in while the liquid is boiling.
Bucht—pen or fold for sheep.
Buffie—fat, purfled.
Burgonet—a kind of helmet.
But—the outer apartment of the house.

Caller—cool, fresh.
Canny—cautious.
Canty—cheerful, pleasant.
Carle—an old man.
Chap—a lad, fellow, boy.
Chiel—lad, fellow.
Chimley—chimney.
Clamjamfrie, a pack of low worthless people.
Cleek—catch as by a hook.
Clishmaclaver—silly talk.
Cogie—a cup, a bowl.
Coof—simpleton, blockhead.
Coutsey—small coat.
Crack—talk freely—familiarly, a sharp blow;—*in a crack*, immediately.
Cramasie—crimson cloth.
Craw—to boast.
Creel—an osier basket, hamper.
Creepie—a low stool.
Croo—a hovel.
Croon—to hum or sing in a low tone.
Crouse—brisk, lively.
Crowdie—a thick gruel.
Crummie—a cow.
Curtch—a woman's cap.
Custocks—cabbage.
Cutty—short.

Daddie—father.
Daffin—pastime, jesting.
Daft—mad.
Deuk-dub—a muddy pool for ducks.
Ding—beat, surpass, excel.
Dochter—daughter.
Dool—woe, sorrow.
Douce—sober, quiet.
Dour—hard-hearted, merciless.
Dowf—dull, flat.
Dowie—dull, doleful.
Dree—endure.
Drookit—drenched.
Drumlie—troubled, dark, muddy.
Dub—mire, dirt.
Duds—clothing.
Dumfounder—astonish, stun.
Dunt—beat, knock.

Eerie—apprehensive, nervous, frighted.
Eident—industrious.
Ettle—aim, strive.

Fash—to trouble, vex; adj. *fashious*.
Fen—a shift, an expedient.

Glossary. 387

Fend—to shift, make a shift.
Ferlie—wonder.
Fidgin—restless, eager.
Fleech—flatter.
Flyte—scold, brawl.
Forpit—the fourth part of a peck.
Fou—drunk.
Foumart—a polecat.
Fouth—plenty, abundance.
Fuff—puff.

Gab—talk, prattle.
Gang—go.
Gar—compel, force.
Gawky — silly, awkward, ill-mannered.
Gear—money.
Gee—ill-humour, sulks.
Genty—neat, light, graceful.
Gerse—grass.
Gilpie—lively, frolicsome.
Gin—if.
Glaikit—mad.
Glaum—to aim at, gaze eagerly.
Gleg—quick, sharp, keen.
Glent—glint, glance, shine.
Gloamin—twilight.
Glower—look intensely, stare.
Glum—sulky.
Gouk—fool.
Gowan—daisy.
Gree—superiority, prize.
Greet—weep.
Gudeman—the head of the family.
Guffaw—a loud burst of laughter.
Guid-willie—liberal, kindly.
Gutcher—grandfather.

Haddin—furniture, stock.
Haffet—side of the head.
Hain—to spare.
Hap—to cover up.
Happity—limping.
Haud—hold, keep.
Haukit—with a white face.
Heeze—to lift up.
Heft—a handle.
Heuch — a low hollow with steep overhanging rocks.
Hirsel—a flock, a herd, a drove.
Hizzie — contemptuous for *lass* or *woman*.
Hool—husk, hull.
Hough—fling a stone as at nine-pins.

Hurkle—to sit crouching.
Husswyfskip—housewifery.

Ilka—every.
Ingle—fire, fireside.

Jade—a low word for *woman*, *lass*.
Jaupit—bespattered with mud.
Jee—move to one side.
Jeel—jelly.
Joe—sweetheart, lover.
Jouk—to move playfully, shift.

Kail—colewort, cabbage.
Kebbuck—a large cheese.
Keel—ruddle.
Ken—know.
Kep—catch, receive.
Kirn—churn.
Kist—chest, trunk.
Kye—kine.
Kyle—a throw at nine-pins.

Laigh—low.
Lave—the rest, remainder.
Lavrock—lark.
Lift—the sky.
Lilt—air, song, ditty.
Lintie—linnet.
Lippen—to trust.
Loaning—a long open green space or meadow.
Lout—bend low.
Lowe—flame.
Lug—the ear.
Lyart—grey.

Maukin—a hare.
Maun—must.
Mavis—thrush.
Minnie—mother.
Mou—mouth.
Murlain—a narrow-mouthed basket of a round form.
Mutch—a woman's cap.

Neist—next.
Neuch—enough.

O'ercome—a refrain.
Owk—week.
Owsen—oxen.

Pawky—arch, shrewd, sly.
Pearlings—laces.

Glossary.

Plack—a small copper coin the third of a penny.
Plenishings—furniture.
Poortith—poverty.
Preen—pin.

Rax—reach.
Rook—a thick mist.
Rowan—mountain-ash.
Runkled—wrinkled.

Sark—shirt.
Sauff's—save us!
Saugh—willow.
Scaud—scald.
Scon—a cake thin and broad.
Shaw—a branch.
Sheuch—a ditch.
Shindy—scuffle, row.
Shouther—shoulder.
Sic—such.
Skyrin—shining, showy.
Smack—an accentuated kiss.
Sodger—soldier.
Sonsy—good-humoured, well-conditioned, well-rounded, plump.
Sough—sob, sigh, panting breath; to blow.
Speir—ask.
Spence—parlour.
Stappit—stepped.
Sten or *stend*—leap, jump, come briskly forward.
Stot—a young bull castrated.
Stour—disturbance.
Styme—a whit, a glimpse.
Sumph—a dull, stupid, boggy-souled fellow.
Swankie—an alert young fellow.
Swarf—swoon, faint.
Swats—new ale.
Syne—long ago, afterwards, then.

Tappit—with a tuft on the head.
Tent—tend, watch, attend to.
Teuch—tough.

Thae—those.
Thowless—weak, faint.
Thraw—twist.
Thud—a blow, a buffet, with cognate verb.
Tine—to lose.
Tirl—spin round.
Tittie—sister.
Tocher—dower.
Toddle—to walk with short feeble steps like children.
Toom—empty.
Tosh—neat, trim.
Totums—little children.
Trews—trousers.
Trig—neat, trim.
Tweel—thread when spun.
Tyce—to go slowly.

Unstent—to loosen—from *stent*, to stretch.

Wale—to choose.
Wame—belly, stomach.
Wanter—a bachelor or widower.
Wat—know, ken.
Waucht—a draught.
Waur—worse.
Weans—young children.
Wee—little.
Whaup—curlew, sea-gull.
Whomble—wamble.
Whyles—sometimes.
Wile—seduce, allure.
Winsome—attractive, pleasant.
Wow or *vow*—truly, certainly.
Wraith—a ghost, apparition.
Wyte—blame.

Yade—a mare.
Yammer—shriek, scream.
Yett—gate.
Yill—ale.
Yont—beyond.
Yowe—ewe.
Yowl—howl.

www.ingramcontent.com/pod-product-compliance
Lightning Source LLC
Chambersburg PA
CBHW020108010526
44115CB00008B/738